Frederick G. (Frederick George) Jackson

The Great Frozen Land (Bolshaia Zemelskija Tundra)

Narrative of a Winter Journey Across the Tundras and a Sojourn...

Frederick G. (Frederick George) Jackson

The Great Frozen Land (Bolshaia Zemelskija Tundra)
Narrative of a Winter Journey Across the Tundras and a Sojourn...

ISBN/EAN: 9783744798716

Printed in Europe, USA, Canada, Australia, Japan

Cover: Foto ©Andreas Hilbeck / pixelio.de

More available books at **www.hansebooks.com**

THE
GREAT FROZEN LAND

(*BOLSHAIA ZEMELSKIJA TUNDRA*)

NARRATIVE OF A WINTER JOURNEY ACROSS
THE TUNDRAS AND A SOJOURN
AMONG THE SAMOYADS

BY

FREDERICK GEORGE JACKSON

FELLOW OF THE ROYAL GEOGRAPHICAL SOCIETY
LEADER OF THE JACKSON-HARMSWORTH POLAR EXPEDITION

WITH ILLUSTRATIONS AND MAPS

EDITED FROM HIS JOURNALS BY

ARTHUR MONTEFIORE

FELLOW OF THE GEOLOGICAL AND ROYAL GEOGRAPHICAL SOCIETIES
AND ANTHROPOLOGICAL INSTITUTE

London
MACMILLAN AND CO.
AND NEW YORK
1895

All rights reserved

PREFACE

OF the two objects which were in view when this journey was undertaken, the first and more important was to experiment with and test a selected variety of equipment, clothing, and food under the conditions of an Arctic winter, in order that the results of this experience might be utilised in the more prolonged and far more difficult journey contemplated to the unknown Arctic area north of Franz Josef Land. As most people are aware, the low Tundras of Arctic Russia and Siberia, although readily accessible and stretching on the east, west, and south to the confines of civilisation, possess a winter climate of a severity so great that it does not merely exceed the rigour of many regions lying farther north, and in the strict embrace of Oceanic ice, but actually reveals the lowest temperature yet recorded in the whole of the Arctic basin. For it is on the frozen Tundras of Siberia that we find what has been called "The Pole of Extreme Cold."

A sledge-journey, then, across the Tundras lying between the Kara and the White Seas—undertaken, too, in the winter season—might well be expected to provide an adequate test of the suitability of the clothing, camp-kit, means of locomotion, and food intended to be taken on an Arctic Expedition. Such very practical and important questions as those involved in clothing for the feet, cooking-stoves for use on the march, the lowest limit of the weight of the sledge compatible with strength, the action of breech-loading and self-ejecting rifles, the most convenient and effectual form of shelter from the snow-gales of the Polar regions—these are but a few of the many problems to be faced, considered, and decided by any one who contemplates an exploration of the unknown areas around the North Pole. Not merely would the Tundras, stiff and stark and lifeless in the deadly grip of winter, provide opportunities of raising and settling these questions, but they would also enable the traveller to reckon on his return to civilisation in the early spring, in time to prepare and complete the equipment which should be the outcome of his experience on those inhospitable wastes.

It is true that the winter visitor would fail to find at his feet the bright if short-lived flowers of the Arctic summer; true that the fortune would not be his to mark the simple nest and priceless eggs of those birds whose breeding-places have never yet been seen by naturalist, but are probably to be discovered on the Tundras; true, too, that the evidences of the geological past and the open book of the geographical present would be largely hidden by the unbroken surface of ice and snow which he would traverse and survey.

But just as the golden harvest of the morrow can alone be reaped through the toil of to-day, so he who would enjoy the delight of Arctic discovery and the glow of a successful wrestle with Nature in her most formidable mood must be content to forego the interest and ease of a summer wandering which fails to stretch the cords of the muscles to a high point of tension or strain the capacity of physical endurance.

Yet here, again, the selection of the Tundras would permit some slight modification; and this book will show that arrival on the scene in the late summer, and a sojourn during the short autumn, enables the traveller to view those solitudes when flushed by the lingering sun, tinged with the hues of vegetation, and broken by the sounds of animated nature.

And this brings me to the second object of the journey, which was to visit and, for some months, to live with that primitive group of the human family, the Samoyads of the Great Frozen Tundra of Arctic Russia; to dwell in their tents, to eat of their food, to go and come with them in their daily life, to share their labour and their rest; to mark their ways and seek their motives, to note their relations to one another, and to learn, if possible, something of their sense of a higher influence. And there was more, too, than the curiosity of a member of a civilised nation in a primitive folk; for—still bearing in mind the coming voyage to lands and seas yet to be surveyed—there were the lessons which a people could teach who simply existed in this rigid wilderness because they had learnt to adapt themselves and all their modes of life to that environment. It is a wise saying and a true which tells us to live, wherever we travel, as the natives of each country can show us how; more especially concerning clothing, food, the ordinary shifts and expedients of the daily round, and regard for times and seasons. And the narrative which this book contains will tell wherein even the rude Samoyad can give knowledge to an Englishman who had already travelled far and well.

Finally, and included in this second object, was the journeying over that Great Tundra, between the Kara Sea and the Pechora River—a solitude through which no Englishman had ever passed; of which no sufficient map existed; whose tale of river-labyrinths, ancient beaches, and lost bays had never been told; of whose winter climate no account was to be discovered in the English tongue.

These, then, were the objects, and these the means which Mr. Frederick George Jackson set before him and achieved in his journey of 1893-94. He went out towards the end of the summer; devoted the autumn to the survey of Waigatz Island, which links Novaia Zemlia to the Ural chain, and opens the gate into the Kara Sea; and the winter to his sledge-journey of near two thousand five hundred miles from the frontier of Siberia across the Great Tundra, the Pechora Valley, the Little Tundra; and then, if haply he might learn of the Lapp what he had not been taught by the Samoyad, through Russian Lapland to the Murmanski Coast. He pulled his own sledge and he drove it behind reindeer and the wiry ponies of Northern Russia; he lived much as the natives lived, and ate with them of their coarse but vitalising food; he stayed in their foul and almost suffocating chooms, and he lay down to sleep, as they slept, on the open snow. And he returned to England with his physical powers and all his great courage and enthusiasm at their highest, and a new store of experience for his very material assistance.

Then the strenuous work of preparing for the great expedition to Franz Josef Land and the unknown area lying north of it, which private patriotism and munificence had rendered possible on a scale we had not looked for, came upon him; and although we had many a talk together on this winter journey and his life among the Samoyads, and together went through his journals, it was not until the fever of preparation was over, and we were steaming up the Norwegian fiords and round the North Cape for the White Sea and Arkhangel, that Mr. Jackson was able to arrange and connect his notes for publication; and, even then, it was found impossible to decide this point and that point, to give final shape to one sentence and another. And so it was left to me to see the work through the press, and make those necessary changes and additions which come within editorial discretion.

If, then, there are errors of opinion, too great insistence on trifles, or scant recognition of that which is important, I trust that they may be set down to my own shortcomings and not charged to my absent friend, for whom I hope and of whom I expect a glorious record of English pluck and Arctic Discovery; and that his readers will remember that for this, his first essay in the literature of travel, I have done what the exceptional circumstances and my own capacity have permitted.

ARTHUR MONTEFIORE.

CHRISTMAS 1894.

[In the following pages I must accept responsibility for the notes, unless otherwise stated, and for the chapters on the Speech and Folk-lore of the Samoyads. And I should acknowledge here the kindness of Mr. Herbert Ward, F.R.G.S., in supplying me with some interesting sketches, and of Mr. J. Russell Jeaffreson, F.R.G.S., in examining and reporting on the birds observed and collected by Mr. Jackson.]

CONTENTS

CHAPTER I

CAMPING AT HABAROVA

The "Ice-blink"—Meeting the ice—The Yugorski Schar—Landing at Habarova—Plans for the winter—Samoyad and Tundra—Habarova—Life of the Tundra—Settling in—Camp kit—Useful stores—Reindeer meat   Page 1

CHAPTER II

WAIGATZ

A Samoyad bargain—Vasili and his babba—Their costume—Across the Schar—Our choom—The Samoyad no beggar—On the march—Waigatz scenery—The Samoyad preference for raw flesh—A sacrificial pile—"Niet dobbera choom"—Dolga Bay—Voronoff Noss—Silk tent a failure—Bolvanski Noss—A Samoyad feast—The eastern slope of Waigatz—Out on the Kara Sea—The Waigatz hills—Ice movements round Waigatz   24

CHAPTER III

AMONG THE SAMOYADS

Learning the Samoyad speech—Dumb show—Character of the Samoyads—Their physical appearance—Average height—Sociability—Kindness—A Samoyad "Aunt Sally"—The man's costume: militza, covcrk, hcnpthcu, and pimmes The woman's dress; its ornamentation Her cap Her pigtails Trinkets and charms The Samoyad "Ski" The reindeer Its food Its fitness for Arctic Exploration, and the difficulty The reindeer's endurance—The Samoyad use of deer flesh, and mode of eating Making bread—The dogs of the Samoyads The lasso The weapons and tools of the modern Samoyad The choom The Holy Island of the Samoyad A burial-place The fashionable religion Half and half The old faith "Yon-pa-ha-pai" Snuff-taking—The calculating stick Money and barter—The common diseases—The Samoyad in brief   Page 48

CHAPTER IV

ACROSS "THE GREAT FROZEN LAND"
(Bolshaia Zemelskija Tundra)

A sojourn among the Samoyads—A story of scurvy—My camp—The current in the Yugorski Schar—A long pull Sport near Habarova—The return of the *Blencathra*—Miss Helen Peel—The attempt to sail to the Kara River—The arrival of winter—Swimming the deer from Waigatz—Rounding up the herds—The start for the Pechora—The first "ducking"—Night in the choom—Putting the baby to bed—A deer's load—A cold bath—Bad weather—The Korotaika River—A Zirian family—Superiority of Samoyad clothing—The art of driving reindeer—The harness—The sledge—The woman's sledge—Gale and frost—Weather-bound in the choom—A Samoyad burial-place—Thirteen in a choom—Raw meat—Weather notes—The rivers—Lost on the Tundra—A night in the snow—Playing the Medicine Man—Breaking in the young deer—The silence of the Tundra—A Tundra gale   97

CHAPTER V

ACROSS "THE GREAT FROZEN LAND" *(continued)*

A new feature—Lost bays—Old beaches—The Pitkoff Hills—Driving a Norwegian sledge—Its great advantages—New landscapes—The Indian snow-shoe—A push for the Pechora—A hospitable friend—The Pechora—Up the frozen river—Ussia—Ivan at

home—Eating "marbles"—An object of curiosity—Pustozersk—
Life on the Pechora—Russian hospitality—Camping out—Cost
of the journey from Habarova—A solar eccentricity—Another
Samoyad burial-place—The pony of Northern Russia—Good-bye
to my Habarova friends Going south—Meeting the tree-line—
The Zirians—A cold morning—Ust-Zilma Roman Okatov—
Madame Okatov—Curiosity of the natives—Twenty-five in a room
—The Ust-Zilma well—Kindness of the Okatovs—My new guide
—Departure from Ust-Zilma—Doorkin—Spill—Another upset—
Stamina of the Russian ponies—A bad track—A drunken Zirian—
Hills and gullies—Pinega and its fair—The English language once
more—The post sledge—Ust-Pinega—Holmagora—Arkhangel—
The British Vice-Consul—Good news . Page 128

CHAPTER VI

ROUND THE WHITE SEA AND THROUGH LAPLAND—HOME

Object—To compare Lapps with Samoyads, and see dog-sledging—
Christmas in camp—Kindness of the Governor of Arkhangel—
Onega—Bad weather—Gales and snowdrifts—Buried in the snow
—Digging the sledge out—Frost bites—" Loshadi nieto "—Eaten
alive—Kem—Cost of posting—Kandalaksha—The Lapps—The
Lapp deer and the Lapp sledge—Costume of the Lapps compared
with that of the Samoyads—Kola—The Ispravnik—Captain
Louschkin—Days at Kola—Sledging to Kirkeness—Vadsö—
Vardo—The return of the sun—Round the North Cape in winter—
Christiania—Mr. Alexander Nansen—The doctor's wife—Norway's
champion skater—Mr. Crichton Somerville—Return to England
—Courtesy of the Russian authorities—Acknowledgments and
thanks . 165

CHAPTER VII

A CHAPTER ON LANGUAGE

The Samoyad speech—Difficulties—Castrén—Parts of speech—A list
of Samoyad words—Mr. Jackson's list—Mr. Rae's list—A contribution from Mr. H. Seebohm—Von Strahlenberg . 189

CHAPTER VIII

SAMOYAD FOLK-TALES

1. The Two Sisters and the Old Woman of the Island—2. The Seven Maidens of the Lake—3. The Old Man of Deceit   Page 208

APPENDIX A

Notes on the Ornithological Results of Mr. Jackson's Journey. By Joseph Russell Jeaffreson, F.R.G.S. .   235

APPENDIX B

Weather Observations kept by F. G. Jackson, F.R.G.S. September 1893 to January 1894   244

APPENDIX C

Topographical Notes to accompany the Map of the Great Tundra. By F. G. Jackson, F.R.G.S. .   254

APPENDIX D

The Jackson-Harmsworth Polar Expedition: Its Object, Method, and Equipment .   263

Index   289

ILLUSTRATIONS

The Author in a Samoyad Sledge	*Frontispiece*
	PAGE
Samoyad Types	12
A Summer Camp	14
A Russian "Pope"	20
The Sacrificial Pile on the South-West Point of Waigatz	34
Camping in the North of Waigatz	37
Bolvanski Noss	41
Samoyad Burial Place	46
At Habarova	58
Skulls of Samoyads (Male Adults)	59
An Old Samoyad	62
Ornamented Leather Belt, showing Knife, Calculating Stick, etc.	65
Samoyad Women	66
The Bonnet of the Samoyad Women	67
Ornaments (Brass or Copper) attached to the Women's Hair	69
The Samoyad and his Dogs	79
Walrus Ivory and Iron Powder-Flask	80
Chaddi	85
Snuff-Boxes and Snuff-Spoon	90
Calculating Sticks	91
Samoyad Knives, with Walrus Ivory Sheath	95
Miss Helen Peel	103
Samoyads on the March	107

	PAGE
The Author in Sealskin Coat (of English Make), and Samoyad Pimmies or Boots	111
The Author in Samoyad Militza and Pimmies, with Bamboo for Harray or Driving pole	114
Chalkis	115
Samoyad Sledge	118
Rounding up the Deer	131
Kuia, the Port of the Pechora	135
A Welcome Wash at Ussia	139
A Wayside Cross	142
Pustozersk	145
A Solar Eccentricity	146
Church at Ust-Zilma	152
Ust-Zilma	153
M. Roman Okatov, Superintendent of Woods and Forests	156
Arkhangel in the Summer	163
A Russian *Mujik*	171
A Lapp Mother and Child	176
A Lapp in his *Pesk* with Bearskin round his Shoulders)	177
A Lapp *Talta* or Summer Tent	179
Kola	183
Samoyad Rosary	205
A Samoyad Doll	234
The Antlers of the Reindeer	243
Last View of the S.Y. *Windward* steaming North in the White Sea	288

Route Map	*facing page*	1
Map of Waigatz	"	32
Map of the Great Tundra	"	262

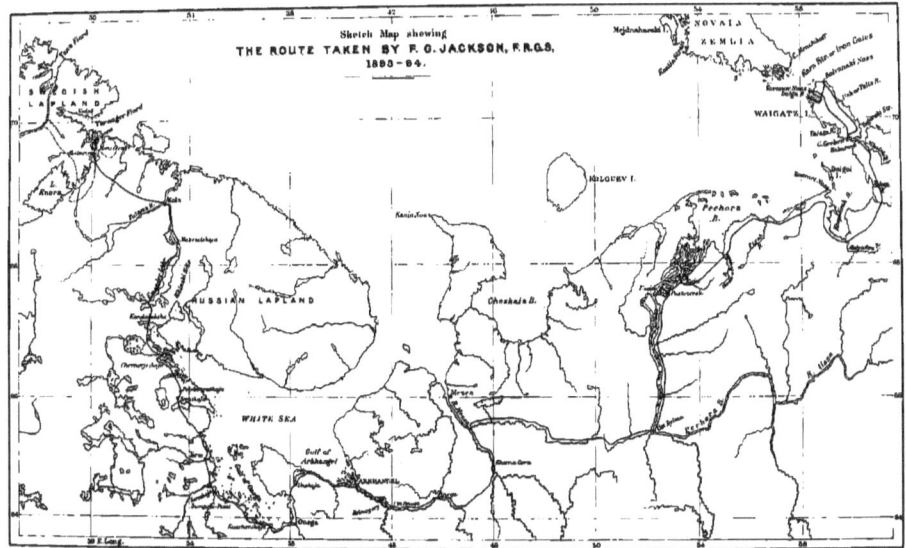

CHAPTER I

CAMPING AT HABAROVA

The "Ice-blink"—Meeting the ice—The Yugorski Schar—Landing at Habarova—Plans for the winter—Samoyad and Tundra—Habarova—Life of the Tundra—Settling in—Camp kit—Useful stores—Reindeer meat.

LAST August, after an interval of seven years, I again found myself in Arctic seas. On the former occasion I had gone westward and spent some six months in Greenland waters: now I was travelling to the east, crossing Barents Sea, and making for that narrow strait which divides the Novaia Zemlian archipelago from the double continent of Asia and Europe, and unites the ice-laden Kara Sea with the more temperate waters named after the gallant Dutch navigator.

Once again I was looking away to the northward for the first sign of ice, and on the 25th, when in 70° 35′ N. lat. and 48° E. long., the "ice-blink" became visible. Above the horizon there was spread upon the sky a map of the ice-fields that lay below upon the sea. There one could trace the wide unbroken stretches of floe-ice — as yet beyond the view — in masses of yellowish-white, and the winding "lanes" of open water in broad veins of dark blue. To many an Arctic traveller this "ice-blink" map has been the means of his escape from an ice-capped sea, but on this occasion to us, who were sailing in a comparatively low latitude, it was merely the indication of the ice-floes lying in our route; floes which we knew, unless our luck was to be bad, were neither so thick nor so packed as to be difficult to navigate.

This harbinger of the ice cannot lie, and on the following morning, away to the northward and windward, we saw the actual sea-scape as it had been mirrored the previous day: long, low fields of ice, the greater part of which would not be more than six feet above the sea, with here and there the turning lanes of open water, and here and there the open patches of blue sea, with a few white blocks of erratic ice floating quietly in their midst, as swans upon a pool. The sun, which now was nearly always with us, gleamed for a little while and called out all the light and colour which lie latent in Arctic scenery, and then there came with sudden swiftness from the north a succession of heavy snow squalls, piling on the deck deep drifts of snow, and making what we could see of the world around us, drear indeed. The rigging stood as a network of white leading upward into the dense mist, which rolled down upon us, wave after wave, as the sea might break upon the shore. Yet in all the world I know no climate so swift to change as that of the Polar regions, and by noon the sun had overmastered snow and mist and was shining upon us with so unclouded a face that the sea was sparkling as if it were liquid light, and the ice-glare became so strong as to try the eyes. Deeper and deeper seemed the blue of the water which lapped the sharp edges of the floes, and more and more beautiful the crystal masses which in an infinity of form and with an endless variety of light and shade drew out of the north and the east, and lay silent on the sea around us.

The ship in which I had taken my passage was the s.s. *Orestes*, and she formed one of a small fleet of vessels which, under the command of Captain Joseph Wiggins, was making for the river Yenisei, and intending there to discharge their cargoes. Our convoy was the *Blencathra*, belonging to Mr. F. Leybourne Popham, and at one time well known as the *Pandora*, and the Arctic yacht of that distinguished explorer, Sir Allen Young. A third vessel was the *Minusinsk*, and accompanying her were three Russian boats, manned by Russian crews, but under the supreme command of Mr. Popham's skipper, Captain Wiggins. The voyage, on which I was merely a passenger as far as the Yugorski Schar, was not so successful as a commercial enterprise as it might have been, but this must be attributed less to the navigation of the Kara Sea and great Yenisei River than to the inadequate arrangements for discharging cargo. Indeed, in favourable years, the Kara Sea presents no insuperable difficulty to the navigator on his outward voyage.

On the evening of the 26th we came within sight of Waigatz Island. Here lay the land which had allured me—the Holy Isle of the Samoyads, standing between the ancient "Samoedia" and the lofty islands of Novaia Zemlia. Here I had come, hoping to do something serviceable, and following in the steps of those early voyagers of the sixteenth century. It was with the deepest interest that I ascended the rigging and climbed into the Crow's Nest, and from that advantageous position—just below the "truck" of the mainmast—looked round the wider horizon I had now obtained.

Owing to the wind being from the north-east, and thus blowing off the land of Novaia Zemlia, the sea was smooth. Away to the northward, the sky above the Waigatz Straits showed a strong ice-blink, and told us that there was but little hope of the *Orestes* passing through those Straits in order to land me, as I had hoped, on the south island of Novaia Zemlia. Moreover, as the ice reached right inshore along the western coast of Waigatz, considerable difficulty would have been experienced in even attempting to reach the mouth of the Straits.

Early in the morning of 27th August we ran into the small bay at the south-west extremity of Waigatz Island and at the entrance to Pet's Straits, or, as it is more frequently called nowadays, the Yugorski Schar.[1] A good deal of fairly heavy ice, not packed but consisting of isolated lumps, was coming through the Straits, and for a while it looked as if the iron steamer would encounter serious difficulty in making the passage. But the *Blencathra*, wooden and very strong, pushed up the channel to reconnoitre, and before long returned

[1] Yugorski Schar means simply the Strait of Yugoria or Ugoria. Arthur Pet, on the 19th of July 1580, entered and passed through the Strait for the first time, and on the strength of this the Yugorski Schar is frequently referred to and was at one time generally called "Pet's Strait." As to the word Schar, its meaning is confined to the true strait between sea and sea, except in the case of the Kostin Schar, which, as a mere arm of the sea, should, according to Lutke (p. 245), be called Kostin Salma. Yet in the days of its baptism this was really thought to be a true Schar. In all probability the word Schar, as several other words used in this region, has a Finnish origin, and Dr. Beke, in his edition of *Barents' Voyages* (2nd edition, p. 31), suggests Spenser (although he calls him "Spencer") as exhibiting an affinity :—

> Upon that shore he spyéd Atin stand,
> There by his maister left, when late he far'd
> In Phaedria's flitt barck over that per'lous shard.
> *Faerie Queene*, II. vi. 38.

In De Veer's account of Barents' second voyage (1595), the following interesting note appears relating to the entrance into the Yugorski Schar: "Then we sailed vnder 70 degrees, vntill we came to the Wey-gates, most part through broken ice; and when we got to Wey-gates, wee cast out our lead, and for a long time found 13 and 14 fadome, soft ground mixed with blacke shels; not long after that wee cast out the lead and found 10 fadome deepe, the wind being north,

with the favourable news that the Straits themselves, right through to the Kara Sea, were practically free from ice.

We had sighted the wooden Russian gunboat *Nayesdnik* lying at anchor south-west of Waigatz, and shortly after the return of the *Blencathra* Captain Pell, her commander, came on board and dined with us. He was good enough to overhaul my Russian vocabulary and write out the Russian alphabet for me. Later on, her lieutenant—Dobrotvorski by name—also boarded us. Apparently he was a capital fellow, but we could

and we forced to hold stifly aloofe, in regard of the great quantity of ice, till about midnight ; then we were forced to wind north ward because of certaine rocks that lay on the south side of Wey-gates, right before vs about a mile and a halfe, hauing 10 fadome deepe ; then wee changed our coarse, and sailed west north-west for the space of 4 glasses, after that we wound about againe east and east and by south, and so entred into Wey-gates, and as wee went in, we cast out the lead, and found 7 fadome deepe, little more or lesse, till the 19 of August : and then the sunne being south-east we entered into the Wey-gates, in the road, the wind being north.

"The right chanell between the Image Point and the Samuters land was full of ice, so that it was not well to be past through, and so we went into the road, which we called the Trayen Bay, because we found store of trayen-oyle there ; this is a good bay for the course of the ice, and good almost for all windes, and we may saile so farre into it as we will at 4, 5, and 6 fadome, good anchor-ground : on the east it is deepe water."

In the foregoing passage the word "shels" is *Stipkens*, and may be translated spots or specks—possibly micaceous debris is meant. The mile and a half is Dutch measûrement, and would equal six miles English. "4 glasses" would be equivalent to two hours, the glass used being a half-hour glass. "Samuters land" is the land of the Samoyads.

not carry on much conversation, as he did not know English. But, on the other hand, he could speak French and German, while, in consequence of having neglected those departments of knowledge when at school, I was unable to do more than what I believe the average Englishman usually achieves on such occasions. Fortunately he found in Miss Helen Peel, who was on board the *Blencathra*, a lady quite capable of exchanging conversational amenities in the French and German tongues. As a matter of fact, it was neither French nor German in which I was just then interested, but Russian and Samoyad, and, encouraged by the help in the former which I had just received from the captain of the Russian gunboat, I forthwith began to practise upon Tiger, a Russian Lapp whom we had on board the *Orestes*. I fear it must be recorded that he gazed at me as if I had sworn at him vehemently.

I should like to mention here that by the kind offices of the captain of the Russian gunboat we were able to send letters home. These were posted at Arkhangel, and arrived a full month after there had been any reasonable expectation of hearing of us.

On 28th August the weather was so foggy that we could not proceed, so we spent the day with our new Russian friends. Among other things I learnt from them was that there is generally a Russian or two on Goose Land. The Russian Government makes a point of maintaining a few Russians there, partly for the purpose of recording meteorological observations, but more particularly with a view to retaining Novaia Zemlia as a Russian country. Deaths from scurvy frequently occur, and consequently new settlers replace the old with rapidity. Nowhere else on Novaia Zemlia is there a permanent colony of Europeans; but the Samoyads who live there may also be found, but in smaller numbers, at the entrance to the Matotchkin Schar. In the summer, however, Russian fishermen as well as Samoyads penetrate the rivers of Goose Land in search of salmon.

On the 29th of August the fog lifted, and early in the morning we steamed to Habarova, where we landed, and found that in addition to a large number of Samoyads there were four Russian traders of the peasant class and a priest. Accommodation, of course, was of the most primitive type, and I was even fortunate in being able to get room for myself and my traps in the log-house of the priest. Captain Wiggins, Mr. Leybourne Popham, Mr. and Mrs. James, and Miss Helen Peel accompanied me on shore; but we had hardly landed when Captain Wiggins thought he could see signs of the ice drifting towards the ship, and, nervous about her safety, he returned at full speed, taking the whole party with him. Immediately the *Blencathra* and *Orestes* were reached, they weighed anchor and steamed up the Yugorski Schar.

A somewhat difficult problem now faced me, and

candidly I was in a bit of a fix. We had landed in a very hurried manner, and my things had been put ashore before I had time to check them. On going through the packages I found that some of my most useful provisions had been left in the ship, and that by some carelessness on the part of those who had the duty of bringing them ashore, all my butter and cheese had gone on to the Yenisei with the *Orestes*. Moreover, the bargain which Captain Wiggins, who knew a little bad Russian, was going to make on my behalf with the Russians and Samoyads never came to maturity, for in the middle of the palaver he had seen the ice drifting, and hurried away. So with a very slight knowledge of Russian, and with absolutely none of Samoyad, I had to make a bargain with these people if I would carry out either one or both parts of my intended journey.

When I left England it was with the intention of penetrating—to some distance northward—the interior of the southern island of Novaia Zemlia, and afterwards of returning south to Habarova. Thence I hoped to go by land or by water to the Yalmal Peninsula.

The interior of Novaia Zemlia and that of the Yalmal Peninsula are entirely unknown: upon the maps they are blanks; of their configuration people really have no idea, and at their flora and fauna we can only guess from observations upon the coast. It was not, however, as a naturalist that I intended to work, and here lies the reason for selecting the winter season for my travels — the fact that it would afford the severest test for my equipment. This test I had elected to apply with one object, namely, to ascertain the best possible equipment for the expedition it was my great desire to take to Franz Josef Land in the following year. Any one who should go to Novaia Zemlia, or cross Yalmal in summer, would probably be rewarded by many interesting discoveries in their topography and geology, flora and fauna; but as I wished to expose my foods, clothing, sledges, and other apparatus to the rigorous test of an Arctic winter, it was obvious that I must be content with general results of a geographical and meteorological character. Of the heights and valleys, of the ranges and plains, the glaciers and rivers, the peaks and passes, the temperature and winds, I might hope to gain some interesting and useful knowledge, while at the same time utilising my experience chiefly with a view to my equipment for Franz Josef Land. Such a journey held out and might have afforded discoveries of no common interest, and I greatly regret that, owing to the timidity of the Samoyads, my plans should have been baffled in both directions. It is true that the timidity was rational—with regard, at any rate, to the Novaia Zemlia journey—for their wretched boats or *lodkas* were fragile things with only three or four inches of freeboard, and utterly unfit to cross the

Waigatz Straits, thirty miles in breadth. Moreover, had I had a good whaleboat with me, I fear my efforts to induce them to accompany me would have been in vain, for when, a month later, Mr. Popham left me one of his whaleboats, I was unable to induce or bribe them to go along the coast into the Kara Sea. But then the Samoyad is no sailor.

Nevertheless, I was fortunate in being able to accomplish a good deal. During the four months spent in company with the Samoyads I learnt much of the manners and habits of a people whose individuality is becoming more and more impaired by Russian contact. Of the primitive folk of this world there are few races so interesting, and none more valuable for supporting or correcting our views on the origins and movements of Early Man than the Finnic people. From the Chukchis in the east to the Lapps in the west, an unbroken chain of evidence is presented by all the intermediate tribes—evidence which goes to establish the antiquity of the Mongolian race, and the persistence of its type. And the careful observation and collection of facts by travellers will one of these days enable some anthropological genius to infer and prove the true history of Prehistoric Man in Northern Asia and Europe. I can advance no claim of giving here a scientific account of the strange people among whom I lived, but I believe it to be accurate, and I know it has been compiled with care;

and therefore I hope that apart from its being taken as a story of travel, just for what it may be worth in

SAMOYAD TYPES.

interest or novelty, some of the facts recorded may prove of use to the ethnologist.

Fortunate, too, have I been in making the first survey of Waigatz Island, and not less lucky to have been the first Englishman to journey from the Samoyad settlement at Habarova across the wild and unknown Tundra which lies between that and the Pechora Valley. Several travellers have visited that river, and a track between the Pechora and Arkhangel has been made by more than one of my countrymen, most noteworthy among whom, of course, is Mr. Henry Seebohm; but the nine hundred miles of Tundra—the heart of the Bolshaia Zemelskija Country—has never been traversed by a predecessor who was my countryman, and, judging from the best Russian and German maps, never been laid down with anything approaching fulness of detail by any one. I hope therefore that my notes on the geography of this region and the information contained in the sketch map accompanying this book will be as welcome to those who seek for knowledge as I trust the account of my daily life among a peculiar people, and the incidents and accidents of a journey in a new land, will be to those who read for pleasure.

Habarova is a small village composed of eight or ten rude huts, with a church and priest's house, and fifteen chooms inhabited by Samoyads. The church and "vicarage" were erected by the Siberian millionaire Siberiakoff, after nearly losing his life on a voyage down the Obi, as a thank-offering for his escape. The huts are mere erections of rough pine-logs brought from the Pechora in Russian sailing sloops, and consist of a single room, about twelve feet by eight feet, with a small entrance room or lobby, which is usually piled up with furs, provisions, and other goods. These huts are occupied by a few enterprising Russian peasants from the Pechora Valley, who sledge every year—in the month of May—to Habarova. It is worth noting

A SUMMER CAMP.

that they bring the Samoyads (who leave Habarova in the late autumn) back with them, and employ them during the summer in hunting foxes, bears, seals, and walrus. The Russians do not pay the Samoyads wages, but buy the produce of their summer hunting from them at prices which, it is needless to say, allow of a wide margin of profit. In addition to the Samoyads of Habarova, about twenty—there were eighteen last year—spend the winter on Bolvanski

Noss, the extreme north-east point of Waigatz, with the object of being on the spot in the early spring to kill bear, walrus, and seal.

The country round Habarova is tundra of the most typical character. Rolling plains of marshy soil are covered on the ridges with coarse grass, a few inches high, and filled in the hollows with shallow lakes and ponds. Walking across this country becomes wading, and, as a matter of fact, it is only when the ground is covered with frozen snow that it is readily passable. So boggy, indeed, is the tundra, that I have walked for miles at a time sinking at every step up to the calf of the leg. The soil is composed of shaly slate and limestones, with calcite veins. I picked out a lamellibranch, of the genus *Pterinæa;* and from the banks of the Nikolski River, near, a *Saxicava arctica*—undoubtedly derived from an old marine deposit. Not a tree is to be seen anywhere, nothing indeed approaching to the dignity of a bush, but here and there, by careful observation, one sees that curious, low, creeping willow, reaching its maximum height perhaps in three or four inches. And here and there in the summer—and particularly in the shelter of the river banks—the eye lights on a small patch of bright but short-lived flowers. Among these I chiefly noted yellow poppies, white anemones, blue forget-me-nots, and a species of pink onion. Other plants that I identified and brought back with me were, among the rushes, *Juncus biglumis;* among the sedges, *Eriophorum polystachyon,* the familiar cotton-grass ; and of grasses, notably *Festuca ovina.* The well-known *Papaver nudicaule;* the common Arctic willow (*Salix lanata*); *Gnaphalium sylvaticum;* the "horse daisy" (*Chrysanthemum Leucanthemum*); and reindeer moss (*Cladonia rangiferina*) were the most conspicuous features of the vegetation.[1] The scrub which one meets on the Pechora is nowhere visible here, and indeed the whole aspect of the country, stretching as it does from horizon to horizon, is one of monotony, cheerlessness, and gloom. This is particularly the case immediately after the first severe frosts of approaching winter, for then the grass turns a dark brown and the flowers disappear. Curious indeed is

[1] Among other plants noted in Mr. Jackson's Journal are:—

RUSHES.

Iuncus triglumis (Linn.)
trifidus (Linn.)
articulatus (Linn.)
squarrosus (Linn.)
bufonius (Linn.)
Luzula campestris (Willd.)
spicata (DC.)

SEDGES.

Carex dioica (Linn.)
leporina (Linn.)
rigida (Good.)
glauca (Mur;.)
vaginata (Murr.)
saxatilis (Linn.)
pallescens (Linn.)
Scirpus cæspitosus (Linn.)
pauciflorus (Linn.)
Eriophorum vaginatum (Linn.)

GRASSES.

Deschampsia cæspitosa (Beauv.)
Molinia cærulea (Moench.)
Poa pratensis (Linn.)

Also—

Allium sibiricum (Linn.)
Arctostaphylos alpina (Spreng.)
Empetrum nigrum (Linn.)
Vaccinium Vitis-Idæa (Linn.)
Vaccinium uliginosum (Linn.)

I am indebted to Professor G. S. Boulger, F.L.S., F.G.S., for confirmation of these plants.

the contrast, for until the green is gone one finds it difficult to appreciate its influence on the landscape; yet, when it is nipped by frost and turns into a dark rusty brown, the green of summer, sombre though it was, seems to the memory a beautiful colour indeed.

The tundra is in many places riddled with lemming holes, and the lemmings are perhaps the most joyous feature of the country. With the activity of rabbits they pop in and out of their holes, and keep the while a sharp lookout for the snowy owl. Contrary to the species of lemmings in other parts of the Arctic regions, it does not change its coat in the winter. I have killed lemmings in December with a perfectly brown jacket. Their enemy, the snowy owl, is a very noticeable object in this bleak country; you can easily see its white plumage two or three miles away, as it softly perches on some stone or hillock on the ground, and patiently waits for a frisky or a careless lemming. Many times have these owls, flying off in alarm at my approach, dropped an unfortunate little lemming to the ground. The Russians call the lemming the "Mus," the meaning of which is obviously "mouse," and treat it with indifference, even when it penetrates into the storehouses much as the common rat might. The lemmings make their nests in the grass, just as the common field-mouse does in England, and as late as September I found many nests with young, which were generally five to six in number. A full-grown lemming is about six inches long from the tip of the nose to the tip of the very short tail. Its rat-like head, with gray muzzle, springs from a body warmly covered with close red-brown hair, and the tail, which is about three-quarters of an inch long, is like a rat's tail, abruptly terminated, but with a covering of hair. Their sight and sense of hearing are, I feel sure, a little defective, for I have often almost stepped upon them as I walked through the short grass, and then, apparently caught by surprise, instead of running away, they throw themselves piteously upon their backs and squeal in a way which would be irresistibly comic were it not evident that the poor little wretches are beside themselves with terror.

Eastward of Habarova towards the Kara Sea the tundra attains a higher average level, and some of the more considerable ridges are looked upon by the Russians and Samoyads, dwellers in plains, as veritable mountains. As a natural consequence of this increase in the mean altitude there is less bog and marsh. These ridges are prolonged in a south-easterly direction, and finally trend almost due south, and I believe—though I am unable to discover any careful survey of this locality—unite with the Urals. Turning to the westward from the top of the ridge which rises behind Habarova, you look down over the Arctic Ocean, while twenty miles to the eastward the shore is washed by the ice-laden waters of the Kara Sea.

Three miles across the Yugorski Schar range the low outlines of Waigatz Ostroff (Island), while sixty miles to the north-west there opens the famous " Kara Gate"—by no means an open entrance to the Kara Sea.

It is unnecessary to explain, perhaps, that there is as yet no hotel at Habarova, consequently I had to find a corner in one of the already somewhat overcrowded huts. I thought myself fortunate in finding quarters in the log-hut put up by Siberiakoff some years before, seeing that it was rather better than the average dwelling of the settlement. It consisted of three rooms, thinly partitioned, and opening into each other. In the first room half a dozen Samoyads were camping, apparently visitors to the place; in the next, three Russian peasants lived and slept and had their being—all on the floor. These were my stable companions, for here I had a corner given me for my goods and myself. In the innermost room the priest, his assistant, and a Russian peasant camped down. The furniture of the room chiefly consisted of ikons and small lamps suspended in front of them burning an evil-smelling grease; some sacred pictures of the most sensational character; and one wooden "bunk" in each room. These bunks were very short, and I much preferred following the fashion set me by the other inmates and sleeping on the floor. I had a small oil stove with me, and cooked my food in the room, while the Russians cooked theirs over a wood fire. I generally breakfasted about eight, while they

A RUSSIAN "POPE."
(From a sketch by HERBERT WARD, F.R.G.S.)

had their tea; and they took their breakfast when I was thinking of lunch.

A few words as to my outfit for travelling in winter through Arctic Russia may be of help to some of my readers. For furs I had a sealskin coat, and breeches made of the young bottle-nosed seal; sealskin boots and mits. In addition to this I had a combination suit of opossum for underwear. Below the fur clothing I wore thick woollen Jaeger underclothing, which was more satisfactory in its way than the sealskin. I carried my baggage on two sledges of the long and narrow Norwegian type, a Canadian toboggan, and an English-built sledge. For travelling over snow I had two pairs of ski and Canadian snow-shoes. I had two ·303 rifles and a double-barrelled breech-loading shot gun—"an old friend"—which had seen service in many parts of the world. I carried a sextant, artificial horizon, a pocket aneroid, prismatic compass, and maximum, minimum, and ordinary mercurial thermometers. Of stores I had a considerable quantity; but I may say at once that during my five months' journey I chiefly used reindeer meat and Scotch oatmeal, and it was my experience that the two made an excellent diet. Owing to the gross carelessness of a firm of Chicago tinned meat and provision shippers in London, my tinned meats had not turned up in the *Orestes* when I went on board, and I was forced to sail without them. Consequently I only had with me a small stock of tinned tongues; no butter, no cheese, no bacon, and no vegetables of any kind. However,

I found in some excellent tea a comfort and a standby, and I strongly recommend any following in my steps to be thoroughly well supplied with this useful and negotiable article. Of cocoa, too, I had a good stock; concentrated Bovril was also found very useful. A small quantity of very fine whisky came in handily for entertainment purposes. But I award the palm to oatmeal among the stores I brought from England; and I should certainly praise the reindeer meat, which I ate in a raw state when circumstances made cooking inconvenient, and with that relish which hunger most happily provides. The best parts of the reindeer—and the reindeer should be young if possible—are the steaks and the fry, and some good cuts may be had from the saddle. It must be remembered that I was alone, and that after travelling for sixteen or twenty hours, making detours across rough country for game, taking observations and recording heights and hollows, winds and temperatures, one naturally felt very unwilling to unpack more goods than were necessary, and bend and twist cords and coverings which had frozen as hard as metal. Consequently the temptation to do with the least one could was not to be ignored, and many a good and wholesome meal I made which simply consisted of a steak of reindeer, half warmed over a blubber fire, a pannikin of oatmeal and a pint of tea. Yet, as I sat on the side of the sledge, with my back to the howling wind which sweeps unbroken across these vast plains, and my eye on a thermometer that often indicated some fifty or sixty degrees of frost, I can honestly say that I was enjoying myself, and felt no irresistible longing for the flesh-pots of England. So thin a veneer is civilisation that man can return to his primitive state of existence without suffering serious inconvenience or requiring any prolonged period of preparation.

NOTE.—The spelling adopted for *Habarova*, the Samoyad village on the Yugorski Schar, may be dealt with here. The initial letters of this name are *Kh*, and have often been transliterated into English as *Ch*, thus leading to the absurd pronunciation of Chabarova (*ch* as in *church*), and even Shabarova. The *Kh* is not peculiar to Russian, but is the well-known Oriental guttural, and thus possesses an interest which would have led to its retention here, if such retention had not been thought misleading. For, as a matter of fact, the *K* is much the weaker of the two letters; it is never sounded fully; and more often than not it becomes mute. When travelling through Northern Russia, the writer particularly noticed that the initial *K* was often slurred; that the common word *khorosho* (= good) was far more usually pronounced as if the *h* were the first letter; and that even the name "Arkhangelsk" was frequently sounded as "Arhangelsk." These considerations, then, have induced the Editor to spell the name *Habarova*, as most nearly indicating to the English reader the ordinary pronunciation of the name.

CHAPTER II

WAIGATZ

A Samoyad bargain—Vasili and his babba—Their costume—Across the Schar—Our choom—The Samoyad no beggar—On the march—Waigatz scenery—The Samoyad preference for raw flesh—A sacrificial pile—" Niet dobbera choom "—Dolga Bay—Voronoff Noss—Silk tent a failure—Bolvanski Noss—A Samoyad feast—The eastern slope of Waigatz—Out on the Kara Sea—The Waigatz hills—Ice movements round Waigatz.

AT last, having got everything ready, I was able on 6th September to start for my journey through Waigatz. Knowing only a few words of the Samoyad language, and not many more of Russian, I had had the greatest difficulty—first, in making the Samoyads understand what I wanted them to help me to do, and next, in inducing them to accompany me at all. The Yalmal Peninsula, on which my mind had been set, had very soon become impossible. The Samoyads would have nothing to do with it. They would say to me that there were " very bad men there "—repeating it again and again with force and assurance, and neither roubles nor much tea could alter this opinion.

Then I tried the Poderata River which runs into the Muddy Gulf—as I translate Multnia Guba—about 700 miles east of Habarova. This again drew blank : "too far" was one plea ; "too bad" was another ; and "no food for reindeer" was the emphatic third. It was evident that advance in the direction of Yalmal was to be *nil*. So, failing this, I next tried to carry out my alternative plan—a visit to the interior of the southern island of Novaia Zemlia. Here again the prudent Samoyad was to checkmate me. *Bolshoi sneark*—" much snow "—and *bolshaia pagoda*—" much bad weather"—were the arguments brought against this, and when I got acquainted with their cranky lodkas, with only a few inches of freeboard, I was obliged to see the force of the arguments, especially as the thirty miles between Waigatz and the south island of Novaia Zemlia are much hampered with ice.

Finally I decided on exploring Waigatz Island,[1]

---

[1] The name of Waigats or Vaigatz has been variously explained. MM. R. G. Bennet and J. G. van Wijk have generally found the meaning in their language by taking *waaien*, to blow, and *gat*, a strait : "a windy passage or strait." The Dutch have certainly applied the name in this sense to other places (*cf.* Waaigat, in Baffin's Bay, and another in Spitzbergen). Again, a German source gives the root as *weihen*, and makes the name equivalent to "holy straits," alluding, of course, to the sacrificial piles, etc., on the southern part of the island. Mr. J. R. Forster considers the Russians the sponsors, and says that "Barents found afterwards in Nova Zembla some carved images on a headland near the straits, in consequence of which he called it *Afgoeden-hock*, the 'Cape of Idols.' Now, in the Sclavonian tongue, *wajat* means 'to carve,' 'to make an image.'

the interior of which had never been mapped, as far as I could learn, though visited by both Russians and Samoyads annually. Even for this work I found it difficult to get companions, but at last a Samoyad and his babba agreed to accompany me in return for "a consideration." And when, after much barter, we made the bargain, we shook hands over it before the Russian "pope," who clasped and then separated our hands, and our compact straightway became inviolable. The Samoyad, whose name was Vasili, was about forty years of age. In height he stood five feet; he was stifily built, but spare of flesh; very strong for his size; swarthy of skin—almost copper-coloured—with a faint patch of red on his high cheekbones, which were almost bare of beard. He had, however, a thin moustache, and a straggling, weak beard on his chin, about four inches in length. His babba was a young

Wajati-Noss would, therefore, be the 'Carved' or 'Image Cape'; and this seems to me to be the true origin of the *Waigats*, which properly should be called *Wajatelstwoi Proliw*, 'the Image Straits.' " Against this argument, Lütke shows that the Dutch did not call the place Waigat but Waigatz, or Weygats; that they changed the Waigatsch of the Russians, substituting *tz* for *tsch*; and that Burrough refers to the name nearly forty years before the Dutch ever went there. Further, the Russian name for the cape in question has always been *Bolwanskyi Muis*, from bolwán, an image of a rude kind. The same writer refers to Witsen, who said that the island received its name from a man named Ivan Waigatsch; and this derivation Dr. Beke, in his edition of *Barents' Voyages* for the Hakluyt Society, seems to confirm. In all probability the original sound of the name might be represented by *Weygats* or *Vaigats*.

woman—not more than twenty years old—and for a
Samoyad distinctly good-looking. She stood four feet
nine inches in height, was built on a sturdy plan, and
her outlines were round and plump. Their conjugal
relations appeared to be of the best; and as she did
as much work as her husband, she seemed to make
him an excellent partner. Although she did not row
the *lodka*—though, bearing in mind the Eskimo custom,
I should mention that Samoyad women frequently do
row the boats—she rounded up the reindeer, harnessed
them, put up the choom, and was very particular in
her care of her husband's skin boots—turning them
inside out, hanging them up to dry, and putting grass
into them in the morning with a constant devotion.
Vasili wore his deerskin *militza* and cap, and when
not wearing sealskin *pimmies* or knee-boots of deer-
skin, used the ordinary Russian sea-boot. His wife
wore similar boots, and, alike with her husband, clothed
her limbs with trousers of a very inferior cloth. Her
coat was of deerskin, which she wrapped across the
breast, and confined at the waist with a strap. It was
highly decorated with "insertion" work, made of long
narrow strips—about half an inch in width—of different shades of reindeer skin and coloured cloth. For
example, there were more than half a dozen strips
placed lengthways on each shoulder; a similar number
were inserted diagonally on the sleeve; while round
the foot of the robe ran a dogskin border. Over her

head she buttoned a tight-fitting skin cap, which formed a sort of travelling cap, as the ordinary head-gear of the Samoyad woman is a highly decorated and voluminous affair with metal ornaments. The regulation pig-tail, however, was much in evidence, with black thread twisted into it, and the usual perforated brass discs attached.

The distance from Habarova to the point where we landed was about six miles, but the strong current which runs through the Yugorski Schar, and the rough sea we met with on the day we crossed, made the journey longer than I had anticipated. We landed at the head of the bay which opens east of the south-west point of the island, and then we dined after our respective fashions: the Samoyads gorging on the raw flesh of the reindeer, finishing up with slices of the raw gullet—a great delicacy of theirs—and I contenting myself with fried steaks of the same useful animal.

Vasili then went off in search of some reindeer which he had been pasturing on the island during the summer—the chief reason, I believe, for his accompanying me—but as night fell before he returned, we camped at the landing-place. Our shelter was the Samoyad's choom (*miahkan*), an erection not unlike in its outline the familiar gipsy tent, the essential difference lying in the material. Some twenty odd fir poles, sharpened at each end, and black with smoke and age, were driven into the ground, and their tops propped and lashed together. Then over these were tied large and roughly triangular pieces of birch bark, reaching from near the top of the poles to the ground, and secured at the latter by lumps of earth and any old stones that might be at hand. The furniture of the choom was then arranged. It consisted of a large flat stone, obtained in the vicinity of the camp, and placed in the centre. On this the small wood fire was made, and over it were to hang the kettle and pot which formed our cooking outfit. They were hung on a wooden hook, itself suspended from two stout sticks, which were fixed across the choom and lashed at their ends to the choom poles. Above was the opening which had been made by simply leaving a space of two feet or thirty inches between the tops of the choom poles and the upper edges of the bark sides.[1] The rest of the furniture began and ended with half a

[1] A well-made Samoyad choom is really a very fine tent. Its one great drawback is the weight which the twenty odd poles (perhaps at least twenty feet long) inevitably add to it. But a clean summer choom, made of bright amber sheets of finely prepared birch bark, softened by being boiled, each seamed and sewn with sinew thread, with the floor soft with thick dry moss, is a very good home indeed for a nomad. As Mr. Jackson has noted, the winter choom is covered with reindeer skin, which, now that the Samoyads trade the skins with the Russians, is apt perhaps to be rather old, and of a patchwork pattern. Yet with this covering, well caulked with moss, and the inside again covered with furs, it forms so excellent a winter home that only its weight remains to disqualify it for use on an Arctic expedition.

dozen deer skins, which served as beds, blankets, carpets, sofas, and chairs for us all. But there was one article, not strictly furniture, which I must not forget — it was the treasure-chest of the Samoyads. Made of pine, and measuring about two feet in length, a foot in width, and nine inches in height, it contained that which the soul of the Samoyad most covets and admires — three or four china cups and saucers. In their appreciation of china, they resemble and indeed imitate the Russians, from whom also they obtain their use and affection for tea. But in addition to the china there were sundry wisps of paper, in which the curious might discover small quantities of sugar, tea, and broken pieces of ship's biscuit. In this chest, too, were carefully laid away the pieces of chocolate and a red cotton handkerchief which I had given them.

I may say here that this handkerchief, which I had been using as a gun-cleaner, was the only thing that any Samoyad ever asked me for, with the single exception of liquor. This rather singular trait I can only ascribe to the fact that the Russians they encounter are so poor that they cannot — and they certainly do not — make presents. Vasili's babba asked me for this wretched little piece of cotton in a most deprecating and deferential way, and her thanks and joy on receiving it were almost unbounded.[1]

---

[1] With reference to this trait, Castrén tells the following story, which at least shows that the Samoyad is not deficient in ingenuity.

Vasili returned from his search soon after dark, but without his reindeer. He was apparently not much put out nor surprised, but he confided to me that his deer were *niet dobbera olen,* which bit of bad Russian when interpreted would mean "not good reindeer." So, early on the next morning—there had been eleven degrees of frost in the night—after a breakfast similar to our dinner of the night before, he again started on his search, and I went out with my gun to walk over the tundra to the south-west point of Waigatz. Snow was scudding from the north-east, and the route might be described as boggy, nobbly, and sousy. The tundra rolled away to the point, the

---

"Give me another cup of vodka," pleaded a Samoyad, vulnerable at any rate on this point.

"What good have you done me that I should give you vodka?" replied Castrén.

"You are travelling with my reindeer."

"But have I not paid you for them?"

"Yes, but I have given you good reindeer."

"But," retorted Castrén, "your son drives them badly."

"Then don't give *him* any vodka," triumphantly replied the Samoyad.

Most travellers agree with Mr. Jackson on the absence of begging among the Samoyads. Rae, in his *Land of the North Wind,* bears testimony to this, and tells an anecdote in which we find the exception recorded (p. 286): "There was a little Samoyad boy standing among a number of his playfellows and elders. As I took a handful of bright silver out of my pocket, the little fellow held out his hand. I drew myself up and looked at him: 'I thought a Samoyad never *begged,*' I said. He hung his head, and looked sadly afflicted when I gave his companions each a small coin. I gave him one, however, by and by."

ridges sometimes reaching a height of thirty feet above the intervening troughs. Along the lowest level of the troughs shallow pools and lakes were frequent, and around their margins there grew coarse yellowish grass, reaching sometimes to two feet in height. The summits of the ridges were, on the contrary, almost bare of vegetation, the deer having nibbled both grass and moss to their roots. Down in the troughs the soil was bluish mud, mixed up a good deal with saturated, decomposing vegetation, and awash with stagnant water, while on the ridges there outcropped the long friable sheets of limestone shale which I found all over the southern part of the island, and on the tundra around Habarova. But it must not be supposed that these ridges were stone dry, for the melting snow had left them in a more or less oozy condition, and it was only by comparison that they could be considered desirable camping-ground.

With the exception of a few lemmings and some snowy owls which I saw in the distance — but they proved too wild to get within gunshot — there was little game, and my bag that day only amounted to a couple of black duck. My gun was an ordinary cylinder breechloader, and I used number two shot with three and a quarter drachms of black powder. This I found useful for all sorts of game on Waigatz, though for the smaller birds number five and six shot was used.

The south-west point, for which I had been

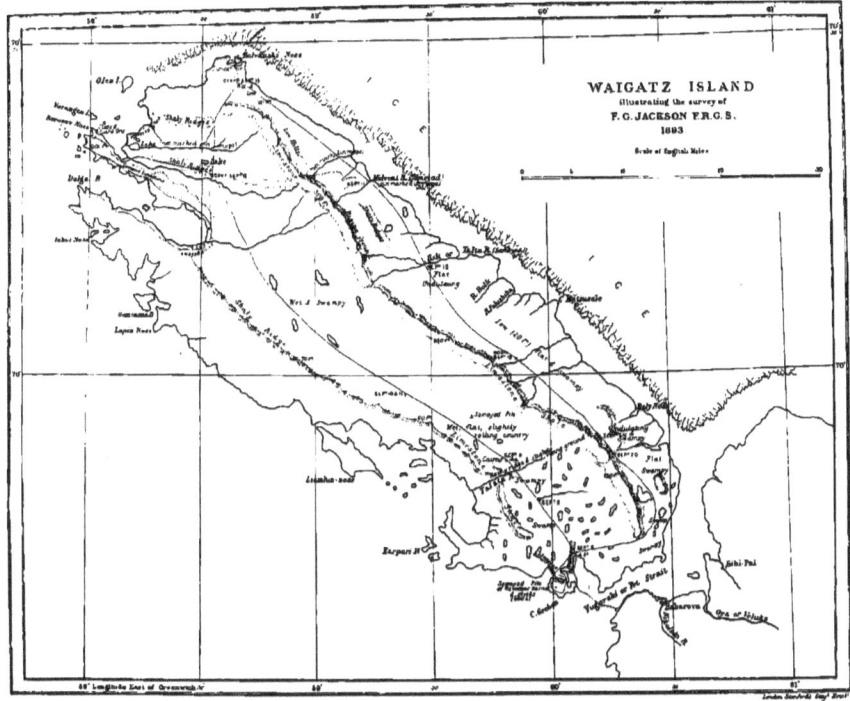

making, proved to be a blunt-ended promontory composed of hard, shaly limestone with many vertical and horizontal veins of calcite running through it, and presenting no special feature of interest. Retracing my steps to our camp, I found Vasili had returned with the deer, so after a hurried lunch we harnessed up and started on our journey north. After a march somewhat impeded by a succession of snow squalls, we camped that night at a choom belonging to a couple of Samoyads whom we found in possession, and on the following morning started off with a strong north-westerly gale in our faces.

By way of giving me a zest for breakfast, Vasili carefully examined his shirt, and proceeded to show me how expert he could be in the destruction of minute animal life; and although there was plenty of boiled meat in the pot, he and his wife made an ample breakfast on raw meat, from which I inferred that the Samoyads will on occasion prefer raw to cooked meat. Of the personal filth of the Samoyads it is difficult to speak; and when at nightfall three Samoyad strangers arrived in a casual sort of way, making in our choom (about nine feet in diameter) a group of five of the dirtiest people one could well imagine, my senses were kept on the alert. Knowing what a zoological garden they carried about, I took—somewhat of a naturalist though I am—very particular care to avoid actual contact with them.

On the 9th of September we sledged for about eight miles through water varying in depth from a couple to eighteen inches, until we reached the Talata River, where the moisture drained off the land. The Talata River at this point—near its head—was rapid, and ran a narrow course through a wide, shallow, rocky

THE SACRIFICIAL PILE ON THE SOUTH-WEST POINT OF WAIGATZ.

bed. Close to it I shot a *pzaitch*, the Samoyad name for all foxes except the brown fox. This pzaitch had its summer coat, which is grayish with a distinct dark cross on its back, from which it gets its name of the Cross Fox. A hawk, three small linnets, and a golden plover completed my bag. Passing the next day through low, undulating country, and having on the west a stony ridge—with dolomite in some quantity —some 170 feet high, we arrived on the 10th at a sacrificial pile of the Samoyads. It consisted of a few posts stuck in the ground, around which a pile of reindeer horns and driftwood had been made. On the top of one of the posts a bear's skull was placed, and several were rudely cut into something resembling the features of the human face. We wanted wood badly, but Vasili would not touch any of that on the pile, for reasons religious of course. Yet, like the rest of the Samoyads, he was nominally a Christian.[1]

On the morning of the 11th I awoke in a very uncomfortable condition, a furious gale having driven the rain right through the choom and almost washed us out. Vasili went to look for his reindeer, but, as in Australia with the cattle, the wet night had made them restless, and he returned about noon after a luckless search. The weather was too bad for marching, so I skinned and boiled a hawk shot the day before, and found it excellent eating. My day's walk —in a circle of which the choom was the centre—

---

[1] It may here be pointed out that until recently the Lapps made the same piles, and set up rude stocks for gods, and fenced them about with reindeer horns. I believe that it was under this form that the Lapps honoured Jumala and other persons they held divine; and, by the way, with much the same ceremonial. But then the Lapps are merely the western members of the great Finnic group, and we may reasonably suspect that they did yesterday what the Samoyads do to-day. Nordenskiöld may be consulted for a note on the sacrificial piles of the Samoyads (*Voyage of the Vega*, chap. ii.)

showed that the last winter's snow still lay in the hollows (we were in latitude 70 N.) and that the tundra character of the island was still maintained. At night Vasili returned with his deer, and I finished a cold, foggy, wet day, by turning into a sleeping bag still soaking from the rain. In the night the temperature fell, and at daylight I found myself covered with about two inches of snow. In the face of this Vasili could not defend the virtues of his choom, and acknowledged that it was a *niet dobbera choom* ("not good choom").

On this day the snow—six inches deep—made our going rapid, although the cold north-westerly wind chilled one through. This perhaps was not surprising, as I had left overcoat and furs at Habarova. At 2 P.M. we struck the head of Dolga Bay, and pushing on towards the coast camped at Voronoff Noss (70° 15′ 22″ N. lat.) Ascending this rocky promontory, and ascertaining by aneroid that it was 300 feet high, I looked over the famous Kara Straits. As far as one could see there was little ice, and that little was of a broken, brashy character. The next day, after an exploration of the Noss, during which I shot a large gray burgomaster gull—a young one—and some snipe, and rowed in my canvas boat round several of the islets lying off the Noss, I loaded a Norwegian sledge and pulled it over the snow towards the mouth of the gulf, passing Samoyad piles and heaps of driftwood, large quantities of which were on the shore, and finding that I could pull 200 lbs. without feeling fatigued. Round Dolga Bay (Long Bay) there is every evidence of the present shore line being of compara-

CAMPING IN THE NORTH OF WAIGATZ.

tively recent existence. A raised beach about twelve feet above the present level runs persistently along the cliffs. The Noss itself is composed of slate and hard grit, while the low range running north and south in its vicinity was formed of compact limestone.

The next day we rested, the reindeer being galled a little. The night was cold, and the thermometer showed 7 above zero. My leather boots were frozen nearly as hard as iron, and it took a good hour to struggle into them. I went out with a sledge, however (myself in the traces), on an exploratory trip, and shot a large bladder-nosed seal in its second year's coat (gray) and some snipe and gulls. It was on this occasion that I came across the most important stream I met with on Waigatz; but, curiously enough, it is not marked on any published map. It rises to the south-east of Voronoff Noss, in the chain of low hills which form the dividing range of Waigatz, and follows a north-westerly course for about five miles. At this point it opens out into a lake about 400 yards across, then suddenly narrows and runs swiftly into the sea.

At night I camped alone in a silk tent which I had taken as an experiment, but a strong gale from the south-east with driving snow soon brought the tent flat upon me, and in the middle of the night I had to turn out in my pyjamas and put it up again. This was a very unpleasant job, and not a little cold. The silk, which was of special manufacture for the purpose, and guaranteed by its maker to be waterproof, was of little avail against either snow or hard rain, and when it became saturated up to a certain point, let the water through nearly as readily as a silk handkerchief. The morning had been bright and frosty, and the sudden change produced by the shifting of the wind from the north-west to the south-east had brought a tempestuous and very cold night. The next morning the weather became even worse, and I returned to the choom to find things still more unpleasant. Vasili and his babba wanted to return at once to Habarova, but I declined in very distinct terms, and as it looked like clearing up, we rounded up the reindeer. Before starting I erected a cairn on the highest point of Voronoff Noss. The promise of finer weather, however, was not confirmed, and we sledged to Bolvanski Noss in the teeth of thick, driving snow, through flat, swampy country with just a few stony ridges to give us some bumps to relieve the monotony of the swishing of the sloshy ground.

On the 16th I sledged down to the extremity of the Noss, which was about two and a half miles from camp, and found it to be a wide leaf-shaped cape of limestone, about 300 yards across, approached by a narrow neck of land hardly forty yards wide. The shape is incorrectly drawn on our Admiralty charts, and I made the latitude 70° 27′ 30″ N. It offers a strong contrast to Voronoff Noss, being only about twelve feet above high water.[1] The dark rocks of

---

[1] The earliest mention we have of this cape is that of Burrough (1556), and although some have thought that he was referring to the south-eastern rather than the north-eastern point of Waigatz, his

which it consisted are limestone. From the Noss I could see nothing approaching the dignity of a hill—only low ridges, and still lower stretches of swamp, limestone being the prevailing rock. Looking seaward, there was a great deal of pack-ice coming in from the Kara Sea—stretching east from Olen Island, which here lies off the coast.

When I returned in the afternoon to the choom in a driving storm of sleet, I found Vasili and his wife in great fettle. He had killed a deer in the morning, and they had been indulging in one of their big feeds. In fact, as I sledged up to the choom he and his wife were only just concluding a three hours' feast. Squatting on skins, they had a rough piece of plank in front of them, on which lay the stomach of the reindeer. This was almost full of blood drained from the deer—in fact, it formed their soup tureen. They

description of the position of the place would certainly point to Bolvanski Noss. "We weyed and went roome with another island, which was five leagues east-north-east from us; and there I met againe with Loshak, and went on shore with him, and hee brought me to a heap of the Samoeds idols, which were in number aboue 300, the worst and the most unartificiall worke that ever I saw. The eyes and mouthes of sundrie of them were bloodie; they had the shape of men, women, and children, very grosly wrought; and that which they had made for other parts was also sprinkled with blood. Some of their idols were an olde sticke, with two or three notches made with a knife in it. I saw much of the footing of the sayd Samoeds, and of the sleds that they ride in." Mr. Jackson notes in his Journal the bolvan or god on this noss—a pole, twelve feet high, set upright in the ground, and steadied by a small heap of stones.

each had a hind leg, on which some of the hide still remained, and cutting off chunks of the meat were dipping them in the crimson soup and then greedily swallowing the *bonne bouche*. As a fitting back-

BOLVANSKI NOSS.
Showing the Bolvan or "God" (12 ft. high).

ground to the picture, pieces of the carcase, still dripping with blood, hung all round the interior of the choom. On the ground were small, dark pools of blood, and my sleeping-bag, though as well out of the way as the size of the interior would allow, was well sprinkled with the same natural dye. As they sat there grinning a welcome to me, with their cheeks and brows all smeared with gore, they looked for all the world like the blood-eating ghouls of one's childish fancy. At any rate I am afraid it was a welcome that touched no vibrating chord in my heart. But man is a strange being, and before long I could look on these often repeated gorges without feeling the suspicion of a twinge.

Travelling down the east coast we came, on the 17th, to an excellent camping spot at the mouth of the Midveat Retchka (River), a river, by the way, which is not indicated in the maps. Our camp was protected on all sides but that on the north-east; the snow had been blown off the ground by the wind; and the thick-growing moss was dry and firm. In common with the other streams of Waigatz, the deeply cut rocky bed of the Midveat was very much wider than the volume of the stream in summer, although there were indications to prove that during May and June the melting of the snow would swell the stream until it fairly well filled its course. The height of the limestone rock-walls on each side is about forty feet, and the gorge they form is precipitous. But just before the river falls into the sea—in fact where we camped—this gorge suddenly ceases and gives way on either hand to low terraced banks through which the stream cuts its way into the sea. While the vegetation on the higher land is sparse and tundra-like in character, the river terrace is covered with a rich spongy moss. This is not in the least like reindeer moss, which is grayish-green in colour and grows in tufts, but of a dark brownish-green, thickly and widely spread, and higher and more luxuriant. A belt of regelated snow lay round the banks at this point, beginning at a height of three feet above the then level of the stream, and indicating pretty plainly the level of the water in the flood of early summer.

In the evening, as it was getting dark, I pulled out into the Kara Sea in the little canvas boat I carried on my sledge, and got as far as the edge of the ice, where I hoped to bag some of the numerous duck to be seen there. But the deepening twilight was against me, and I was only able to secure one fine bird. Trying to follow up the others, I found that the ice was so brashy and the foothold so insecure that little good was likely to result, so I reluctantly turned the seven-foot skiff toward shore. It was a calm and a beautiful evening: the sea all round me lay silent and quiet; the Kara Sea—the great Ice Cellar as it has been called—was the very embodiment of loneliness and desolation; not a single sound fell upon my ears—not even the distant note of a calling gull; Vasili and his babba, and the dilapidated choom which formed our common home, were hidden by the darkness, and their reindeer had strayed away beyond the low hills; a sudden sense of my solitariness fell swiftly upon me, and I realised for one short moment how much I should have gained had I had a companion to whom I could have spoken and have been understood. But the next second I had grasped my sculls, and with the swish of the water about the bows of the skiff called myself back from what threatened to become an ineffectual reverie.

During the next four days we travelled in a south-westerly direction, keeping near the eastern coast of the island. The country was almost uniformly swampy and undulating, and we seldom found a dry camping-place. Until the 20th we met with a succession of low ridges and wide intervening swamps; but on the afternoon of that day an easterly spur of the main range, which proved to be 200 feet at the highest part, was reached. After travelling for about half an hour in a south-westerly direction we crossed the main range itself. At no point in the whole of the range did I find an altitude exceeding 300 feet, and the greater part of it, of course, is much lower. The northern half has a greater average elevation than the southern; I should place the average of the former at 200, and the latter at 150 feet. Snowstorms and cold winds followed us until we got quite close to the Yugorski Schar, when the weather became suddenly mild. The change was all the more marked as a few miles further north we had crossed a stream which was frozen over, and the snow which had been some eight inches in depth was now rarely deeper than an inch. I may notice, in passing, that the name of one of the rivers was *Usk*—a strange example of the persistence with which this name (meaning "water") clings to rivers in many parts of the world.

On arriving at the south-west point (our original landing-place) after a complete detour of the island, I went to visit a Norwegian derelict sloop, and by a piece of good luck came across an ancient Samoyad burying-place, the description of which I will leave to my chapter on the Samoyad and all his ways. I merely mention this now to show how easy it would be for a traveller to pass through the Samoyad country with natives, and yet miss some of the most interesting of its features. Any one who follows in my steps would do well to have a thorough understanding with the natives on this matter, and I would suggest that a small reward might be profitably offered for everything of interest to which they might bring one.

With regard to the ice movements around Waigatz, I may say that the Kara or Waigatz Straits are more or less open during the winter; and this affects the climate so noticeably that a small number of Samoyads —about twenty—winter on Bolvanski Noss in preference to Habarova, where the Yugorski Schar is frozen. The object of their so wintering is to enable them to be on the spot in the early spring for their pursuit of the bear and seal. If the wind is from the south-west or south, such ice as there is leaves the shores of the northern end of Waigatz, and may be found on the Novaia Zemlia shore; but if the wind is

SAMOYAD BURIAL PLACE.
Showing the broken Sledges and Harrays (Driving Poles).

from a northerly quarter, you find the ice packed up against Waigatz. Thus it is obvious that the Waigatz Straits are not available for sledges at any time of the year, while, on the other hand, you can sledge across the Yugorski Schar during January, February, March, April, and May. Ice begins to form on the sea between Habarova and Waigatz as early as October; and on the 10th of that month there was thin ice for some distance from shore, and the rivers were frozen to their mouths. On Waigatz the snow is very deep, except on the ridges and hills, which are swept bare by the gales which accompany the snow. Thus the reindeer of the Samoyads are able to get at their food all the winter through.

CHAPTER III

AMONG THE SAMOYADS

Learning the Samoyad speech—Dumb show—Character of the Samoyads—Their physical appearance—Average height—Sociability—Kindness—A Samoyad "Aunt Sally"—The man's costume: militza, soveck, lieupthieu, and pimmies—The woman's dress: its ornamentation—Her cap—Her pigtails—Trinkets and charms—The Samoyad "Ski"—The reindeer—Its food—Its fitness for Arctic exploration and the difficulty—The reindeer's endurance—The Samoyad use of deer flesh, and mode of eating—Making bread—The dogs of the Samoyads—The lasso—The weapons and tools of the modern Samoyad—The choom—The Holy Island of the Samoyad—A burial place—The fashionable religion—Half and half—The old faith—"Yon-pa-ha-pai"—Snuff-taking—The calculating stick—Money and barter—The common diseases—The Samoyad in brief.

On my return to Habarova on 21st September I set to work to study the Samoyad and all his ways. The insight into this peculiar people, which the journey round Waigatz had given me, made me keenly desire to see more of their manners and customs, to understand their code of morality, and something, at any rate, of the motives by which they were swayed. Unfortunately I had at the outset little knowledge of the

Samoyad speech :[1] I only knew a few Russian words, which became a medium for acquiring a Samoyad vocabulary. Gradually, however, I was able to increase

[1] The spelling of the name Samoyad is very various. Samuter and Samoit are archaic, and Samoed has a respectable antiquity of more than 300 years. Samoied, Samoyed, Samoyade, and Samoyede persist to this day, and the last is perhaps the most generally accepted form. Mr. Jackson left England, adhering to this spelling and its pronunciation, *i.e.* of the first *e* as the English *a*, and the second *e* mute (the combination *ede* being sounded as *ade* in *wade*), but he told me on his return that he could not confirm the pronunciation by his experience. He had numerous opportunities, of course, of ascertaining how the people themselves pronounced it, and it seems that they not only did not sound the first *e* in the way generally believed but rather in a manner which is almost new to us. He states that the word is pronounced as Sam-o-yad, and so quickly that the *o* is much slurred, and the phonetic form might even be Sammyad. I have therefore adhered to his view throughout this book, although I have nowhere, in my notes, ventured to alter the spelling adopted by the writers quoted.

The idea that the name of the Samoyad means self-eater is of long standing, and we find a curious instance of it in the contemporary account of Frobisher's *Third Voyage,* by Captain George Best of the *Anne Francis.* He is referring to the Eskimo : "These people I judge to be a kind of *Tartar,* or rather a kind of *Samoed,* of the same sort and condition of life that the *Samoeds* be to the north-eastwards beyond *Muscovy,* who are called *Samoeds,* which is as much to say in the *Muscovy* tongue as 'eaters of themselves'; and so the Russians, their borderers, do name them. And by late conference with a friend of mine, with whom I did sometime travel in the ports of *Muscovy,* who hath great experience of those *Samoeds* and people of the north-east, I find that in all their manner of living, those people of the north-east and these of the north-west are like." The text is that of Hakluyt, and the modernisation Mr. Edward John Payne's (*Voyages of the Elizabethan Seamen to America,* p. 185).

It was the Finlander Castrén who gave the name of Ural-Altaic to that family of the great Mongolian race which dwells, not in

my knowledge of Russian with the help of the few Russian peasant-traders at Habarova, and with their aid to add to my stock of Samoyad, as Russian is fairly

Central, but in Northern Asia; in the lower basins, as opposed to the upper courses of the Siberian rivers; in the wide-reaching swamps of the Arctic Tundras rather than on the high and dry steppes beloved of the true Mongolian. But it may be pointed out, as M. Lefèvre has emphasised in his *Race and Language*, that the term Ural-Altaic describes neither the present geographical limits nor the continuous distribution of the race, but, on the contrary, merely the area of its primitive occupation. And although this term includes five branches, the Tungus, the true Mongols, the Tartars, Finns, and Samoyads, it is more correct to place the Samoyads in the section of the Finns, and so reduce the divisions of the Ural-Altaic family to four in number. But it will be well to remember that Dr. Brinton, followed by other ethnologists, has called all those races north of the Altai Mountains and the Caspian Sea with a discontinuous distribution from the Atlantic to the Pacific Ocean, the Sibiric, as opposed to the Sinitic branch of the Mongolian race. He rightly places the Samoyads with the Finns, but he has added a so-called "Arctic" group in which we find the Chukchis and Kamschatkans, and a sixth division devoted to the Ainus, Japanese, and Koreans.[1] I think we should protest against the application of the word "Arctic" to a mere moiety of those races who dwell within the Arctic Circle and in areas and under conditions practically uniform in their character and influence.

On the present occasion, however, I am only concerned with the Finnic Group, and, to speak more particularly, with but one branch of that group—the Samoyads. We may take it, I suppose, as generally conceded that the evidence of Tacitus to the existence of the Finns in Northern Europe may be safely received, and this would at once give us for the westward migration of the race a minimum antiquity of more than 2000 years. They came from the upper waters of the Siberian rivers, and anthropologists, following Castrén, place their primitive home in the highlands of the Saiansk

---

[1] *Races and Peoples* [New York, 1890], pp. 197, 214.

well understood by nearly all these people. Naturally
I made the most absurd mistakes at first—as every
traveller has done again and again—but owing to

range, which lies west of Lake Baikal and immediately east of the
head waters of the river Yenisei.¹ Our knowledge of the philology
of the Finnic Group as a whole is in a state of accretion, and there
are gaps, frequent and wide, which the anthropologist might well
endeavour to fill; yet, by means of its language, the greatest
authority on the matter has traced the Finn to the Saiansk range.²
For example, in the Yenisei basin you have Oja, Yoga, Kolba,
names of waters, and in both modern Finnish and Lapp they recur
bearing the interpretation of brook, water, and fishing water.³
Again, the upper course of the Yenisei is called Kem, and in that
form, and in those of Kemi and Kymi, we meet with the names of
rivers in the district of the now Europeanised Finn.

Further, we find in Lapland even to this day a tradition of their
westward migration, and, curiously, in one locality we find the Lapps
calling themselves by the very name by which the Finns are still
known among themselves and the Samoyad is only known to
civilisation. And again, the southern Samoyad, separated from his
northern kinsfolk by the Tungus on the middle course of the
Yenisei and the Ugrians on that of the Ob, still clings, though as a
miserable remnant, to his highland home between Lake Ubsa, in
Chinese territory, and the south-west point of Lake Baikal, in the
Russian Empire.

Common to the whole Finnic Group we find those characteristics
which, as Professor Keane has shown us, are "fundamentally and
typically Mongolic."⁴ We find, in particular, the yellow or yellowish-

---

[1] Peschel, *The Races of Man and their Geographical Distribution* [London, 1876], p. 387.

[2] Castrén.

[3] The agglutinative and polysyllabic languages of the Finns and Samoyads are of all the Finnic Group most nearly related. The flexion, together with the foregoing strongly developed characteristics, remove them even from the agglutinative and polysyllabic tongue of the Tungro or Tartars. The verbal affinities between the Finn and Samoyad are very close.

[4] *Journal of the Anthropological Institute*, vol. xv. p. 218.

my sojourn and subsequent prolonged journey to the Pechora, in company with a Russian and several Samoyads, I gradually corrected these, and added new

brown hue of the skin, the stiff, black, cylindrical hair; the absence or scantiness of beard; the prominence of cheek-bone and flatness of nose; the lowness and breadth of skull; the obliquity of the eyes. The further west we go, the more mixed we find the race become; or, at any rate, the more dissimilar are the elements of infusion. So it happens that while the Samoyad of the Tundra, east of the Pechora and Urals, may be to some extent composed of other elements, which are, after all, at least Mongolian, the Finn and the Lapp, and even the wretched specimens of Samoyads met with west of the Pechora, are largely impregnated with Teutonic and Slavonic blood. Thus the eastern branches of the Finnic Group retain almost without exception the broad heads and other Mongolian characteristics, while the western branches frequently and in certain localities generally exhibit the long heads, fair skins, light hair, and eyes of Gothic type.

I now pass to the geographical distribution of that sub-division of the Finnic Group which is occupied by the Samoyad, and I may mention at once that the Samoyad race itself is divisible into two branches—the Southern Samoyads or Soiots, and the Northern Samoyads or Hasovo. The Southern Samoyads may still be found at the headwaters of the Ob and the Yenisei, in the region of Lake Ubsa, on the northern slopes of the Saian Mountains, and at the south-west extremity of Lake Baikal. Around Lake Ubsa they are called Soiots; Lake Baikal, Koibals; in the Saian range, the Kamassintzi and Karagasses. As I have said above, the remnant is small, and at the present time probably so intermixed as to have lost their tribal idiosyncrasies.

The Northern Samoyads or Hasovo are divided into two sections: the Yuraks, who may be found from Mezén to the valley of the Yenisei, although the name more properly belongs to a small tribe in the delta of this river; and the Tawgi, who inhabit the wastes between the Yenisei and the Khatanga River, east of the great northern peninsula of Asia. The Yeniseians (sometimes called Ostiaks, but improperly, and causing confusion with the Ugro-Ostiaks

and, I think, correct words and phrases. I always had a small note-book in my pocket, and nearly wore it out in the good, if self-sacrificing, service of philology.

of the Ob) who still cling to the comparatively elevated country between the Ob and the Yenisei, are not Samoyads. It is with the first division—the Yuraks—that Mr. Frederick G. Jackson lived and travelled during the five months' journey he made in 1893 and 1894.

The name of the Samoyad is frequently but erroneously stated to mean self-eater or cannibal. For a considerable period, philologists vexed themselves about its meaning; hypotheses became conclusions, and conclusions lapsed into discredit over and over again in the case of the Samoyads' name as, I suppose, in the case of almost every name in the world. First came the classicists with their Lithuanian Samogitæ;[1] then followed the Germans, intent on making capital out of "Sam," self, and "ged," eat.[2] So widespread is this belief that the generality of the Russians to this day are convinced that the Samoyads have been, if they are no longer, cannibals, and so recently as last year I could obtain no other derivation from that highly educated Russian, the Governor of Arkhangel.[3] Yet it was long since shown that the derivation must be sought in the Finn language. Throughout the various branches of that tongue, we find the root *Suomi* or *Samé*, meaning a marsh or swamp; and *lats* or *laisats*, meaning men. Finland, be it noted,

---

[1] Latham, *Native Races of the Russian Empire* [London, 1854], pp. 114, 115.

[2] Herberstein, *Rer. Muscovit. Comment.* p. 81.

[3] Compare for this and many other matters closely connected with the Samoyads, *Mémoire sur les Samoiedes* (*Hist. Gén. des Voyages*, xxiv. 66) 1762. Dismissing the theory of their having been cannibals at some former time, and the interpretation of their name in that light, the author continues: " Others pretend the word Samoye signifies, in the language of these people, *an inhabitant of the country*, and that their denomination is deduced therefrom. This origin would appear sufficiently natural, if the supposition which is the base of it was not destitute of proof. But as in their language there is no word to be found resembling Samoye, and as in their dialect they give themselves the names of Minez and Chasowo, it is clear this latter etymology is purely chimerical, like many other derivations adopted without discussion.

" It will therefore be proper to seek for a word in the language of the neighbouring nations which may have affinity thereto. Now, as it is well known that the Finns formerly inhabited the greater part of the countries of the north, the

I lived for weeks at a time precisely the same existence as that of a note of interrogation; for I did nothing but ask questions. My eyes and ears were always

is a foreigner's name for that country, and its natives still call it Samé-ädnam, and themselves Samé-lat or Samé-laisat. Similar terms may be found among a small group of the Lapps, now inhabiting a region which does not justify the name. The Samo-yad then, is the Fen-man of that Arctic belt which stretches from near Mezén even to the valley of the Lena; he is the wandering lord of the Tundras of Russia and Siberia, at once the master and the victim of the dreariest swamps in the world.

The Samoyads call themselves Hasovo, which is equivalent to *men*, and Nyenech, which has the same meaning. The Ugrian Ostiaks style them Yergan-yach; the Zirians, Yarang; the Voguls, Yorran-Kam; and the Russians, and indeed all civilised countries, give the name of Samoyads. I am aware that it is more usual to pronounce the name as if it were spelt Samo-yede, but Mr. Jackson, starting with this practice, found by experience that the Yuraks of the Trans-Pechora country invariably pronounced the name as if it were Samo-yad or even "Sam-yad."

Something has been done to elicit the history of the Samoyad. Castrén, Winkler, Pallas, are names that occur to one as original authorities; and one or two of our countrymen—notably Mr. Henry Seebohm—have dealt in a general way with their results. But the fact remains that our sources of knowledge are slight, though the race was mentioned by its present name in Russian Chronicles dating as far back as 1096 A.D. There is but little that we know for certain to put against the much we can only hazard. We have ascertained the meaning of his name, and we have traced him back to the highlands of Central Asia; we have established his place and connections in the human family; and we are approaching a com-

---

word *Sooma*, which signifies in the Finnish language a marsh, may very well have served as an origin for the name Samoiede; it is also very likely the root of the name *Samalantsch*, which the Laplanders give themselves in their own tongue, and that of *Somaemayes*, which the Carelians call themselves by. In the Russian chancellary the Samoiedes are designated by the title of *Sirogneszi*, eaters of raw meat" (Pinkerton. vol. i. p. 529).

wide open, for I knew by experience in other countries that I might learn more by observation than by speech.

plete knowledge of the habits and manners of the Samoyad as he now exists—a demoralised and pitiable remnant. The inhabitant of the Arctic Tundra, he has learnt to accommodate himself in a rude fashion to his environment; but his craft as a hunter has waned since he became the owner of a gun, and his claim to be an expert artificer with the disappearance of his bows and arrows. The peasant-trader has brought him gas-pipe guns, vodka, and the diseases of his civilisation, and the Samoyads are decreasing in numbers and idiosyncrasy with such rapidity that the observant notes which Mr. Jackson made during his sojourn among them are valuable, not only for their own interest, but also as a permanent record of a race that is passing away.

The land of the Samoyads or Samoedia in the early voyages was always the country lying between the mouth of the Ob and that of the Pechora. I will quote a passage from the Commission given Pet and Jackman by the Russia Company, which was incorporated in 1559 as the "Fellowship of English Merchants for Discovery of New Trades," and further established by Act of Parliament in 1566. The date of the Commission is 1580. "And when you come to Vaigats, we would have you to get sight of the maine land of Samoeda, which is over against the south part of the same island, and from thence, with God's permission, to passe eastwards alongst the same coast, keeping it alwayes in your sight (if conveniently you may) untill you come to the mouth of the river Ob." This limit was subsequently found to be incorrect, and the peninsula of Yalmal was added. We may therefore take it that the "Samoedia" of the sixteenth, seventeenth, and eighteenth centuries extended from the valley of the Pechora to that of the Yenisei; although as we advance through the centuries, we find a growing appreciation of the fact that the Samoyads may be found, represented by one tribe and another, from the Mezén peninsula to the Lena River. Only it should be added that the further one travels west of the Pechora, the more mixed with Slavonian blood and less true to their original type the Samoyads become.

Habits and methods were enacted in dumb show before me by the good-natured Russians, and I jotted them carefully down as a painter might transfer a moving scene to his sketch-book—partly by rough sketches, and partly by descriptive notes. As an example of how I learnt some of the strange things to which the Samoyad still clings, I remember that when I was inquiring about the little image of Chaddi, which I noticed in the possession of Vasili's babba on Waigatz, the Russian peasant to whom I was speaking went through a whole series of pantomimic signs. First of all he wrapped a rag round his hand to show how the image was dressed; then he placed the rag on the floor, and lay down and drew his hand across his neck and ankles to show how the Samoyad cut off the head and feet of the reindeer, and placed them before the image to propitiate Chaddi;[1] then he went through dumb show to indicate how the Samoyad smears the mouth of

---

[1] Mr. Seebohm, on good hearsay evidence, describes another method of killing the deer to be sacrificed to the Numa of the Samoyads. A noose is thrown over the antlers and another round the hind legs of the deer, and these are then pulled in opposite directions. While the deer "is thus held at full stretch, he is stabbed in both sides with two pieces of wood (not with a knife)." In this way and only in this way can the spirit of the reindeer attain to Olympus. I may also add that William Gourdon (*Purchas, his Pilgrimes*, lib. iii. ch. xii.) relates—and he wintered at Pustozara 1614-1615—that the Samoyads were not Christians. He declared that they "worship blocks and images of the deuill, unto which they strangle tame deere."

Chaddi with blood; finally he turned over towards the image and pretended to go to sleep. I was extremely glad to get this information, as the Samoyad never performs the ceremony before strangers—not even before Russians—and always chooses night-time to carry on the service in secret. My informant obtained his knowledge from a Samoyad servant, who being much more real in his Christianity than others of his race had a fine contempt for the heathen practices which still obtain among the Samoyads.

If I were asked to describe the Samoyad people in a word, I should certainly use the word "dirty," but it would be only fair to add a second word, and that would be "honest." In support of the first I think I may say with confidence that they never wash their bodies during the term of their natural lives. Rarely, too, do they change their clothing—only, indeed, when it is worn out. As the result they simply swarm with vermin, and possess an inextinguishable stench. In the evening in the choom they used to sit round in a semicircle—I took care that they did not complete the circle—and rolling up their trousers, or turning back their shirts, would for an hour at a time set themselves to destroy the animal life which luxuriated there. The women would take the sheath knives they invariably wore, and passing them under each other's hair, so that the back lay flat against the head, would proceed with a dexterous thumbnail to annihilate a multitude of minute organisms. I was under a constant dread of contagion, but managed by unceasing watchfulness to escape from the pestilence untouched. The peculiar odour I attribute entirely to dirt, although I must not forget to say that on certain rare high days a slight ablution of the face and hands

AT HABAROVA.

was performed by filling the mouth with water, squirting it out into the hands joined together, and then carrying it to the face.

In appearance the Samoyad is decidedly Mongolian. His head is flat and wide; the shape of the face is short and broad; the forehead slopes back, sometimes at a very considerable angle; the eyebrows are slightly arched and almost pencilled; the eyelid is full and heavy, and the dark, sloe-coloured eyes, which are long and almond-shaped, are set obliquely—in some cases very much so—and far apart. The nose in profile is of the Chinese type—straight, but flat.

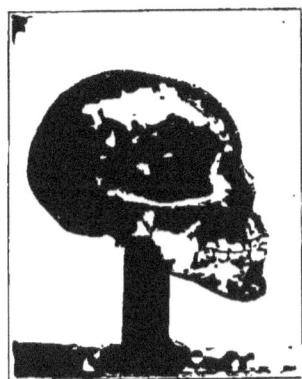 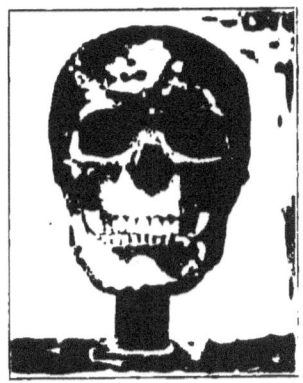

SKULLS OF SAMOYADS (Male Adults).

The region of the mouth is only moderately prominent, the lips are thick and everted, and the teeth are white.[1] The profile of the Samoyad's face is flat and the cheek-bones are very conspicuous. It is never easy to determine the exact hue of a savage's skin, and when it

[1] The white teeth of the Samoyad have been attributed to his fondness for chewing the resin of the red pine (Seebohm, *Siberia in Europe*, p. 73). This, however, would scarcely apply to those Samoyads who dwell continuously beyond the tree limit, although, of course, it would not be impossible for them to obtain the resin. Yet it is probably unlikely that they would go to the trouble of obtaining a regular supply of a luxury of this character, and I do not find any general confirmation of the statement.

wears a deep and ancient coat of dirt the task becomes difficult; but from careful inspection I came to the conclusion that the colour of the Samoyad is yellowish-brown as a rule, but reddish-brown not infrequently. In childhood and adolescence the cheeks are often ruddy, but this generally disappears at middle age. The hair is black—by which I do not mean dark brown—and straight, coarse, and rather luxuriant. The cheek is almost bare; the moustache slight, but from the chin a thin beard hangs for about three inches. I succeeded in obtaining from a Samoyad's head a lock of hair for anthropological purposes; he was not aware that I had robbed him of a tress, which was so very rich in zoological life that I consigned it to hot water immediately his back was turned.

I measured for height twenty male Samoyads, nine women, and four children of five, seven, eight, and nine years of age, with the following results:—

MALES.			FEMALES.		
5 feet	5	inches.	4 feet	9	inches.
5 ,,	2	,,	4 ,,	10	,,
5 ,,	0	,,	4 ,,	9	,,
4 ,,	$10\frac{1}{2}$	,,	4 ,,	$10\frac{1}{2}$	,,
5 ,,	$4\frac{1}{2}$	,,	5 ,,	$0\frac{1}{2}$	,,
5 ,,	$3\frac{1}{2}$	,,	4 ,,	8	,,
5 ,,	4	,,	4 ,,	7	,,
5 ,,	2	,,	4 ,,	11	,,
5 ,,	$0\frac{1}{2}$	,,	4 ,,	9	,,
5 ,,	$1\frac{1}{4}$	,,			
4 ,,	$8\frac{1}{2}$	,,	43 feet	2	
5 ,,	2	,,	Average		
5 ,,	$2\frac{1}{4}$	,,	height, 4 feet	$9\frac{3}{9}$	,,
5 ,,	$3\frac{1}{4}$	,,			
5 ,,	5	,,			
5 ,,	1	,,			
4 ,,	10	,,			
5 ,,	$5\frac{3}{4}$	,,	CHILDREN.		
5 ,,	1	,,	Height.	Sex.	Age.
5 ,,	$2\frac{1}{4}$	,,	2 feet $10\frac{1}{2}$ inches.	boy	5
103 feet	$2\frac{1}{4}$ inches.		3 ,, 4 ,,	boy	7
Average			3 ,, $3\frac{1}{2}$,,	girl	8
height, 5 feet	$1\frac{3}{4}+\frac{13}{20}$ in.		3 ,, 8 ,,	boy	9

I also measured a very old Samoyad of 91 years of age—deaf and almost blind—and his height was exactly five feet.

No one could be more sociable than the Samoyad. He is extremely hospitable to his tribesmen and to strangers; he delights in gossip; his smile is almost continuous, and his harsh laugh loud and frequent. Visiting each other seems the favourite social occupation—a Samoyad will go a long way out of his road in order to put in an appearance at a choom which he knows to be in the neighbourhood; and during the whole time I was in their country I never saw a blow struck, or even witnessed a serious squabble. It will be interesting to some of my readers, perhaps, to hear that the women are also on the best of terms with each other, and, as far as I could learn of course, there was no wrangling and little backbiting. There was a good deal of twaddle with tea, and I am afraid I somewhat

An Old Samoyad.

aided and abetted them in this, for when their tea fell short I replenished the supply. I may mention here, too, that the Samoyad sometimes indulges in the civilised luxury of toast, and this he makes by spreading his lump of rye-dough on two or three sticks and holding it in the fire. Thence it issues either very much smoked or very much burned, and invariably a pungent morsel.

Both father and mother are kind to their children, who, on their side, do not show any fear of their parents.[1] The only toys which I saw the children playing with were a miniature model of a reindeer sledge and bows and arrows. On the former they dragged each other, romping about not unlike puppies, and turning head over heels with all the adeptness of youth.

Almost the only game at which the Samoyads play is one which combines the main features of "Aunt Sally" with those of the good old game of "Nine Pins." They roughly trace upon the ground an oblong space about sixty feet in length, and placing the pins at one end, throw at them from the other with short, stout sticks, in almost every particular identical with those familiar to the frequenters of country fairs in England.

Up to a certain point men and women dress alike;

---

[1] The Samoyad is by almost every one described as amiable and kind. There is a good story told of his unselfishness in Rae's *Land of the North Wind* (p. 244): "As the canoe came out with us, attached to the side of our boat, we handed to the youngest of the three Samoyedes in it, a youth of eighteen, evidently the son of one and the brother of the other, half a loaf of bread; and I watched how he would divide it. He broke it into two equal halves, and gave one half to his brother. He broke the remaining half into two, giving about two-thirds of it to his gray-headed old father, and kept the little piece that was left for himself, poor fellow!"

but then the woman shows her natural taste by going in for decoration. A red cotton shirt and thin cloth trousers are affected by both; the *lieupthieu* or skin-stocking is also common to the sexes; and, with the exception of the cross-bar being just above the instep rather than just below the knee, the *pimmies* or long deer-skin boots of the women are identical with those of the men. For wet snow, such as they get in the autumn, they wear pimmies made of sealskin, as, owing to its fatty character, it is more waterproof than deerskin. If the Samoyad has not been lucky enough to buy an old cloth coat from a Russian trader, he puts on his chief article of clothing, the *militza*, next to his shirt. This militza is a smock-like garment of reindeer skin, having the hair inside. It is cut very full, and is absolutely closed from the hem to the neck, through which he thrusts his head on putting the garment on. Attached to the neck is a close-fitting skin hood, hair inside; and sewn with sinew on to the end of his sleeves are his *rukavitza* (mitts). In order to prevent the cold air from passing up underneath this loose tunic, and at the same time to retain the warmth given out by his body, the Samoyad pulls up his militza until he has it in voluminous baggy folds above his waist, and then girds it tightly with rope or leather belt (the latter often much ornamented with brass and copper buttons). This is a simple and effectual plan which may be commended to

Arctic explorers. In very bitter weather he wears over this a white deer-skin, cut on the same pattern as the militza, but with no rukavitza, and usually ornamented with bands of red flannel round the wrist. Moreover, the *soveek*, as this is called, has the hair outside. The militza is often enhanced in appearance by bands of different-coloured deerskin inserted round

ORNAMENTED LEATHER BELT, SHOWING KNIFE, CALCULATING STICK, ETC.
(One-sixth of natural size.)

the bottom edge, and this is also done to the soveek, but at a height of eighteen inches from the bottom.

The woman wears no soveek, but her robe is very warm, and often bears evidence of much time and trouble having been expended on it. Roughly, it may be described as a long, loose, buttonless skin-coat, reaching to the calf of the leg, folded over the breast, and secured round the waist by a belt. At regular intervals bands of eight or nine stripes of white deer-skin, often with intervening pipings of red and green flannel, are laid horizontally round the sleeves, and vertically down the back and front. The effect is rich and bright, and must certainly appear to the Samoyad woman as well worth the trouble she has taken in producing it. Dog-skin flounces, usually two, but sometimes three, are sewn round the garment at the bottom and at intervals of six inches upward. These give a heavy effect which somewhat takes off from the brightness of the insertion work, and certainly makes the little fur-banded Samoyad women more dumpy than ever. As they waddled along leaning forward—and I would lay special emphasis on this universal characteristic of the Samoyad woman's gait—I was over and over again strangely reminded of the Chinese women.

SAMOYAD WOMEN.

The cap worn by the Samoyad woman is detached from the robe, invariably has the hair outside, and is often as highly ornate in its own way as a Parisian bonnet. But the "fixings" are not the same, for the Samoyad inserts strips and frillings of different hues of deer and dog skin and attaches strings which tie nowhere, but have metal ornaments, which are numerous and heavy, suspended on them. The Samoyad bonnet is indeed no light or vain thing, and it has a valance stitched round the base of the hood which comes well down over the shoulders. From below this flounce—or what you will—there fall two long tails of black, coarse hair, which are made up partly of hair and partly of the coloured strips of cloth of which they appear particularly fond. These tails are adorned with a set of brass discs (about three inches in diameter) and other ornaments, such as brass charms, beads, and buttons. While I am talking about Samoyad jewellery I might mention the vast buckles sometimes used to fasten the belt; they are made of brass, stamped out with patterns, and are often nine inches in diameter. Of brass, too, and copper are their rings; and they even wear reindeer bells, each weighing at least half a pound, hanging from their elbows.

THE BONNET OF THE SAMOYAD WOMEN.

(One-eighth of natural size.)

The Samoyads are not above ornament, as the

reader will have seen, and they also affect the use of charms. The most common of these is a bear's tooth, which is hung with a bundle of other odds and ends from the belt.[1]

---

[1] In the Second Voyage of William Barents, related by Gerrit de Veer of Amsterdam, we meet with an interesting account of the Samoyads, which, although it was published in 1598, yet remains substantially correct:—"The maner of their apparell is like as we vse to paint wild men; but they are not wilde, for they are of reasonable iudgement. They are apparelled in hartes skins from the head to the feete, vnlesse it be the principallest of them, which are apparelled, whether they bee men or women, like vnto the rest, as aforesayd, vnlesse it bee on their heads, which they couer with certaine coloured cloth lyned with furre : the rest wear cappes of hartes or buckes skinnes, the rough side outwardes, which stand close to their heades, and are very fitte. They weare long hayre, which they plaite and fold, and let it hang downe vpon their backes. They are (for the most part all) short and low of stature, with broad, flat faces, small eyes, short legges, their knees standing outwards; and are very quicke to goe and leape. . . . And after they were gone from vs, and were somewhat within the land, one of them came ryding to the shore, to fetch a rough-heawed image, that our men had taken off the shore and carried into their boate; and when he was in our boate, and perceiued the image, hee made vs a signe that wee had not done well to take away that image; which wee beholding, gaue it to him again; which, when he had receiued, he placed it vpon a hill right by the sea side, and tooke it not with him, but sent a stead to fetch it from thence. And as farre as wee could perceiue, they esteemed that image to be their god : for that right ouer against that place in the Wey-gates, which we called Beelthooke [Image Point], we found certaine hundreds of such carved images, all rough, about the heads being somewhat round, and in the middle hauing a litle hill instead of a nose, and about the nose two cuttes in place of eyes, and vnder the nose a cutte in place of a mouth. Before the images, wee found great store of ashes, and bones of hartes; whereby it is to be supposed that there they offered vnto them."

The Samoyad, it should be noted, has *ski* of his own making and type. They are wider than the Norwegian and shorter; though, on the other hand, longer (they are about six feet long) and much narrower (their width is six inches) than the Indian snow-shoe. Made of light wood, they have deerskin, with the hair left on, stretched over the sole, and this is said to greatly improve the shoe. Personally, I preferred the ski if the snow was in good condition,

ORNAMENTS (BRASS OR COPPER) ATTACHED TO THE WOMEN'S HAIR.
(One-third of natural size.)

but if the temperature rose, or when one was shooting in scrub, the Canadian snow-shoes were certainly more handy and useful. It is on this account that the traveller in Arctic climates should be recommended to take the one and not leave the other. But the Samoyads did not think much of my shoes, and boasted the long journeys they could make in their *olen loegia* or *kammus loegia*, with their turned-up toes. Certainly the Samoyads could make with them a march of about thirty-five miles in the day without fatigue.

Children are dressed just like the adult sexes: if a boy, he is a tiny reproduction of his father; and if a girl, of her mother. The effect is comic, but it is a rational dress all the same.

The reindeer[1] is the camel of the Arctic desert; without his deer the Samoyad would—well—not be a Samoyad. He has no industries: he does not till the ground; he has ceased to smelt ore and weld iron; it is only in one or two localities—on the Korotaika and one or two other rivers further west—that he takes the trouble to fish; his women neither weave nor spin; of carving or making pottery they know nothing. It is on the reindeer that he lives. It is his chief, almost his only food; the skin protects him from the Arctic winter—is stretched over the poles of his winter home, and forms the sole material of his winter clothing. The reindeer carries him great distances along the vast Tundra, and allows of the oscillation of the tribe between the White Sea and the Lena. The Samoyad does nothing with his life: he finds his sole interest in his deer; his only exercise in rounding them up. Yet he has little if any affection for them. He will find amusement in their dying struggles, and when a deer falls dead in the traces he only laments his loss from a pecuniary point of view.

---

[1] Male (stallion) reindeer = *hora tu*; the cut reindeer = *hab tu*; the female reindeer = *ya tu*. Thus it will be seen that *tu* may be regarded as the Samoyad specific term for reindeer.

Many people seem to think that the only food of the deer is reindeer moss. But this is by no means the case. In some parts of the Arctic regions—in Greenland, for instance—reindeer moss or lichen occurs in such sparse quantity that the deer takes to other food. Even in the tundra country, where it is plentiful, they eat the grasses of the tundra. But they prefer the lichen. In fact, the deer would be very difficult to feed on any food other than that to which he has been accustomed. Artificial feeding is practically unknown, and only obtains in the case of those which have been made pets when very young ; and even these are sent during the summer to feed with the herd. The only instances I met with of this petting of the young were in Lapland and the White Sea locality. I do not think that in the Pechora and Malaia Zemlia country there is a single pet reindeer.

There seems to be a belief that the reindeer uses his horns to help him to his food. This is a heresy. He invariably paws away the snow with his hoofs, and I have seen him shovel away two feet and more of snow in order to reach the moss. But, as I have previously said, when you get snow in the tundra you also get wind, and this sweeps bare the long, rolling ridges on which the moss chiefly grows. I have seen the deer greatly hampered by the first snows of autumn, which melt and then freeze again ; for the layer of ice thus formed makes it difficult for the deer to reach their food. Last winter, for example, I was obliged to proceed from Pustozersk—the northern limit of habitation in the Bolshaia Zemelskija Tundra—by horse (although anxious to continue to drive reindeer) owing to the poor condition of the deer in the neighbourhood, a fact which was largely due to this cause. The reindeer at home is a manageable and most useful animal, but this food difficulty makes it impossible to take him to a country to do useful work where there may be no grass or lichen; and as our knowledge of Franz Josef Land does not at present reveal the presence of the proper food, I reluctantly decided not to take reindeer on my expedition. It would have been impracticable to convey sufficient quantities of moss and keep it sweet; and it is only by domestication that the reindeer could be trained to eat it when compressed and dried. If I had had two or three years to prepare for the Polar Expedition, I should most certainly have had a number of deer taken when very young and brought up on artificial food; they would have been invaluable for my purpose.

There is another common mistake about the reindeer which I may perhaps point out. Many people think that the deer is brown in summer and white in winter. This is not so; a brown deer is always brown, and a white deer always white.[1]

[1] It may be here mentioned, for the benefit of those who are not naturalists, that there are several points on which the reindeer differs

The endurance of the reindeer, when we remember his light weight and slender proportions, is most remarkable. Well-authenticated instances of the long distances they have been driven are not uncommon: I have in a marked degree from other members of the *Cervidæ*. Apart from the peculiarity of the hoofs, elsewhere referred to, the female is alone, of all the deer tribe, adorned with antlers. Moreover, the reindeer bears his antlers in a totally different way : instead of these fine coronals springing from the brow, and low down at that, as with other deer, they originate in the higher part of the skull—someway, of course, behind the eyes, and over the ridge of the occiput. Again, the very form of the antlers is unique. For while one reindeer differs from another so commonly as to result in great specific variety, there is a clear line of demarcation from other genera in the great development of the brow tines. These tines, indeed, project so far forward, and descend at an angle so inclined towards the face, that the under edges of their branched and palmated extremities occasionally only just escape touching the nose. A further distinction of the reindeer is the hairy muzzle ; and yet another is the fact that it has the smallest ears of the whole deer tribe.

It may be interesting to add here a further note on the antlers. The main shafts of any antlers are called the beams, and the branches tines. The number of tines differ in the various genera and species, and also, of course, according to the age of the individual ; but the lowest tine on the under edge of the beam is called the brow tine, the second the bez tine, and the third the trez tine, and occasionally the royal tine. All three will be found in the red-deer. Then there are the tines on the summit of the beam, which vary in number, and are known collectively as the sur-royals or crown. Now the reindeer have the brow tines projecting far forward over the face, with their extremities palmated : the palmated bez tines similarly project forward, and the beams run backward for about half their entire length, and then bend upward and gradually forward, being finely palmated on the posterior edge. I may mention here, also, that while the brow tines of the reindeer of America are highly developed and palmated, the individual has but one brow tine, the other being aborted.

myself driven three reindeer a distance of one hundred and twenty versts within twelve hours without feeding them, and I heard of a case when a Zirian drove three deer from Ishma on the Pechora River to Obdorsk on the Obi, a distance of three hundred versts, within twenty-four hours. In my case they went the last ten versts as gamely as the first, and I was told that this was also the case with the Zirian's team; but his died the following day, while mine were perfectly fresh after two days' rest. A "Reindeer" or Samoyad verst, by the way, is equal to four Russian versts.[1]

The Samoyad shows his sense in selecting the reindeer as the object of his appetite's affections.

[1] The special fitness of the reindeer's feet for crossing the swampy tundras and traversing wide regions of snow is known to the naturalist, but may be brought to the attention of the general reader. Every one has noticed that in the sheep the higher part of the lateral metacarpal bones is represented by two small excrescences or splints above the foot, apparently having no further function to perform than to remind us that they are the remnant of those bones which at one time supported the lateral toes. But that which in the sheep is now a mere survival without usefulness, in the reindeer is in actual existence and of great utility. For it is the lower part of the lateral metacarpal bones that we find in the reindeer, and their function is still the support of the toe-bones. Thus, while the main hoofs of the reindeer are large in size, wide in shape, and so deeply cleft as to spread asunder when pressed on the ground, the lateral pair are also brought down to the ground level and grasp the snow or swampy peat. By this quadruple arrangement the weight supported by the leg is distributed over a wide base, and does not in consequence break through the soft ground, which would prove impassable to an animal, used as a beast of burden, with the more common shape of hoof.

Cuts off the haunch of a young reindeer I found to be capital eating and the steaks tender. But if not hung, or when cooked in an artless way, the old reindeer makes a very tough morsel. The Samoyad himself eats all parts with voracity, and drinks the blood by the quart. He undoubtedly prefers the meat raw, and will eat it in this condition even when cooked meat is hanging in the choom. In fact he eats the cooked flesh just as we eat dessert. The raw brain and windpipe are his tit-bits. I tried the brain once and the windpipe on several occasions in order to find out where the attraction lay, but failed to discover any great charm. Under press of circumstances, however, I often ate the steaks and haunch raw, and having got over one's natural repugnance I should not find any particular hardship were I compelled to subsist upon it for a time.

The method of eating in vogue with these interesting nomads is simplicity itself. The Samoyad usually cuts off with his knife a large chunk of meat—too large indeed for even his mouth; but then, like other children, his eyes are often bigger than his stomach. Having crammed this chunk well into his mouth, he cuts off the part protruding beyond the teeth, and steadily chews what is in his case a literal mouthful. He repeats the dose as required, that is to say until he is surfeited and feels that it is a physical impossibility to continue; but the amount of meat which disappears before this point is reached is so enormous that if I gave any maximum records my readers would be inclined to regard them as specimens of folk-lore—and fairy tales. His other method is simply to take up a hind-leg, say, of a reindeer, and gnaw away at it until the bone proves his master. Yet there is one other way he has, and at which I felt compelled to draw the line—licking my plates and frying-pan! I had but to turn my back and he was down on his knees, with all the bones, fat, gristle, and skin that had been left, packed into his mouth, and rapidly polishing with a tongue, that darted about with the speed of a snake's, the top, bottom, and sides of my dinner service.

Left to themselves, the Samoyads would probably never dream of troubling to make bread, but as the Russians are much addicted to black or rye bread, the Samoyads make a considerable quantity from time to time. They mix the rye-flour with water, and then slowly heat the dough over a stove or a hot stone and leave it to ferment. I think that this fermentation accounts for the bitterness so noticeable in black bread, and by way of ascertaining whether it was the case or not, I baked an Australian damper, made out of the same rye-flour, and found that it was perfectly free from the bitter flavour. Though capable of stewing and frying, and making certain not unattractive "potages" when circumstances demand it, I am not sufficiently experienced a cook to say whether my theory as to the cause of this bitterness in black bread be correct or not; but the evidence of the Australian damper should carry some weight.

The dogs (*voinaika*) of the Samoyads have a strong resemblance to the familiar Eskimo dog of Greenland, but in several points they are superior. The most striking characteristics which they have in common are the thick woolly coats which enable them to withstand such a rigorous climate, and the wild and savage temper they display toward each other. If you chained a number of these dogs together and left them to their own devices, I am confident that they would speedily develop a feeling so grimly fraternal that one half (the weaker half) would be absorbed with the least possible delay into the bosom of the other half of the family. When trained and educated, however, even by that unskilful pedagogue their master, they become exceedingly useful and, on the whole, well-behaved members of Samoyad society; and as the proof of the pudding is in the eating, so I may fortify this certificate of good character by the assertion that while you may buy a wild young puppy, and welcome, for a rouble and even less, you may have to give sixty, seventy, and sometimes a hundred roubles for a trained adult. But it is such hard work for the indolent Samoyad to bring his dog to the stage required for driving large herds of reindeer in the best manner, that I very much doubt your being able to persuade him to sell such a dog at all. The rounding up of the deer when teams have to be selected, is an interesting sight. Round and round they gallop, kept in a compact mass by the trained dogs. Now and again a Samoyad will drive out, or run out, and approach the wheeling, galloping multitude—perhaps seven or eight hundred deer will be in motion—and lasso the animal he wants. There will be a short, sharp struggle, ending in the deer being thrown backwards to the ground, where it will lie without making any particular effort to rise. And so the process is repeated until the number required is obtained. It takes some time, particularly as the Samoyad is a poor hand at the lasso.[1] No one with any experience of South American or Australian lassoing, could praise this Mongolian for his skill with the rope; and although some writers have seen fit to call him an expert in this connection, I have every reason to believe that they were not capable of judging, being ignorant of the art they beheld for the first time.

For the bows and arrows with which they were at

---

[1] The lasso is called a *tinzé* and varies in length, reaching perhaps its maximum at thirty-five yards. It is made of deer-hide and usually is a twist of two thongs, about half an inch in diameter. The rope thus formed is passed through a stout piece of bone or walrus ivory, pierced with two holes. The end of the rope is secured by a pin to one hole, while it travels without friction through the other.

The Samoyad and his Dogs.

one time excellent performers, the Samoyads have taken to the trashy "gaspipe" guns sold them by the traders. It is a pity, depriving the race of some of their individuality, destroying a native industry which compelled care, thought, and skill, and not adding materially to their power of procuring food or defending themselves. There is, however, an element of picturesqueness which the Samoyad has introduced into his use of inferior firearms; he fires with a gun-rest not unlike that of the old matchlock days. It is made of wood, is about two inches in diameter and four feet long, and reminds you more particularly of a dwarfed billiard-rest.

WALRUS IVORY AND IRON
POWDER-FLASK
(Probably of Russian make).
(One-third of natural size.)

The Samoyad has few tools —indeed they are only three in number: an axe, a borer, and a knife. Yet with these he can do almost anything in the way of simple carpentry, and he will make a mortice as neatly as an English carpenter. The women too are dexterous with these tools, and no one could cut up a reindeer into "prime joints" more deftly than the Samoyad housewife. At sewing she is especially expert, her only thread being the reindeer sinews, prepared by a tedious process of chewing. When on my way through the Bolshaia Zemelskija country, I desired to make some alterations to the sealskin coat made in London, and gave a Samoyad woman a formidable pair of high sealskin boots to cut up and introduce into the coat. She did the work very well indeed, and was evidently delighted with the sixty kopecks she received in payment. The neatness of the work put into their clothing, especially their pimmies, is deserving of all praise; and one never met with threads coming undone or anything fastened on coming off. I would recommend the Samoyad woman and her sinew thread to those gentlemen who wear shirts with buttons.[1]

[1] Their primitive customs are fast dying out, and it may be well to note that the fashionable method of arranging a marriage used to involve a visit of the groom to the paternal choom of his beloved, when he would first tap the parents on the shoulder with a short stick, as a sheepish young lover might, and then invite them to drink and eat of what he had brought. Alacrity to partake meant a cordial reception, and this in its turn was an encouragement to renew the visit. On the second occasion the suitor would arrive tricked out in all the splendour of Samoyad costume and plentifully provided with vodka. On entering the choom he would sit down by the maiden's side and begin his love-making. This chiefly assumed the form of a prodigious gorge on raw meat and a great drinking of vodka. The young man would take a pull and then pass his cup under his left arm to the young woman, who with commendable tact would promptly empty it. The same order attended the devouring of raw meat, and then the maiden took the initiative and, with that difference, the ritual was repeated. After some hours of this game at Paul and Virginia, the *shaman* would be called in—human nature craves for priestly sanction even among the Samoyads—and the groom was expected to inquire of the priest if he knew aught

Of the choom which forms the Samoyad's home there are two kinds, one for summer and another for winter. They do not really differ in construction, nor, as far as the poles are concerned, in material. But the birch-bark covering, which consists of strips about eighteen inches wide stoutly sewn together with sinew, gives place in winter to what is often a wonderful piece of skin patchwork. The Samoyad has the Russian peasant-trader too much in view to use up good skins unnecessarily, and his choom is frequently covered with worn-out pimmies, lieupthieu, and odds and ends and waste pieces of skin. This choom is practically impervious to snow and wind, and can be made really hot as long as the fire which burns in the centre is kept up. It becomes almost suffocating and blinding when the smoke, as in a gale of wind, does not escape through the large hole in the top. If it

against the woman he desired. If that intermediary knew nothing, or, knowing anything, did not choose to tell, he kept that silence which is golden (often prompted, one does not doubt, by previous arrangements with the anxious groom), and instead of reading the impatient pair a homily, would begin to beat loudly upon a drum. This concluded the marriage ceremony. I may add that when the *shaman*, for one reason or another, reported unfavourably of the gay lady, two courses would be open to the lover: he might at once retire with perfect self-respect, or, if he preferred his own opinion to that of the priest, he might take the girl on trial for any reasonable period, and if discontented at its termination, send her back whence she came.

As with the Eskimo, marriages are contracted at an early age, girls frequently becoming brides at thirteen years, and mothers before they are fourteen.

were not for its great weight, it would make the best Arctic tent that I know.

The Holy Island of the Samoyad is Waigatz, and he still desires to be buried there. The ancient burial-place, which I had the good luck to stumble against on the south-west point of Waigatz, is one of many, and a short description of it will practically describe all. At that time it consisted of three tombs above ground. The first, which is evidently very old, was nothing more nor less than a wooden box of timber three inches thick. It is six feet long, three feet nine inches broad, two feet six inches high. The sides are faced, both outside and in, but the top consisted of split logs, placed longitudinally and pinned together. In order to brace this structure more firmly together, four heavy uprights with cross pieces at top and bottom encased the box. The other two merely consisted of the Samoyad's domestic chest, flat-bottomed, ark-shaped, a heavy box, which during his life served to keep his worldly possessions. Their lids were nailed down with four nails, and on one of them four stones were placed. Their length was three feet six inches by two feet six inches; and the red paint which the Samoyad invariably puts on them was here still fresh. I am inclined to think that one at least of the two formed the last resting-place of a woman, because one of the sledges, which were placed near each of them, was of the pattern used by the women. Whenever you find a tomb or coffin — for it is the same thing — you also find a sledge (*hán*), and in almost every instance the sledge is overturned; though at this particular place one of the three lay on its runners. Beside the sledges were three *harrays* (reindeer driving-poles), and I particularly noticed that each sledge and each pole was broken. This I also noticed at other burial-places, and I have little doubt that it is a deliberate action on the part of the Samoyad to indicate that their owner has no further use for them here, although the sledges are placed there with the distinct purpose that they may be useful to their owner when he awakes in another world. How the Samoyad expects to get them mended I do not know, but he probably relies upon his god to do this piece of carpentry for him.

The fashionable religion of the Bolshaia Zemelskija Tundra and the Waigatz Samoyads is Christianity, but in the vast majority of cases it is only skin-deep. As long as things go well with him he is a Christian, but should his reindeer die, or other catastrophe happen, he immediately returns to his old god, Num or Chaddi. The Russian peasant-traders with whom he comes in contact are very thorough-going Christians, and impress upon him the necessity of Christianity. So much so that the Samoyad conducts his heathen services by night and in secret, and carefully screens from sight any image of

Chaddi.[1] For example, when I was travelling with the two Samoyads on Waigatz, Vasili's babba, in turning out

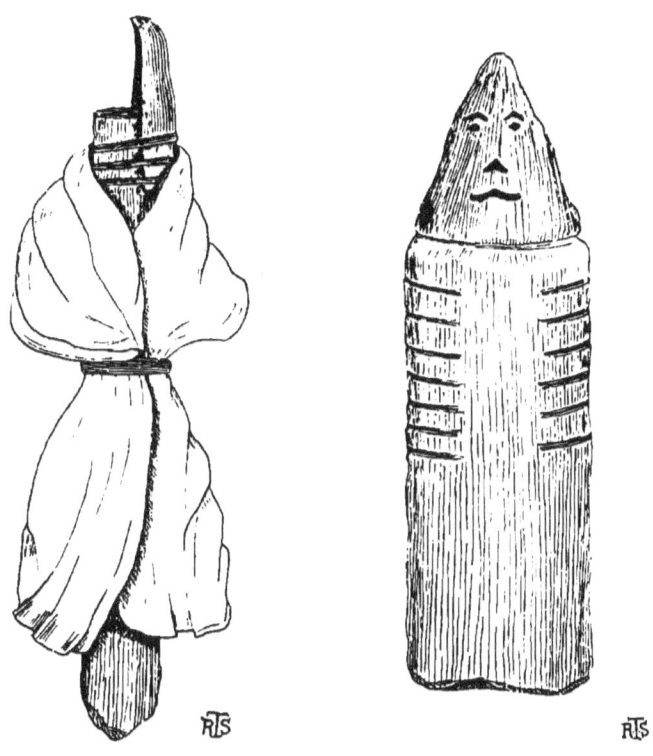

CHADDI.

Wooden images secretly carried about by the Samoyads. These are survivals of that nature-worship which, finding its highest development in *Num*, the Creator, also venerated and even idolised trees and stones of uncommon shape. The rude figures called Chaddi are usually models of the larger "bolvans" found *in situ* in Waigatz, the Holy Island of the Samoyads, and other places. (One-half the natural size.)

a bag of odds and ends, accidentally exposed a little image of Chaddi—a stick dressed in red flannel, with

[1] A curious account of the priestly functions of the Samoyad may be found in "Certaine notes vnperfectly written by Richard

the upper bill of a duck lashed to the top to represent the head—and on seeing I had noticed it, immediately pushed it away with a very shamefaced look. At the

Johnson, seruant to Master Richard Chancelour, which was in the discouerie of Vaigatz and Nova Zembla, with Steuen Burrowe in the Serchthrift 1556, and afterwarde among the Samoedes, whose deuilish rites hee describeth."

"And East North East of Russia lieth Lampas, which is a place where the Russes, Tartars, and Samoeds meete twise a yeere, and make the faire to barter wares for wares. And Northeast from Lampas lieth the countrey of the Samoeds, which be about the river of Pechere, and these Samoeds bee in subiection to the Emperour of Russia, and they lie in tentes made of deere skinnes, and they vse much witchcraft, and shoot well in bowes. And Northeast from the riuer Pechere lieth Vaygatz, and there are the wild Samoeds which will not suffer the Russes to land out of the Sea, but they will kill them and eate them, as wee are told by the Russes ; and they live in heards, and haue all their carriages with deere, for they haue no horses. Beyond Vaygatz lyeth a lande called Noua Zembla, which is a great lande, but wee sawe no people, and there wee had Foule enough, and there wee sawe white Foxes and white Beares.

"And the sayde Samoeds which are about the bankes of Pechere, which are in subiection to the Emperour of Russia, when they will remoue from one place to another, then they will make sacrifices in manner following. Euerie kinred doeth sacrifice in their owne tent, and hee that is most auncient is their Priest. And first the Priest doeth beginne to playe vpon a thing like to a great sieue, with a skinne on the one ende like a drumme ; and the sticke that he playeth with is about a spanne long, and one ende is round like a ball, couered with the skinne of an Harte. Also the Priest hath vpon his head a thing of white like a garlande, and his face is couered with a piece of a shirt of maile, with manie small ribbes, and teeth of fishes, and wilde beastes hanging on the same maile. Then hee singeth as wee vse heere in England to hallow, whope, or showte at houndes, and the rest of the company answere him with this Owtis, Igha, Igha, Igha, and then the Priest replieth againe with his voyces. And they answere him with the selfesame

same time Vasili was wearing conspicuously round his neck a little metal cross, which had been given him by Russian traders. On more than one occasion

wordes so manie times, that in the ende he becommeth as it were madde. and falling downe as hee were dead, hauing nothing on him but a sheet, lying vpon his backe I might perceiue him to breathe. I asked them why hee lay so, and they answered mee, Now doeth our God tell him what wee shall doe, and whither wee shall goe. And when he had lyen still a litle while, they cried thus three times together, Oghao, Oghao, Oghao, and as they vse these three calles, hee riseth with his head and lieth downe againe, and then hee rose vp and sang with like voyces as hee did before: and his audience answered him, Igha, Igha, Igha. Then hee commaunded them to kill fiue olens or great Deere, and continued singing still both hee and they as before. Then hee tooke a sworde of a cubite and a spanne long (I did mete it my selfe) and put it into his bellie halfeway and sometime lesse, but no wounde was to bee seene (they continuing in their sweete song still). Then he put the sworde into the fire till it was warme, and so thrust it into the slitte of his shirt and thrust it through his bodie, as I thought, in at his nauill and out at his fundament: the poynt beeing out of his shirt behinde, I layde my finger vpon it, then hee pulled out the sworde and sate downe. This beeing done, they set a kettle of water ouer the fire to heate, and when the water doeth seethe, the Priest beginneth to sing againe they answering him, for so long as the water was in heating, they sate and sang not. Then they made a thing being foure square, and in height and squarenesse of a chaire, and couered with a gown very close the forepart thereof, for the hinder part stood to the tents side. Their tents are rounde, and are called chome in their language. The water still seething on the fire, and this square seate being ready, the Priest put off his shirt, and the thing like a garland which was on his head, with those things which couered his face, and he had on yet all this while a paire of hosen of deeres skins with ye haire on, which came vp to his buttocks. So he went into the square seate, and sate down like a tailour and sang with a strong voyce or halowing. Then they tooke a small line made of deeres skinnes of four fathoms long, and with a small knotte the Priest made it fast about his necke

I noticed this compromise between the old religion and the new. For instance, about a mile from Ussia,

and vnder his left arme, and gaue it vnto two men standing on both sides of him, which held the ends together. Then the kettle of hote water was set before him in the square seat, at this time the square seat was not couered, and then it was couered w^t a gown of broad cloth without lining, such as the Russes do weare. Then the 2 men which did hold ye ends of the line still standing there, began to draw, and drew til they had drawn the ends of the line stiffe and together, and then I hearde a thing fall into the kettle of water which was before him in the tent. Thereupon I asked them that sate by me what it was that fell into the water that stoode before him. And they answered me, that it was his head, his shoulder and left arme, which the line had cut off, I meane the knot which I sawe afterwarde drawen hard together. Then I rose vp and would have looked whether it were so or not, but they laid hold on me, and said, that if they should see him with their bodily eyes, they should liue no longer. And the most part of them can speake the Russe tongue to bee vnderstood: and they tooke me to be a Russian. Then they beganne to hallow with these wordes, Oghaoo, Oghaoo, Oghaoo, many times together. And as they were thus singing and out calling. I sawe a thing like a finger of a man two times together thrust through the gowne from the Priest. I asked them that sate next to me what it was that I sawe, and they saide, not his finger; for he was yet dead: and that which I saw appeare through the gowne was a beast, but what beast they knew not nor would not tell. And I looked vpon the gowne, and there was no hole to bee sene: and then at the last the Priest lifted vp his head with his shoulder and arme, and all his bodie, and came forth to the fire. Thus farre of their seruice which I sawe during the space of certaine houres: but how they doe worship their Idoles that I saw not: for they put vp their stuffe for to remoue from that place where they lay. And I went to him that serued the Priest, and asked him what their God saide to him when he lay as dead. Hee answered, that his owne people doeth not know: neither is it for them to know, for they must doe as he commanded. This I saw the fift day of Januarie in the yere of our Lord 1556, after the English account" (Hakluyt, vol. i. pp. 317, 318, ed. 1809).

on the Pechora, I saw above a grave in a Samoyad cemetery the wooden cross of Christianity together with the overturned sledge of Chaddi-ism. More commonly, however, the grave of a Christian Samoyad is marked by an upright stick. The rings of stones which I frequently met with in Waigatz are the sites of their midnight services, and made of course by the Samoyads. They are called *Yon-pa-ha-pai*. It is possible that within these circles the human sacrifices with which the Samoyad used to propitiate Chaddi were offered up; and although these are things of the past now, it was only a few years ago that a Samoyad living on Novaia Zemlia sacrificed a young girl.

Although he does not smoke tobacco, the Samoyad is an inveterate snuff-taker. He makes the snuff by grinding down tobacco (which he has purchased from the Russians) in a wooden mortar which he constructs for this special purpose. Yet his abstinence from smoking I attribute to the influence of the Russians, for on the Pechora River tobacco is looked upon as the devil's weed, and I have never seen a Russian in that locality use it in any form, though no hesitation is shown in selling it to the Samoyads for snuff-making. The box in which the snuff is kept is generally hung to the belt, and is made of birch bark with the top and bottom of pine. The top comes off for the purpose of filling, but when the box is in use the Samoyad merely draws out a slender peg which is inserted in the top, and through the hole shakes out sufficient snuff for his use. Occasionally he also takes it out with a small slender spoon, made of walrus ivory.

For making up his accounts, and reckoning

SNUFF-BOXES AND SNUFF-SPOON.

1. Made of birch-bark, with pine top and bottom, and peg to draw out.　　2. Made of pine. (Both are two-thirds of natural size.)

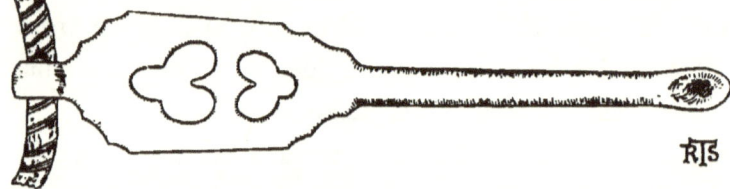

The spoon is made of walrus ivory, and used for getting the snuff out through the small hole in the top of the box. (Natural size.)

numbers generally, he uses the calculating stick, with the aid of which he proves a very accurate if not particularly rapid accountant.[1]

[1] With reference to these calculating sticks, Dr. George Harley, F.R.S., has been good enough to furnish me with his views. They

This side of the Urals, money is a very great matter with the Samoyads, but in Northern Siberia

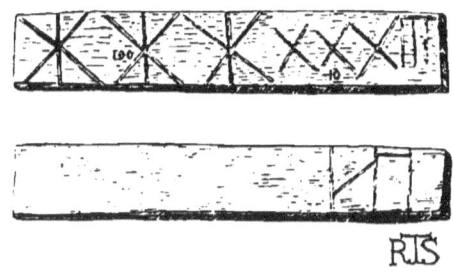

CALCULATING STICKS.
(One-third the natural size.)

I believe this people have little if any use for it. There the currency is that old-fashioned inconvenient

are the more valuable because he has studied the subject for a number of years :—

"First. All the primitive tribes of Northern Europe used wood, bone, and stone to write and cipher upon. The remnant of the practice is still to be seen in the notching of the tally-sticks used at the present day by our Scotch fisher-folk in counting their fish when selling them.

"Second. Du Chaillu, in his *Viking Age*, tells how the ancient Norsemen wrote upon staves and whalebone, and how they tied hair to their letters of communication—just, strange to say, as the aboriginal Australians do to-day. I have some Australian 'talking-sticks' with hair tied on the end of them, so that the recipient of the letter might the more easily know who sent it to him.

one of barter; and although here one could certainly engage in barter, a few shining silver roubles would do far more than many pounds of excellent Demerara sugar or whole-fruit jam. Indeed I have known the rouble conquer when the allurements of "Mixed Ceylon Souchong" (whatever the grocers mean by that) proved of no avail. But it was my policy to hide the fact that I had much money with me, for I was travelling alone and did not wish to add their cupidity to the difficulties which already existed. So I was always very short of roubles when bargains had to be made, but very ready with my stores. And when it came to reckoning very small articles of consumption at a fixed market-rate, and adding them

"Third. Stranger still is the fact that the writing on two of my native Australian 'stick-letters' is identical with *old* Irish Ogam writing.

"Fourth. The Australians, like the Norsemen, write also on bones as well as wood. Miss Fenwick of Leeds, from whom I got some of my talking-sticks, showed me a bone—the fibula of a kangaroo—with Ogam characters on it.

"Widely separated though the Australians are from Scandinavia, the combination of all these facts suggests the possibility of some form of intercourse having existed between them in early times. Just as I showed at the Bath Meeting of the British Association, a quarter of a century ago, that the natives of Guiana, in South America, had come from Borneo by their not only using the same peculiarly constructed poisoned spikes, but with a blow-tube made of identical fashion. For though men in different quarters of the globe may easily invent the same kind of instrument—be its nature what it may—no two men can invent a consecutive series of combinations, in an identical way, of anything whatever, so as to produce a precisely similar result."

all up and on to a previous account, the Samoyads displayed a keenness and perception of which the casual observer might have judged them deficient. When I was asked for money I used to say: "'No money—not a stiver; it's all at Arkhangel. I can only give you tea, biscuits, and sugar."

The traveller who follows in my steps may like to know the exchange value of the stores which he may have with him, and be able to barter with—indeed, it would be a good plan to take a quantity of tea, condensed milk, and jam for the express purpose. But he should remember that food is very cheap in these regions, and high-priced articles would be not only thrown away upon the natives, but also prove unmarketable at a fair rate. Tea was readily taken as payment in kind, at the uniform rate of two roubles a pound. Ship's biscuits at twenty kopecks and fifteen kopecks a pound; sugar at twenty kopecks; for a small tin of condensed milk seventy-five kopecks were allowed. Jam, especially marmalade, was a fairly satisfactory article of barter—a three-pound tin being considered equivalent to a rouble. Biscuit has a ready sale, but it is too bulky an article to form a satisfactory means of exchange. From these few figures it will be seen that if a traveller cared to burden himself with extra stores, he could travel on them to a considerable extent. I usually paid about three-quarters of the sum agreed upon for services reindeer, etc., in stores. Tin plates would also find ready acceptance and be handy to carry with one.[1] Moreover, there is the humanitarian view; for sound, wholesome food can do nothing but good to the Samoyad, while the money he would otherwise receive would probably be spent on the vile vodka which the Russian traders sell him at exorbitant prices. The Russians chiefly trade vodka with the Samoyads, and I well remember when visiting a Samoyad in his choom, his bitter lamentations over a fine bear-skin which he had just sold to a Russian for half a bottle of that spirit.[2]

The more common diseases of the Samoyads appear to be small-pox, syphilis, bad eyes, colds and

[1] Richard Finch, writing in 1611 to the Worshipful Company of English Merchants trading into Russia of the trade on the Pechora, refers to the Samoyad regard for tin plates—a taste which has remained in vogue ever since. "Among these were some which seemed to be Merchants, who asked to buy Lists, remnants of Cloth, Cap-clothes, *Aqua vita*, especially they asked for small Pewter Dishes, which I understand to be a commoditie sold by them to the Samoyeds, at a great rate."

[2] In the event of disputes, no trace was found of the oath described by William Gourdon, who wintered at Pustozersk in 1614-1615, and has left us a description of the Samoyads which should be read (*Purchas, his Pilgrimes*, iii. pp. 555, 556). The following passage on a form of Trial obtaining among these people will be welcome here: "If any Controuersie bee which cannot bee decided or the truth knowne, then one of the two betwixt whom the Controuersie is, must bee sworne, which is in this manner; they will make an Image of a Man of Snow, bringing a Wolues nose, diliuering a Sword to him that must sweare, he rehearsing by name all his Friends, desiring that they might all bee cut in peeces in that manner, as hee doth cut that Image of Snow. Then he himselfe,

diarrhœa. They are often terribly marked and disfigured by the ravages of the first two. I prescribed for the sore eyes with apparently fair results, and was in constant demand as a Medicine Man for affections

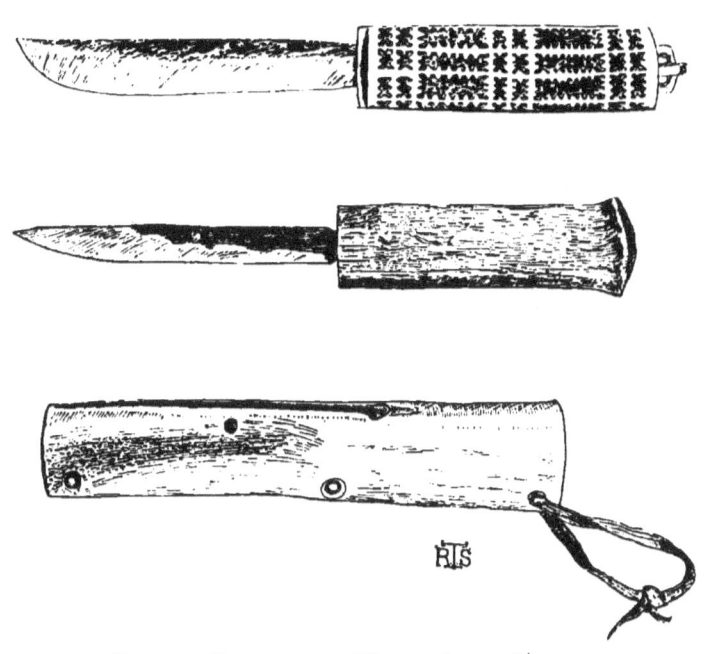

SAMOYAD KNIVES, WITH WALRUS IVORY SHEATH.
(One-third the natural size.)

of the stomach and bowels. I should say that the Samoyad is as free as any one on the face of the earth

doth cut the Image of Snow all to peeces with the Sword; then after, the Wolues nose being layd before him, he desires that the Wolfe may destroy all his tame Deere, and that hee may neuer more take or kill any wilde Deere after that, if hee speaks not the Truth, so cutting the Wolues nose in peeces, there is no more to bee sayd of that Controuersie."

from nervous diseases. Yet it is my duty to record that on one occasion when a mouse made its appearance in the choom, the Samoyad ladies behaved in a manner identical with that which is said to obtain among more civilised members of their sex. At any rate, I feel certain that had there been such things as chairs in the choom, the Samoyad ladies would have immediately mounted upon them.

Of the Samoyads as a race I noted what I think might be said of any race in the world: they reflected all shades of character. For there were the energetic man and the inert; the industrious and the idle; the intelligent and the village fool; the brutal and the kind; the dandy and the sloven. In a Samoyad named Stefan I found united nearly all the qualities of a good man. He was sober, honest, industrious, well-mannered, kind to his wife and child, careful of his reindeer, and neat in his appearance. What more could you have?

CHAPTER IV

ACROSS "THE GREAT FROZEN LAND"

(*Bolshaia Zemelskija Tundra*)

A sojourn among the Samoyads—A story of scurvy—My camp—The current in the Yugorski Schar—A long pull—Sport near Habarova—The return of the *Blencathra*—Miss Helen Peel—The attempt to sail to the Kara River—The arrival of winter—Swimming the deer from Waigatz—Rounding up the herds—The start for the Pechora—The first "ducking"—Night in the choom—Putting the baby to bed—A deer's load—A cold bath—Bad weather—The Korotaika River—A Zirian family—Superiority of Samoyad clothing—The art of driving reindeer—The harness—The sledge—The woman's sledge—Gale and frost—Weather-bound in the choom—A Samoyad burial-place—Thirteen in a choom—Raw meat—Weather notes—The rivers—Lost on the Tundra—A night in the snow—Playing the Medicine Man—Breaking in the young deer—The silence of the Tundra—A Tundra gale.

THE Samoyáds having refused to go with me to Yalmal, or indeed any distance east of Habarova, it became clear that the only course left to me was to stay at Habarova and wait until the heavy snows and frosts of winter made it possible to sledge across the Bolshaia Zemelskija Tundra, "The Great Frozen Land," as the literal translation might run, which stretches from the shores of the Kara Sea to the Pechora River.¹ This was really the only direction in which the Samoyads would go, for they annually migrate south to avoid the wild winter weather of the Straits and trade their furs with the Russians of the Pechora.²

Meanwhile I took up my abode in the log-house which Siberiakoff built some years ago for the accom-

[1] From the Yugorski Schar to the river Pechora there stretches the Great or Greater Tundra, called by the Samoyads, Aarka Ya the Greater Land, and by the Russians, Bolshaia Zemelskija Tundra. Waigatz and Dolgoi (= long), the only noteworthy islands off its coast, are generally similar in their features to the Tundra mainland. Both as regards its topography and its rigorous climate, the Great Tundra is allied to the Siberian Tundra, and lying wholly within the Arctic Circle, presents phenomena exceptionally severe even in the Polar Basin. West of the Pechora, and extending from that river to the Mezén, is the Little or Lesser Tundra, which the Samoyads call Njude Ya and the Russians Málaia Zemlia. Off this tract there lies the island of Kolguev, which is annually visited by Russians for purposes of trade, and has on several occasions been traversed by Englishmen and travellers of other nationalities. The character of the Little Tundra is less defined and typical than that of the Great Tundra, and of course its climatic extremes are not so severe. There remains yet another Tundra in Europe, and that is the small tract on the Kanin Peninsula. The deteriorated Samoyads who occasionally visit it call it Salyé, but this term is rather descriptive of the promontory it occupies than of any characteristic it may itself possess.

[2] This has been the custom for centuries. *E.g.* in 1611 Richard Finch wrote: "The Samoyeds inhabiting upon the mayne land ouer against Vaygatz, trauelled in the Winter time with their Reyne Deer to the parts of Mongosey, to kill Sables and other beasts; and doe carrie their Furres from thence to Mezén, to sell there" (*Purchas, his Pilgrimes*, iii. p. 540).

modation of a few monks; and hereby hangs a tale which those interested in the study of scurvy may be glad to read. There were in all at this tiny monastery —a log-house about twenty feet long by fifteen feet wide, excluding the out-house—six Russian monks, and one lad who acted as general servant. They belonged to the strictest sect of the Russian priesthood, and were bound by their vows to abstain altogether from meat. This obligation, however, did not apply to the lad, who was kept busy and in constant exercise, and lived on fresh reindeer meat. At the end of the second winter (in May) the Russian peasant-traders and Samoyads came back from the Pechora to find all the six priests dead of scurvy and the boy of twelve in perfect health. The poor little fellow had buried his masters one after the other in the snow, and was the sole inhabitant of Habarova. I knew him well, and used to chaff him a good deal by telling him he had killed six monks; and he had sufficiently got over the gloom of that trying time to laugh at the accusation.

This house was divided into three portions—one room of moderate size and two small ones leading out of it. The stove formed the principal feature of the outer room, and in addition there were a table and a bench. In the small room where I camped there was a five-feet wooden bedstead of very primitive make, but finding it impossible to deposit in it with comfort my seventy-three inches, I slept on the floor. There was also one chair. Around me lay several Russian peasant-traders and a Samoyad. It was a case of over-crowding, but to this I should have had no objection had not my companions been so odoriferous and "animated." But we were really very comfortable, and soon got on excellent terms with each other. Each did his own cooking and maintained a separate larder; went to bed when he liked and turned out as he felt inclined. We conversed in monosyllables, and signs supplied the missing words. The atmosphere was thick, and my companions were dirty, but I had a swim every morning in the Straits—to the great astonishment of the Russians and Samoyads alike, who both tried to impress upon me the fact that it was very cold. One Russian in particular, Ivan Berzumoff, I found a first-rate fellow. He was of course rather a savage in his habits and perhaps a little inclined to play the Shylock at a bargain; but really he was honest, good-hearted, very manly, and he never got drunk—indeed he was a teetotaller. These Russian peasants are generally one thing or the other; if they drink at all, they drink hard. The honesty and straightforwardness were not shared by all the others, and I had to keep a sharp lookout after my goods.

The day after we had returned from Waigatz I spent in rowing back to the island in order to photograph the burying-place already described, for I had not a camera with me when I stumbled upon it. I left about noon by myself in a fourteen-feet lodka which I borrowed of a Samoyad - the sea being a little too rough for the seven-feet canvas boat. As the wind and current were favourable, I reached the spot in about two hours, and took a number of photographs of these interesting relics. But the wind and sea were rising quickly, and I hurried back to the shore to recross as soon as possible before the weather got worse. But it was too late: the current and wind were carrying me out into the Arctic Ocean, and it was as much as I could do to make any headway at all. After a couple of hours of hard pulling I found myself near the mouth of the Straits, and saw that if I ceased my efforts for a moment my position would be still more awkward. So I steadily pulled on, hour after hour, and finally managed to make shore, just at the very last point of land. I was so exhausted that I lay down on the beach in my wet and more or less frozen clothes. When a little rested, I launched the boat again, and, keeping only a few yards from the shore, pulled back to Habarova. It had actually taken eight hours to accomplish what had been done in two hours earlier in the day. This will give an idea of the power of the current running westward through the Straits with the tide. The average rise and fall of the tide at Habarova is thirty-three inches, although the highest tide-mark, frequently reached no doubt, in the full spring tides is fifty-six inches.

There were few days when I did not explore the surrounding country, but the best results, as far as game was concerned, were obtained in the valleys of the Nikolski and Oya Rivers. Sport, however, was limited to a few Arctic owls, duck, and snipe, with occasionally some golden plover. The former were very wild in the summer and autumn—that is, as long as there was plenty of food about—and I had to use a rifle to get them at all. But when the country was frostbound and covered with snow, their food became scarce, and they could then be easily bagged with a shot-gun; for they live almost entirely on lemmings (which the Russians call *mus*), and these little animals keep a good deal at home during the severe frosts of winter. Cross-foxes are plentiful, and as cunning as our old friend at home. I followed one for about eight miles one day, and eventually lost him in the hills that lie south-east of Habarova. These hills, by the way, are described in some of the maps as mountains, but they are mere elevations of the Tundra, and do not exceed four hundred feet.

On 25th September, about 2 P.M., a Russian peasant ran into my den exclaiming " Angliski parrahod masheerum "—this " pidgin " Russian by the way was for my personal benefit — " An English steamer is coming." I went out to find the steam yacht *Blencathra* coming through the Straits on her way home from the Yenisei. So I picked up the canvas-boat and carried it down to the shore, and pulled out to where the *Blencathra* lay anchored. The voyage to the Yenisei, as far up as Golchika, had been safely accomplished, and I was able to congratulate Mr. Popham, the owner, on his having on board two ladies, the first to

MISS HELEN PEEL.

sail through the Kara Sea—an honour, I am pleased to add, which had fallen to our own countrywomen. One of these was Miss Helen Peel, who has since described her voyage in such an interesting manner in *Polar Gleams*.

Mr. Popham was kind enough to insist on leaving

a whale-boat for me, in case I should have trouble with the Samoyads, and be compelled to make my way to the Pechora by sea. I may mention here that I gave two cross-foxes into the charge of the captain of the *Blencathra*, and asked him to deliver them to Dr. Sclater, of the Zoological Society, feeling sure that they would be acceptable in the Gardens.

On the following day the *Blencathra* sailed for England, and I began to see what I could do with the whale-boat. A short voyage to the Kara River would have been extremely interesting, and this I could well have managed in the boat; but here again the lack of a companion defeated my wishes—for the Samoyads refused to go with me. *Bolshaia pagoda* ("much bad weather") was the prevailing argument with them, and *Bolshoi sneark* ("much snow"), *Bolshaia Otchin halodna* ("much cold"). They were not far wrong, for when I eventually started by myself—a Samoyad who had promised to go having failed me at the last moment—I encountered such a gale of wind, that after going fifteen miles, the only course to avoid being drowned was to run ashore. As it was, with the sheet in one hand and the tiller in the other, I was fairly tied up in a knot. However I managed to land without damaging the boat, made it secure, and then walked back by the coast to Habarova. It blew and snowed hard for four consecutive days, and winter set in from that date. But I hired a

Samoyad to help to bring the boat to Habarova, and then with the assistance of about twenty of his tribe, and with a maximum of grunting and a minimum of hauling, they brought her at last to Siberiakoff's empty store, where she is now safely housed.

It was really surprising how suddenly the whole country changed from an autumnal to a winter condition. Only four days came and went, and the rivers were all frozen hard, the snow was lying deep around, and although the wind-swept ridges of the Tundra were certainly bare of snow, the slatish-green grasses and rushes had changed to a dark brown. With the exception of the snowy owl, all the birds had migrated, and even of the owls there were few left. The lemmings were no longer running in and out of their holes, and the only cheery feature of the Tundra had disappeared. Constant storms with high winds swept across the country, making even its bleakness indistinguishable; and the Samoyads and Russian traders began to make preparations for their long sledge journey to the south. It is only when the winter has well set in that you can get big game at Habarova. When the sea, however, is all frozen over, and the snow is some four and five feet thick, then the white bear comes up to the settlement, and may be readily stalked. On the other hand the small game will have disappeared so completely that you could scarcely believe it had ever been plentiful.

Some little time before the Great Migration was made, a number of deer—some four hundred head were swam over the Straits from Waigatz, and on 13th October all was ready for our start. A party of the Samoyads had left on the previous day, and another followed ours later in the day. There was a great rounding up of reindeer; and the groups of Samoyads in their warm-coloured garments, and with their high sledges, heavily laden with furs, blubber, bundles of goods and their chooms, made an interesting scene.[1] My party consisted of one Russian peasant, four Samoyads —afterwards as many as eight or nine and occasionally many more—eleven sledges, and at first fifty-five reindeer, although this number increased to several hundreds before we reached the Pechora.

Starting just before noon, we made a southerly and then a south-westerly course, crossing the Nikolski River about three miles from Habarova. Shortly after crossing this river a Samoyad stupidly drove four sledges and ten or twelve reindeer across a small lake which was fed by a running stream. The ice broke and let the sledges and reindeer in, with the unpleasing result that all my goods, including my

[1] It is interesting to compare this passage with one in De Veer's narrative, 1595, describing the laden sledges of the Samoyads: "Diversche sleden met velwerck, traen, ende dierghelijcke waer" ("several sledges with skins, train-oil, and such-like wares").—*Vide Barents' Voyages,* edited by Dr. Chas. T. Beke, p. 53, 2nd edition, 1876.

SAMOYADS ON THE MARCH.

(The middle sledge has the household treasures; that on the right is a woman's sledge.)

sleeping-bag, were soaked through. They were in the water quite two hours, and it was only after a lot of trouble that we got the reindeer and sledges out and resumed our journey. We had been so delayed by this accident that it was some time after dark before we halted at a choom belonging to the Samoyad named Stefan, where we camped for the night. As we found three Samoyads there, we made in all a party of nine in a choom nine feet by ten. And I must not forget—indeed I cannot forget—that in addition to these, there was a Samoyad baby of about eighteen months, who kept up a vigorous crying and made itself generally felt. My companions, including the Russian, were soon deep in a feast on raw reindeer, and the Samoyad lady on my right comfortably seated herself on the ground and placed the stomach of a deer on her lap. It was full of blood, and she dipped in it the pieces of raw meat she was eating. As the coloured candles—the same as they use before their ikons—flared and flickered, the blood-smeared faces of these hungry eaters framed in a strange circle of primitive life. However, hunger provided sauce and overlooked surroundings, and I supped well, and then tried to thaw the sleeping-bag, which had frozen hard after getting wet (we had been driving in 14° F. of frost), but the attempt was not very successful, and I had eventually to sleep on the ground in my clothes. It was amusing to see the baby, which had been sitting up and had eaten a fairly good supper of raw meat, put to bed by its mother. She first wrapped it in furs, then placed it in a box shaped like a coffin, and laced it in with narrow strips of hide, so that it was not only impossible for it to fall out, but also very difficult for it even to move.

The following morning we broke camp about noon, having had 23 of frost during the night. Berzumoff, the Russian peasant, here took on four hundred of his reindeer and sixteen more sledges, fourteen of which were loaded with deer-skins. A deer will draw a load of four hundred pounds (ten poods)—of course over snow; and to a sledge on which there was quite eight hundred pounds of blubber only two deer were harnessed. Our progress, though rapid, was not continuous, for at least once in half an hour the Samoyads pulled up for a feed on raw meat and a prolonged gossip. I was driving my own team, but in the afternoon, by way of a change, I joined Berzumoff. It was undoubtedly a change for the worse, for shortly afterwards he drove straight on to a lake which was only covered with rotten cat-ice—owing to a stream running into it. The next moment we were all—Berzumoff, myself, the four reindeer and the sledge —mixed up in the water in a heap, and having a very lively time. As far as my memory serves me, the language used just then (both Russian and English) was fluent and to the point. Partly by our own efforts, and partly by those of the others, we got out of this mess, and had a minute or so for reflection. My first thought was that all my clothes as well as my sleeping-bag were already wet through and frozen hard. I, too, was freezing hard as I stood; there were 14° of frost, and though I moved rapidly about and shook myself well, my clothes became in a few minutes as stiff as a board. There was nothing left for it but to camp, so camp we did. Comfort is of course not to be expected on such trips, but there was something more than discomfort in this little episode, and the most annoying thing about it was the ease with which it might have been avoided. And, to make matters worse, the fire in the choom smoked so abominably that, although it was naturally necessary to dry one's clothes, it could only be done in a very piecemeal fashion. The thick clouds of smoke rose, and failing to escape at the top, wreathed round and round the choom until one could scarcely see or breathe.

On the next day we made good travelling, the country being rolling tundra covered with deep snow now hard frozen. In crossing the Gushina River, I had a view of the sea with young ice upon it. The country beyond the Gushina we found less undulating, and indeed very flat and wet, although of course it was now frozen. On camping this night the Aurora was very bright in the sky.

On 16th October, although it was blowing hard from the north-east, the snow driving across the tundra like a blizzard, we started about ten, crossed the Talata, and travelled for about twenty versts,

THE AUTHOR IN SEALSKIN COAT (OF ENGLISH MAKE), AND SAMOYAD PIMMIES (OR BOOTS).

when even the Samoyads thought it best to camp—seven or eight miles north of the Korotaika. The wind was very keen and stormy the next day, but the weather being less dirty, we pushed on to the

Korotaika River, which we found hardly sufficiently frozen to enable us to cross it safely. So we camped and waited for the night's frost, which we reckoned would make the ice firm enough. This proved hardly the case, although we ultimately got across without any serious mishap. At the spot where we struck the river, about nine miles from the sea, the Korotaika occupied a bed about one mile across, although the actual stream did not exceed three hundred yards in width nor twenty feet in depth. Parallel to the main bed of the river there runs a second and much narrower channel. In the early summer, after the melting of the snow, this river would be a very considerable body of water—indeed it is the most important river east of the Pechora. About eight miles up from our camp I found some *Koropatki*—the *rüper* of Norway, and our own ptarmigan—on a patch of scrub. This was the first time I had met with it, and as far as my own journey is concerned, the Korotaika marks its north-eastern limit. On this day we also crossed the Viseha River, which, after running for some time in a south-westerly direction, falls into the Korotaika. The channel is about two hundred yards in width.

After crossing the Korotaika River we paid a visit to the choom of a Zirian—a sort of cousin by race to the Samoyad, but dwelling in a more southerly latitude. This good fellow hospitably laid before us a dish of raw fish, which proved exceedingly high. Berzumoff appeared to enjoy its flavour hugely, and I managed to make a struggle with it to avoid giving offence. I should think that my companion and the Zirian ate between them about six pounds. The fish, which was like a large roach, had a dark back with silver scales on flanks and belly. It was caught in the Korotaika, and I saw several of different sizes which I should say varied from two to ten pounds. Our host was a genial, hospitable fellow, standing about five feet eight inches, well built, with broad face, high cheekbones, very dark eyes, clean-cut straight nose and a thin black beard. His wife was plump, rather fair, oval of face, quite five feet six inches in height, and in manners pleasant and gentle. In her choom the Zirian woman was clothed in a species of dressing-gown (of the most primitive make), but in her walks abroad she almost invariably wore a rough soveek, with hood and all. The soveek of the Samoyads, I should add, becomes a "park" with the Zirians. There were no fewer than seven children in the choom, and consequently there was not a little crowding. I noticed among other articles of furniture two large copper bowls, clearly of Russian manufacture. From this Zirian I bought a militza of the type worn by the Samoyads, and very soon found out what an admirable garment it was for the cold, rough weather we were experiencing. It was much superior to the bladder-nosed sealskin, which I had had made in London, and for the rest of my journey I was only too glad to wear the Samoyad militza. I had already taken to the pimmies, or long skin boots, finding them very much lighter and more suitable

THE AUTHOR IN SAMOYAD MILITZA AND PIMMIES, WITH BAMBOO FOR HARRAY OR DRIVING-POLE.

than those I had had made of sealskin. The pimmies were bought from the Samoyads at the rate of three roubles a pair.

As by this time I had become something of an

expert at driving reindeer, I may perhaps be permitted to describe the method employed by the Samoyads. Either two, three, four, or five reindeer are driven abreast; I have never seen more than five,

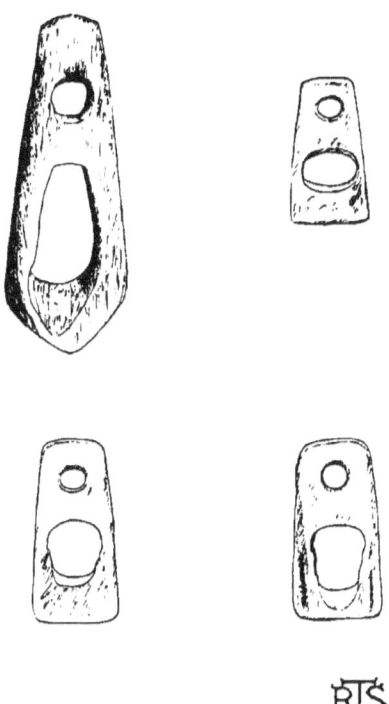

CHULKIS.
The largest is of wood; the others of walrus ivory. (One-third the natural size.)

or less than two. They are harnessed to the sledge by means of running traces of seal-hide, by a capital arrangement which makes each deer do his share of the work. This is the *chulki*, of which there is one at each side. It is a kind of tackle-block made of either wood or walrus ivory, through which the trace runs from the near to the offside reindeer. If you are driving a team of four, two more chulkis, called *piatsa*, are attached for the traces of the two deer inside, but this time not to the sledge, but to the part of the first trace which travels between the chulkis fixed on either side of the sledge. When five are driven the odd deer has a single trace attached to the middle part of the second trace between its chulkis. These traces are all attached to the respective deer by a broad flat band of hide which passes round the chest, and is held in place by another over the withers.[1] The deer are driven by a single seal-hide rein (*milanai*), which leads from a light halter (*siahn*) along the near-side of the near-side deer. If you pull this rein, the rest of the team follow the one so guided.[2] The difficulty comes

[1] The collar (*podija*), saddle (*yodijina*), and traces (*sa*) are very simply designed, and in practice answer admirably. The first is of hide, about three inches broad, and passes round the neck to be fastened in front by the single trace which leads from the sledge through the hind-legs, along the belly (there kept in place by the belly-band) and between the fore-legs up to the collar. The saddle is nearly three times the width of the collar, and usually hangs down free to about six inches below the belly. At the place where it leaves the flank a twisted or, at any rate, double thong of hide is fastened by means of a horn, bone, or ivory button (*schorlak*), roughly rectangular as a rule, but sometimes round and pierced with two holes. These buttons have occasionally a diameter of three inches, and are usually curved to fit the swell of the flank.

[2] This single rein travels through a bone catch called the *halsa;* and the halsa itself is the most varied part of the reindeer's harness. It is made of ivory or bone, sometimes in the form of a simple hook,

in when you want them to go to the offside. It took me some time to find this out—I had to learn almost everything by keeping a sharp lookout—and I at last discovered that by lightly and sharply jerking the single rein over to the right, you could manage pretty well. But the offside is always the weak point in reindeer driving—even with Samoyad experts—and a Samoyad sledging-team is not the kind of turn-out one would care to steer down Piccadilly on an afternoon in the season. A great help, however, in driving is the *harray*, or long driving-pole, which the Samoyads call the *toor*. It is about fifteen feet long, two and a half inches in diameter at the thickest part, and then tapers to a fine point, on which there is fixed a knob (*toormal*) often made of walrus ivory. At the butt end is a spear-shaped piece of iron, which is used for trying the ice when crossing rivers. Although the actual weight of this harray is considerable, the weight in the hand is very materially reduced because the heavy end, which is allowed to extend some five feet behind, acts as a weight to adjust the balance.

The Samoyad sledge varies in size, but is generally about nine feet long and thirty inches wide. It is made of pine, and may be described as having two large thick runners curved up at the front end to a

often in that of a double hook, the hooks being back to back, and frequently these forms are rendered elaborate by a serrated upper edge or a number of piercings in the solid ivory.

height of two feet. On each side four uprights, placed rather close together towards the rear, slope upward and inward until at a height of two feet from the runner, when they are united together by stout bars, which act as cross-overs and make the floor of the sledge. The long pieces extending from the top of the bend of the runners to the rear end of the sledge

SAMOYAD SLEDGE.

are called *bereznias*, and give the required rigidity to the structure. Baggage is put on this floor and heaped up against the high back of the sledge, while the driver generally sits on this baggage, or on a seat just in front. The woman's sledge is larger, and is ornamented by long strips of hide painted red, which hang from the bereznias and form a fringe.

On the 19th and 20th we had very bitter weather,

high wind and snow driving in our faces. All the 19th we waited for some deer which had been left behind at the Talata River. The wind increased to a gale, and the snow came down without ceasing. The high wind drove the snow into the choom until there was a very sensible deposit, while just outside the hide walls the snow piled up three or four feet. All the morning my Russian companion carried on a wild flirtation with the Samoyad woman—a most hideous small-pox-riddled beldame — but in the afternoon he drove off to visit some Zirians in the neighbourhood. To make matters rather worse, he came back hopelessly drunk, and was ill all over the choom. But no one noticed it or attempted to clean our reeking floor. Throughout the day the baby hallooed loudly, and as it was suffering from dysentery, I have no doubt that it was not without justification. Yet it contributed to the making of an exceedingly unpleasant day for me. Towards the evening of the 20th there was a rise in the temperature to only five degrees of frost, which made the snow very wet and troublesome, as it penetrated everything.

In the course of the next day we passed a Samoyad burial-place with four wooden vaults and broken, overturned sledges. About thirty yards from these there stood a stick driven into the ground. Stefan, one of the Samoyads, explained that the stick marked the grave of a Christian Samoyad, and that the vaults were those of Samoyads who were not Christians. We were very heavily laden with skins, blubber, etc., but made fifteen miles, which, considering the high wind and the bad condition of the snow in the afternoon, was very fair under the circumstances. Had we been travelling light we could have made sixty miles a day without injury to the deer, but on this journey we were really hauling what were heavy loads. This night, I find from my Journal, we passed very cheerfully, owing to one of the Samoyads having brought some driftwood from the sea-coast. For the last two nights we had been entirely out of wood, and consequently had not had a fire in the choom; but as it had been crowded with Samoyads and Zirians — thirteen in a space nine feet in diameter — there had been maintained a certain oily heat, which, I suppose, now I look back upon it, was not without its advantages.

It had been cold all the way from Habarova, as may readily be supposed from our being compelled to cut our meat into the chunks required for cooking with an axe. But cooking was often quite out of the question, and on these occasions raw frozen reindeer meat had to be gnawed. It was always a great business to unpack one's baggage, owing to the ropes being frozen so hard that they felt more like steel rods. We used to place the meat in the wood fire, and actually keep it there for fifteen minutes before it thawed to the point when we could cut it easily up into chunks.

Elsewhere I give a fairly complete account of the weather experienced, but as an indication of that which we met when crossing the Great Frozen Land, it will be more convenient perhaps to give here just a few jottings on the weather and temperature during the last ten days of this month. Oct. 22nd.—Stiff north-west breeze, temperature 4° F., bread frozen so hard that it required half an hour's thawing close to fire. Oct. 23rd.—Light west wind, snow − 2° F. Oct. 24th.—Very light north breeze, fog at night, temperature − 13° F. Oct. 25th.—Very light north breeze − 5° F. Oct. 26th.—Light breeze, foggy, temperature − 14° F. Oct. 27th.—Light north breeze: at night south-east and heavy snow, temperature − 21° F. Oct. 28th.—South-east wind and heavy snow, temperature 15° F. Oct. 29th.—From zero to freezing-point, light southerly breeze, with snow later. Oct. 30th.—Heavy wet snow, south-east moderate wind, temperature 30° F. Oct. 31st.—Temperature rose to 34° F., snow in very wet state and heavy going. The Samoyads were in great disgust at the state of the snow, and the Russian poured out an almost unceasing string of oaths throughout the day. The traces were continually breaking, and the deer laboured heavily. During the entire journey the sky was usually overcast and snow-laden, and indeed I only saw the sun two or three times between Habarova and the Pechora.

The rivers, which are short but evidently much flooded in the early summer, are very numerous. Between the 21st and 31st of October I crossed the following: Talata, Tambiha, Nosiyaha, Yaha (this does not flow into the sea as marked in the Admiralty chart, but into the Hyputhra), Hyputhra, Eraya, Hannawayaha, Sonsida, Lobbergonway Yaha, Charnayaha, Ichvit, two rivers both called Nahwul, and the Gostroma. The common characteristic of all these rivers was the wide, shallow bed, at that time only partly occupied by the stream.

The 23rd was another drunken day. The Samoyads in the choom were in an advanced stage of liquor, and those who had been visiting Zirians in the neighbourhood were driven back lying across their sledges like dead logs. If it had not been for the cold weather, these days in the choom would have been intolerable, for its condition had become indescribable.

On the 24th, the Russian peasant, a Samoyad, and I went to visit an encampment some way off, the object being to buy skins. So long a time was spent in haggling over a matter of three roubles, that when we started back it was quite dark, and owing to a thick fog the Samoyad soon lost his way.[1] We wandered over the Tundra for some hours, and by

[1] The Samoyads know the trackless Tundra well; but the more experienced among them are able to shape their course by the stars, and when fogs or clouds obscure the sky, they are said to be able to ascertain their locality by examining the moss. They have been

way of varying the monotony, drove over a bank of snow, which, as it turned out, dropped almost vertically to the frozen bed of a stream some fifteen feet below. The sledge shot forward on to the backs of the deer, and, throwing them down, capsized. The next moment we were all struggling in a heap together—sledge, deer, furs, and ourselves almost indistinguishably buried in the deep snow. However, we soon rearranged our relations to one another, and then decided to sleep on our sledge and wait for daylight. The thermometer was down to thirteen degrees below zero, and it proved difficult to keep warm on the sledge, so I dug a long hole in the snow, and lying down in it in my militza, covered myself over with snow and was soon comfortably asleep. We started early in the morning, and after some hours' travelling regained our camp. I should like to add that in these tumbles—and they must be expected in a journey of this kind—a team of reindeer is in many respects preferable to one of horses. The latter would probably have kicked us soundly and have inflicted very serious injuries.

During our progress across these wastes of snow we kept falling in with other Samoyads, and often when we out-spanned our choom was inconveniently crowded. One night we had as many as thirteen

seen on such occasions in winter-time to scrape and kick away the overlying snow until they reached the moss, and then shape their course in accordance with the nature of this lowly signpost.

in the choom—about three yards in diameter be it remembered—and as the temperature had risen a good deal, the result was almost overpowering. But they were extremely interesting people to watch, and in addition to the interest, I often found great amusement in closely noting their peculiar habits. As is so often the case with an ignorant race when it comes into contact with a representative of a civilised people, they seemed to regard me as a great Medicine Man, and soon got into the habit of coming to me for relief in all their aches and pains. Sore eyes and colds were the chief complaints for which I prescribed; but I did not attempt the hopeless task of extinguishing the myriad animal life which clung so closely and intimately to them and their clothing—much as I should have liked to remove this plague.

Throughout this part of my journey, sport was very indifferent, and even the young snowy owls were not plentiful, while the old birds had entirely disappeared. I had not seen one since leaving Habarova. The lemmings (*mus*), were also rather scarce, but those I saw still gave no sign of changing their brown coats.

From time to time as we journeyed across the frozen Tundra, the Samoyads would divert themselves by breaking in some of their young deer. It is almost needless for me to say that the method was of the roughest, and made no allowance whatever for the personal feelings of the deer. The animal to be broken in is lassoed, and then has a rope tied round its neck with the end of it fastened to the rear of the sledge. The Samoyad then stirs up his team and starts off at a rapid rate, the terrified young deer pulling back until he is nearly strangled. I have seen them exerting their whole force against being thus dragged along, and when their legs gave way under them, lying on the surface of the snow while they are rapidly towed by the skimming sledge. It is true that the Samoyad will usually stop when a deer falls down; but the only reason, of course, is his fear that the animal will die of strangulation. After a few courses of this treatment the young deer either gets used to following close behind the sledge, or, for obvious reasons, elects to run in preference to being dragged after it. When he has done this to the satisfaction of the Samoyad for a little time, he is placed on the offside of the team, with one old deer outside him. It then becomes a question of going with the rest, and like that perfidious creature, the average man, the reindeer usually prefers to be found with the majority. Should he show, at the outset, any leanings to individualism, the banging of the runners against his hocks, and a prod or two from the sharp end of the long driving-pole, will probably bring him back to his senses and the state of life to which he has just been called.

Nothing that I know in nature can equal the dreariness and solitude of the Tundra. Mile after mile as you travel along there is no break in the monotony of this great frozen land. Everywhere is snow, everywhere the vast white plains. In the perspective of distance the very ridges melt into the general level, and as you look around, everywhere you are met with the same great mantle of unbroken snow. The country lies before you as an earth that is dead, so still, so motionless, so rigid is the landscape. Life has fled before the icy winds which draw out of the north, and the land you traverse is surely the land of death. There is scarcely the cry of a single bird to break upon the ear in this untenanted wilderness; the very streams are motionless masses of ice. Track there is none, and you may wander east, west, north, and south without landmark to set you right. Day after day and week after week your deer will gallop along their frozen way, and your compass or, if the gray clouds will lift for a while, the stars in the heaven above will be your only guide. But yet there comes a break now and again even in this silence. When perhaps the stillness is most oppressive, when you would welcome with all your heart even the wild, harsh scream of a wandering gull, then there comes from the north a murmuring of the highly rarefied air, and a short while afterwards sudden gusts of an angry wind. The clouds grow darker and droop close overhead, and the sharp, white horizon becomes dim and then disappears. With the howl of the demon of your childhood's fancy, the storm-fiend of the Tundra leaps upon you. The snow drives and the wind shrieks, and you are suddenly wrapped in a furious cloud of whirling snow. The eye cannot pierce it, and the antlers of the cowering deer are the utmost limit of your landscape. Hour after hour the gale continues, and the cold becomes so intense that even to breathe is painful. But you continue to urge the deer forward, with voice and rein and harray, and at last the wind suddenly swerves half round the compass and gradually drops. Then you take counsel with your common sense, and, calling a halt, outspan the plucky little deer, raise the poles of the choom, and after a supper on some frozen flesh, compose yourself to that sleep which is Nature's medicine for weariness.

CHAPTER V

ACROSS "THE GREAT FROZEN LAND" (*continued*)

A new feature—Lost bays—Old beaches—The Pitkoff Hills—Driving a Norwegian sledge—Its great advantages—New landscapes—The Indian snow-shoe—A push for the Pechora—A hospitable friend—The Pechora—Up the frozen river—Ussia—Ivan at home—Eating "marbles"—An object of curiosity—Pustozersk—Life on the Pechora—Russian hospitality—Camping out—Cost of the journey from Habarova—A solar eccentricity—Another Samoyad burial-place—The pony of Northern Russia—Good-bye to my Habarova friends—Going south—Meeting the tree-line—The Zirians—A cold morning—Ust-Zilma—Roman Okatov—Madame Okatov—Curiosity of the natives—Twenty-five in a room—The Ust-Zilma well—Kindness of the Okatovs—My new guide—Departure from Ust-Zilma—Doorkin—Spill—Another upset—Stamina of the Russian ponies—A bad track—A drunken Zirian—Hills and gullies—Pinega and its fair—The English language once more—The post-sledge—Ust-Pinega—Holmagora—Arkhangel—The British Vice-Consul—Good news.

WE had been steadily travelling across the frozen Tundra for eighteen days when, on 1st November, we crossed the Piatsoworyaha River, and on the following day, about eight miles west of the river, entered a most interesting region. Right in front, and away to the northward, there spread the amphi-

theatre of an old bay, whose width would be about
fifteen miles, and its inmost reach at least nine miles
from the present sea-shore. Step above step there
ranged the old sea-beaches, following the lines of the
higher land immediately behind them, and girding with
a terraced rampart the level basin of salt marsh into
which the waves once rolled. The beaches themselves
were now thickly covered with grass, and the grass
with snow, but walking along the terraces I found
several pools of salt water, and a number of recumbent
pine-trees—one of which I measured, to find it was
forty feet long and two feet in diameter at the thickest
end. They had evidently lain there for a long time.
It is my belief that these trees which I found in a
treeless country were carried down the Pechora and
washed round to this former coast line. On the higher
beaches the wood was clearly much older than on the
lower; and there was no trace of mud, or of immersion
in mud, even on the most recently deposited trees.
No other explanation will account for their presence
at this point, or for the various other signs I found in
abundance of this having formerly been a marine shore.
These old sea-beaches, I may add, continued at intervals for many miles westward—notably that which
is now six miles from the sea, and lies just to the east
of the Pechora River—and most certainly would repay
the attention of a geologist if he could visit them in
the summer. For in the winter, as I found, not even

the most determined "picking" could make the ground, frozen as hard as metal, yield up the shells which I feel it must contain. But I think he would find it no easy matter to reach the spot, as, owing to the shoals and sandbanks on the coast, nothing but a vessel of the lightest draught could approach it from the sea, and during the summer season the Great Tundra is practically impassable.

On the 3rd we skirted along the northern face of the Pitkoff Hills, which rise to nearly six hundred feet, and are the most considerable heights we had yet seen. In character, however, they do not differ from the ordinary elevations of the tundra, being rounded hills with smooth dry slopes dropping to a boggy base. Up to this point there had been, south of us, rolling tundra of the ordinary type, while between us and the sea the country had been quite flat, grassy, and with a considerable amount of ancient driftwood. When the Russians go north to Habarova in May they travel by night, in order that the surface of the snow may be hard enough to bear their sledges. On the other hand, they could not well travel at an earlier date, as the depth and frozen character of the snow make it impossible for the deer to get at the moss.

I now tried a Norwegian sledge instead of the Samoyad sledge which I had been using. It was ten feet six inches long, one foot six inches wide, and six inches in height from the runner to the top of the sledge.

ROUNDING UP THE DEER.

It went rapidly and well; but, owing to its narrowness, and being so little raised from the ground, it is not so suitable for use with reindeer as the higher sledge. Yet, at the end of a drive of about one thousand versts, during which I had many spills with it, occasionally skidding down the ice-slopes of the high banks, and arriving anyhow on the frozen river below, it was just as strong and sound as ever. One of the great reasons for this lies in the pliability and elasticity of the sledge. For apart from its lightness, and the toughness of the usk or ash wood of which it is made, the sledge had not a single nail, not a piece of metal, to keep it together. All the parts were firmly lashed together with raw hide, which would give and yield a little, and yet not break under a serious strain. To this I attribute its adaptability to rough work. The runners, which are nothing else than a pair of ski, travel over the snow with the least possible friction, and are immeasurably superior to the flat toboggan, which was at one time so popular. Unquestionably it is the sledge for pulling by hand or driving with dogs.

The land was all so white and comparatively smooth that, just as it often is at sea, it was extremely difficult to judge distances. Low elevations of the tundra would sometimes appear like high hills, and the mirage at times was most deceptive. But on the 8th we crossed the Posanka River, and the country underwent a great change. Deep gullies and scrub became frequent, the former proving rather awkward places to gallop down into and out of; and on the 9th we reached the highest elevation we had actually found, lying directly before us in our route—the Heisadahoi Hills—about two hundred and fifty feet above the sea-level. I should mention that *heisada* is Samoyad for hill. At this point Pustozersk, the first outpost of comparative civilisation, and on the western frontier of the Great Tundra, lay about one hundred versts from us; and Ivan, the Russian, found the slow travelling of the heavily-laden sledges so wearisome that he asked me to accompany him on a rapid run to that place. I was very glad to go, and joined him with pleasure.

Just before striking camp, I started out on Canadian snow-shoes to stalk *koropatki*, and soon bagged three fine birds. A little later I winged a fourth, and, running after it, found that one could come a very fair "cropper" in the snow-shoes, by first selecting short rough scrub partly covered over with frozen snow as a running path, and then forgetting this hard fact. But plunging headlong into deep snow is not such unpleasant exercise; what is far less pleasant is searching for anything in it! On this occasion, for example, I dropped a pipe which, when I left England, my friend M. had slipped into my pocket, and as I had in consequence a sort of regard for it, I was determined not to lose it. Yet although the splash I had made in my snow-bath was certainly less than six feet in diameter, it was rather over an hour before I found the object of my search. By that time the temperature had itself become searching, so I "shoed" back to camp at a good round rate, only stopping to bag with a right and left another brace of koropatki.

We started about 11 A.M., I driving three deer harnessed to the Norwegian sledge, and Ivan having four deer harnessed to his sledge, on which a fair amount of baggage was packed. We drove at a gallop through a country which showed us clearly enough that for a time we had left the Tundra behind. The hills were frequently of considerable elevation; instead of wide, wet, flat marsh with shallow pools, we met with narrow valleys and deep lakes. At 2 P.M. the sun set, and the cold, keen wind became very bitter. With the thermometer registering 42° of frost, and the wind right in our faces, the rapid gallop at which we drove made the cold decidedly severe. One's face naturally suffered: my eyelashes were blocked up with snow and ice; my forehead and nose lost all feeling, and I was continually rubbing them to prevent very serious frost-bite. I could not reach my mouth—it was caged over with ice which had formed on my moustache; and, as a matter of fact, the whole of my face was more or less covered with a mask of ice. However, we kept on, and at 5 P.M. reached Kuia, a very small village which hardly wears the air of comparative importance which the Port of the great river Pechora, which it really is, might be expected to possess.

Here a friend of Ivan very hospitably entertained us with hot tea and fish-broth, before which, however,

KUIA, THE PORT OF THE PECHORA.

Ivan went to the church to give thanks for his safe return from the Tundra. At tea, the fish-broth was placed on the table in a large bowl, and each person was given a spoon or ladle with which he dipped into the common dish. It was very agreeable to sit in the warm hut and pour some hot food down, but we

were anxious to get on, and would not accept our
host's pressing invitation to stay the night. So at
7 P.M. we started off again in perfectly execrable
weather. The night was so dark and the gale so
severe the snow driving straight into our faces that
Ivan very soon lost his way. After wandering about
for two hours I at last induced him to accept the indication of my compass, as I knew that the Pechora
must lie to the west of us. The virtue of the compass
was soon established in his eyes; for shortly after this
we struck the river, and driving on to its frozen surface, made a course right up the middle of the stream.[1]
It was very evident that before the river consented to
remain solid it was broken up time after time by the
rising tide.[2] This made it extremely rough and

[1] The river Pechora, the most considerable of all the Tundra
rivers, rises in the Urals, close to the frontiers of three govern-
ments—Vologda, Perm, and Tobolsk, and runs in its lower course
through the government of Arkhangel. It is two thousand versts in
length, and, though navigable from the mouth to near its source,
has comparatively little navigation. This is doubtless owing to the
short period which intervenes between the breaking up of the ice,
with its ensuing floods, and the setting in of the long winter. It
runs through very large and dense forests, while here and there
stretches of rich pasturage occur. The Pechora simply swarms
with fish, and its salmon are justly famous: for while they reach the
enormous weight of eighty pounds, they do not lose their peculiar
delicacy.

[2] The account which Mr. Seebohm has given of the breaking up
of the ice on the Pechora and similar rivers should be read by every
one interested (*Siberia in Europe*, p. 111, and Presidential Address,
Section E, British Association Meeting at Nottingham, 1893, pub-

hummocky, and we often in the darkness drove over rough blocks, which landed us down a drop of three or four feet on the other side. I trembled for the safety of my light sledge, but it bore the trial magnificently, and behaved like the proverbial cork upon the water—perhaps almost too much so for the comfort of the driver. After five or six miles of this we turned off the river and drove across the country until we arrived at a village of five huts called Ussia, and about three miles from Pustozersk. And here an incident occurred which revealed to me that my knowledge of Russian, though rapidly improving as far as my own speech was concerned, was far indeed from the stage at which I could wish it had arrived, with regard to comprehending the voluble dialogue of my companion. It turned out that so little had I understood the amiable conversation of my friend Ivan, that I was thunderstruck (a powerful word is needed here) to find the next morning, when getting ready for another start, that he was going no further, and had in fact reached his home! From this the reader may be able to gather how difficult it was sometimes to

lished in the *Geographical Journal*, October 1893). Here is a sentence: "Cracks running for miles, with a sound like distant thunder, warned us that a mighty power was all but upon us, a force which seemed for the moment to impress the mind with a greater sense of power than even the crushing weight of water at Niagara, a force which breaks up ice more than a mile wide, at least three feet thick, and weighted with another three feet of snow, at the rate of one hundred miles in the twenty-four hours."

know what was going on round one; and it was my ignorance which often made me suspicious and over-watchful when no harm, I now feel sure, was intended.

During the journey from Habarova there was only one day when the meat was not frozen so hard that an axe was required to chop it into chunks for cooking. As we experienced such bad weather—high winds combined with low temperatures—I came to the conclusion that the mid-day meal would be less of a trouble if one made some provision for it before breaking camp in the morning. So I generally took a good-sized piece of partially-thawed deer's flesh and cut it up—a painful process and a slow—into small cubes of a size that would go comfortably into one's mouth. When, later on, I grew hungry, I used to transfer one of these at a time from my pocket to my mouth, and so, in the course of an hour's sledging, managed to absorb a fair amount of nourishment. I can hardly say that hunger proved on these occasions so good a condiment as it is proverbially supposed to be, for although I was decidedly hungry, I never got over the sensation that I was putting marbles into my mouth. Still, it never does to indulge in the luxury of growling when you cannot mend matters, and I derived a certain sort of cold comfort by remembering that an ancient philosopher used to preach and, what is strange for a philosopher, actually tested the virtue of keeping stones in his mouth.

A WELCOME WASH AT USSIA.

I had a general washing of clothes, etc. The Russian villagers crowded round, and kept up a fire of questions and gaped generally at my things. They said I was the first foreigner who had come through the Bolshaia Zemelskija country to Pustozersk, although both Germans and English have visited the Pechora Valley during the summer; and gave me to understand that they thought our run of one hundred and ten versts of the day before was something very good in the way of driving, especially as they seemed to consider the Norwegian sledge a light and altogether too absurdly fragile a thing for such rough and rapid work.

Towards the end of the day I went out for a look round and stretched my legs on ski, and, as the snow was in excellent condition, made good going. Nothing, however, falls more quickly out of condition than snow, and on the following day when I started for Pustozersk, ski were impracticable, and Canadian snow-shoes proved just the very things. Pustozersk,[1] the most

[1] From *Pusto*, shallow; and *Ozero*, a lake (Russian). Josias Logan gives us a good account of the main events which took place during the winter of 1611-12, which he spent at Pustozersk. He notices particularly, that early in December "the Townsmen of Pechora went overland into Jugoria, to trade with the Inhabitants there, and the *Samoyeds*"; and that on 19th January they returned, having had "but an hard Voyage" owing to the Samoyads of Yugoria being then at war with the Samoyads of the Ob, whence came the finest Sables; and he further mentions in a letter to Hakluyt, written from the Pechora, that "there use to come hither in the Winter about two thousand Samoieds with their Commodities, which may be such as we dreamed not on yet" (*Purchas, his Pilgrimes*, iii. pp. 544-546).

William Pursglove, who spent part of the winter of 1611-12 at Pustozersk with Josias Logan, confirms and amplifies many of the observations made by the latter: and it is interesting to note

important settlement of the district, is a compact village of fifteen log-houses and a church. It lies on the south side of a lake about six miles long, at a distance of about three or four miles from the Pechora. The inhabitants—Russians, Zirians, and some Samoyads—live chiefly by fishing,[1] but the most flourishing people of this and the neighbourhood are the enterprising peasant traders who push north every spring to deal with the Samoyads of the Great Tundra. The better-class Russian house here is of two stories, the ground floor being devoted to stores, and the upper floor to living rooms. Entrance is effected by a sloping wooden way, which reaches to the first story, and up which horse and sledge can be driven. Within there are no passages, but you pass through compartment after compartment—I can hardly say room after room—each with closely-fitting doors, and thus you gradually leave all the cold air behind. It is considered very neglectful and discourteous if you do not close each door carefully as you go through. The custom of erecting crosses near their houses to com-

---

that the Russians on the Pechora prevented him from travelling eastward into Yugoria and trading direct with the Samoyads, as he had wished to do. Pursglove describes Ust-Zilma as "a pretie Towne of some sixtie Houses: and is three or foure dayes sayling with a faire wind against the streame from *Puztozer.*"

[1] The great business of man on the Pechora is to fish, and that of woman is to spin yarn and make of it fishing-nets for her lord. But she does not make a bad housewife, and can knit a very good pair of stockings from wool she has herself spun.

memorate dead friends, I first met with here, where I found it in full vigour; but these crosses very soon became one of the most familiar features of the landscape, and before I was well into settled Russia I had ceased to notice them.

A Wayside Cross.
(From a sketch by Herbert Ward, F.R.G.S.)

No one could be more hospitable than these rough, simple, genial Russians. They invited me to tea continually, and I was overwhelmed with attentions. I learnt afterwards that some of these people were descendants of men of good family and position, but that many years ago their forerunners had been sent for "political reasons" up to this part of the world, which, by the way, is considered a degree worse than Siberia. Indeed I received everywhere—with the single exception of a Zirian—such uniform kindness, that my surprise was great when I heard at Arkhangel that communications had been sent from somewhere on the Pechora to the Governor of Arkhangel, reporting that a man named Jackson was travelling in that district, and that he had been sent there by the British Government to spread cholera amongst the inhabitants. What were they to do with him? The only explanation that I can possibly give was the profound impression which my spirit cooking-stove everywhere seemed to make; and it is quite possible that the blue flame which I had contrived with some trouble to imprison in the white metal cylinder, through the wire gauze holes of which its gleam was visible, excited some superstitious awe.[1] The peasants

[1] It is probable that the great plague of cholera which visited Northern Russia about a generation ago has left an indelible impression upon the minds of the Samoyads and Zirians; especially as the disease, which subsequently more than decimated the reindeer of the Tundras, is generally traced to this epidemic. More than 50,000 head are supposed to have died from its effects. Mr. Henry Seebohm (*Siberia in Europe*, p. 56) refers to the opinion of residents on the Pechora as bearing out this belief; and a similar experience even befell Mr. Rae, who mentions that he and his companion were taken for Germans, and that the Samoyads he met with on the Kanin peninsula declared that "we Germans were notorious for our dirty habits, and for carrying cholera about" (p. 274).

in that region are in the depths of ignorance, and their ideas of the world beyond the Pechora were misty indeed. I told them I had come from London, and they thought London some far country, at least the other side of the world. During April and May the Pechora has plenty of water, and steamers can go up to Pustozersk; later in summer they cannot go beyond Kuia.

I stayed at Pustozersk about three weeks, seeing much of the people, and having, on the whole, a good deal of sport. On one occasion I went off for two or three days with a Samoyad after a pack of wolves, whose tracks, as they passed near us, were visible in some short birch scrub. We were travelling light and took no choom. In fact I had only a small quantity of raw meat and my spirit stove. At night my former plan of scraping out a hollow and sleeping in the snow was followed without the least harm ensuing. We were, however, unsuccessful, not having the good fortune even to see any bigger game than some koropatki (the ptarmigan), an Arctic hare, and some tit-like birds—samples of all of which I bagged. I found the magpie very common here, as indeed it is throughout the whole of Northern Russia. It is not easy to shoot koropatki in the morning when they are feeding, as they post sentries in the branches; but when they have done their repast on the twigs of the uraa or scrub, they lie close or perch on the branches.

You can get within shot of them then, and I have often shot several brace in a very short time. The crops of the koropatki were full of the twigs and shoots of the uraa scrub and enormously distended.

During my journey from Habarova I had made a fair amount of way with my Russian. Every word I

PUSTOZERSK.

captured with some difficulty, but directly I was sure of the meaning, it went into my pocket vocabulary. And at Pustozersk, through the medium of Latin, I obtained from the pastor a number of new words. The cost of the hire of the reindeer and the services as guide of Berzumoff all the way from Habarova amounted to 225 roubles (about £23 : 10s.), which seemed to be a fair price, especially as much of it had been paid in kind.

When I was returning from a fruitless stalk after wolves on 28th November, I was rewarded by a curious sunset, the peculiar arrangement of lights being different from any of the solar eccentricities I had witnessed in Greenland seas. The sun was just above the horizon, and to the east and west of it, at a

A SOLAR ECCENTRICITY.

distance of about ten degrees, there appeared two great lights similar to that which spread upward and outward from the sun itself. Had these lights been less fiery, they would have reminded one of short sections of a rainbow, with the colours all mingled, if that were possible ; but as it was, they were extremely ruddy, and lit up the darkness, although only extending for some six degrees upwards. The phenomenon lasted for fifteen minutes.

A mile east of Ussia there is a Samoyad burial-place, but here of course it is the Christian Samoyad that one finds entombed. Over one grave there was a Russian cross (☦) six feet high, on which was cut an inscription in Russian; but the other graves were simply marked by upright poles or even sticks, some being quite rough, and with the bark left on, and others being shaped with an axe. Yet, so strongly does the old faith cling to these rude inhabitants of the Tundra, I saw at a short distance from the graves two overturned reindeer sledges, symbols of the old belief in the hunter's paradise to come.

On 1st December I started on the drive to Pinega, distant one thousand versts. I had been extremely anxious to use reindeer, but their proprietors declared that they were in poor condition, and unfit for so long a journey, while the ice now covering the land prevented them from getting at their food. So I was reluctantly compelled to use horses, although afterwards I regarded my new experience as a very valuable one. The horse of the country is a little shaggy animal, standing about fourteen hands, and extremely hardy. He is rarely stalled at night, even in the severest weather, and I have seen these ponies, as I might call them, often turned out after a long day's march, with nothing but a small bundle of hay thrown to them for food. So after a long barter—these traders are fair Shylocks —I agreed with a Russian to supply horses for the journey to Arkhangel for the sum of thirty roubles as far as Pinega; a ridiculous price from our point of view, but a very fair sum from his. At starting, I had to say a final good-bye to my Yugorski Schar friends—both Russian and Samoyad. Our leave-taking was of the most affectionate nature, as they were good enough to manifest a strong liking for me, and, beyond any doubt, an insatiable interest in all my doings and plans; while, for my part, I was sincerely sorry to see the last of these capital fellows—undeniably filthy though they were. But the longer I lived with them the more I grew to understand them, and throughout the whole of my sojourn and subsequent journey with them, we had not had one single serious hitch, nor one instance of unpleasantness. Their timidity or natural sluggishness—perhaps a little of both—had deprived me of a most interesting journey to the Yalmal Peninsula; but their subsequent behaviour had, to some extent, condoned this, and, as far as they were concerned, I have little doubt that they thought they were only acting an entirely friendly part to an eccentric stranger.

After travelling for eighty miles, we left the land beyond the forest for the next zone in the geographer's category, and came upon the tree-line, here represented by a species of willow, about fifteen feet high, and six inches to eight inches in diameter at the butt. This is the first indication that you have reached the Pechora basin; and the second is given by the inhabitants. For they are largely composed of Zirians, whose strongest characteristic perhaps is the number of children they rear. This particularly strikes the traveller who seeks the asylum of their dirty one-roomed huts, if I except the sort of half loft which projects from the walls, on which some of their family sleep without appreciably thinning the crowd which occupies the floor. I have slept in Zirians' huts when twelve or thirteen people have been crowded into a space not so many feet in length and half as many in width. I may mention that during my journey I always cooked for myself, and carried my food on my sledge. Throughout this time the weather was very cold, and on 4th December 28° F. below zero was registered. This I took shortly after sunrise, at the end of a long and very cold drive through the night; and when the night again came round, the temperature fell to so low a point as 35° below zero, or 67 degrees of frost.

After following the course of the Pechora, only leaving it occasionally to take a short cut through the forest, in which dejected-looking pines were now making their appearance, we arrived on 5th December at Ust-Zilma, a large Zirian village of three thousand inhabitants.[1] Here I looked for the person for whom

[1] Ust-Zilma = Ust, at the mouth of; Zilma, the river Zilma. Compare Ust-Ussa, Ust-Pinega, and many other similar combinations in Russia. For sense, our Avon-mouth, and, for order, our Aber-avon, would be examples of some dozens of names of like construction.

Pustozersk gossip had vouched a knowledge of English, but, somewhat naturally perhaps, I failed to find him. In his stead, however, I learnt that it was French and Italian which the wife of Roman Okatov, the chief officer of the woods and forests of this northern district, could speak. Though no master of these tongues, I sent a message to M. Okatov, begging permission to be allowed to call, and received a most cordial invitation to come immediately. With those fine fragments of Anglo-French, however, which cling to one fifteen years after leaving an English school, I plunged into conversation, and I owe it to my instructors (may their shades be blessed!) to acknowledge that I was able to make myself understood. Madame Okatov spoke fluently and well. We managed to converse most agreeably, and so usefully that I learnt a great deal

When Ust-Zilma was visited, in 1611, by Josias Logan, it was a village of "some thirtie or fortie houses." Both barley and rye were cultivated, and Logan considered the barley "passing faire and white almost as rice." Ust-Zilma was, for some weeks, the centre of Mr. Seebohm's ornithological wanderings, and he describes the main street—practically the only street—as about two miles long. Each house stands on a considerable area of ground, and the better houses have outhouses and even a bath-house in their own yards. For seven months Ust-Zilma is frost-bound; and the advance of summer is annually heralded by the floods caused by the bursting of the ice-dam of the Pechora. Then Ust-Zilma becomes a navigable part of the earth; and you may boat from house to house, if you will; if not, you must swim. In 1875 the summer population was less than two thousand; but this was increased in winter by the accession of the Samoyads who came, and still come, south from the Greater Tundra at that season.

about the place, the people, and the conditions of life and travel in the district.

Here, as elsewhere in uncivilised parts, the natives displayed the most unbounded curiosity in my goods and my person. I was staying at a peasant's hut, where accommodation of course was very primitive, and my host and a wide circle of his acquaintances would crowd into the room staring at me with as much surprise, and examining me as minutely as if I were a newly-discovered animal. My stove, my canteen, everything in my kit, in fact, was a source of interest and astonishment. They even came—women as well as men—into the room where I was having my sponge-bath, and pressed closely round me without evincing so much as a sign of bashfulness. I treated them as the savage children they really were, and found it much the easiest plan to go on with my washing without taking the slightest notice of their presence. I did not see the force of going without my bath, because they chose to make themselves spectators ; and, at any rate, it formed a sort of object-lesson of which, one and all, they stood in great need. They seemed much surprised at my having a sponge-bath at all, and called me *Taplia Chelavek* (the warm man), but this was more particularly with reference to my going about the place in tweed clothes. I found my thick Jaeger underclothing so great a protection that, while I was taking exercise, and the temperature was not far below zero, I could easily dispense with the militza. And a bath was a luxury which I would not forego at any price, after the enforced abstention from it on the march. Indeed, the life in the reeking Russian huts made it one of the greatest pleasures of the day. The

CHURCH AT UST-ZILMA.

Russians smell badly, the Zirians worse, and the Samoyads worst of all. When, one night at Ust-Zilma, no fewer than twenty-five Zirian peasants were crowded together in one small room, the atmosphere was very nearly insupportable, and the stench became so *solid*, that I felt I could have cut it like cheese.[1]

Ust-Zilma is built on the right bank of the Pechora, opposite the point where the Zilma River

UST-ZILMA.

runs into it. With the exception of the officer of the woods and forests and the chief of the police,

[1] At Ust-Zilma accommodation was sometimes rather more than scanty. One night, for example, the hut in which I was staying—a mere rectangular room, some twelve feet by ten feet, with log-walls—provided sleeping-quarters for twenty-five peasants, most of whom were on their way to the Pinega fair. The state of the atmosphere may be partly inferred from the temperature, which the huge furnace in the room had raised to 85° F.; and partly when I add that the

the inhabitants are all Zirians.[1] The people grow rye and barley, the former with the better results; and one of the commonest features of the place are the windmills on the hills, which lie to the north of the town. Higher up the Pechora, east of Ust-Zilma, is a village called Ishma, where Okatov told me kerosene is found in considerable quantities; and it is here that one comes in touch with the ore-producing region of northern Russia. Ust-Zilma itself boasts

whole party had been feasting on fish, which was not merely "high," but absolutely decomposed. These Zirians—the great mass of the Pechora population is Zirian—delight in malodorous dirt, and they have their seven months of hard frost to thank for a comparative immunity from disease. Ust-Zilma itself reeks with offal and foul refuse, and when the temperature rises to any marked extent, becomes almost impossible to the stranger.—F. G. J.

[1] I am indebted to Mr. Henry Cooke, M.A., our capable and courteous Vice-Consul at Arkhangel, for translating the following paragraph relating to the Zirians from a Russian pamphlet on the geography of the Province of Arkhangel: "The Zirians live in the Pechora country, along the river Pechora and its tributaries the Ishma, Zilma, and others. In aspect and constitution the Zirians differ but little from the Russians, their skins only being slightly browner. They are quick-witted, intelligent, honest, and are particularly noted for their great hospitality. In their habits they resemble the Russians more closely than any other race, and their whole style of living is but little different from that of the Russians. But the Zirians are poorer, are averse to cleanliness, and not remarkable for industry. Their villages are as a rule extremely dirty, and built in a haphazard manner. Their clothing is made up of a shirt, boots, militzas, and soveeks. As early as the fourteenth century they were converted to the Orthodox Faith by St. Stephen Velikopermoki. But the Pechora Zirians are chiefly Dissenters or Rasskolniks. Their main occupation is fishing, agriculture, hunting fur animals, and herding reindeer."

but one long winding street, with one or two short roads lying at right angles to it. Of course everything is most primitive, but it was with interest that I noticed the appliance for drawing water from the wells, for I had seen it in other countries, and was to meet with it everywhere in Russia. My readers, too, will recognise it — the long pole working on a pivot at the top of a post, and with a heavy log hanging from the lower end, while the bucket is suspended by a rope from the other. Towards evening, when the horses are being watered, and the household supply is being drawn, the creaking of some dozens of these heavy but ingenious levers makes a great noise, and strikes the stranger particularly. The Zirians of Ust-Zilma live on the grain they grow, the fish they catch, and the skins they obtain from the Samoyads by trade. What they do not eat or use, they sell in the markets of Pinega and Arkhangel. I was offered at Ust-Zilma a large portion of a mammoth tusk, weighing seventy lbs. Russian. The Zirian owner wanted to sell me the lot at two and a half roubles a pound; but as I could not carry so much additional weight, and as he would not sell a part of it, we made no deal.[1]

[1] "Likewise being at Pechora, Oust Zilma, or any of those parts, there is the Winter time to bee had among the Samoyeds, Elephant's teeth, which they sell in pieces according as they get it, and not by weight."—Richard Finch (1611), *Purchas, his Pilgrimes*, vol. iii. p. 538. The similarity of experience is interesting.

With the kind assistance of R. Okatov, I engaged a Zirian named Doorkin, with two sledges and two horses to carry myself and baggage as far as Pinega, distant seven hundred versts. The sum I paid for this was twenty-four roubles, by which it will be seen that money is dear in these parts, although in all probability the fact of the fair being in progress at Pinega had a good deal to do with the lowness of the figure. Leaving Ust-Zilma, I bade farewell to my kind friends the Okatovs, of whose hospitality and kindliness I cannot speak too highly. Mrs. Okatov was good enough to bake some excellent white bread—the first I had tasted since landing at Habarova—and cook me some rissoles of reindeer meat. This I found a very convenient way of carrying meat when travelling in cold weather. I may add that M. Okatov was very much interested in my account of the Bolshaia Zemelskija Tundra country, which is quite a *terra incognita* to the people here.

M. ROMAN OKATOV,
Superintendent of Woods and Forests.

On the 8th of December, about seven o'clock in the evening, I left Ust-Zilma, and, travelling all night, got over about fifty versts before daylight. The country was covered with fir and birch of small size, and was, on the whole, hilly. The road was decidedly bad, and the farther we drove, the worse it seemed to get. But as we were travelling night and day, we covered the country rapidly. On the night of the 10th, Cyprian Doorkin was pitched out of the sledge by one of the exceedingly sharp jerks which were due partly to the rough road and partly to our rapid pace, and, owing to the darkness, and perhaps a little to my sleepiness, I did not miss him for a mile or two. I then stopped the horses and waited for him to come up. We found the road on the 11th a little better, but this amelioration was not destined to continue, and by night we were galloping down long hills over a most abominable track. At the bottom of one of these descents my sledge suddenly swerved and turned right over, fairly pinning me down on the ground. The weight of my baggage alone was about three hundred lbs., and the total weight of the heavy Russian sledge and baggage must have been not less than seven hundred lbs. Fortunately I got off very easily, owing chiefly to the yielding snow into which I had been pressed, and as I had not let go of the reins, I managed to stop the horse and crawl from underneath in a pretty ruffled condition.

By the 12th we had driven two hundred and forty miles, and such are the courage and stamina of these hardy little Russian horses, that, although we had only given them two rests of two hours each during that time, they were full of spirit at the end. We had scarcely shut our eyes, I believe, and even though I often felt very sleepy, the incessant jerks and plunges of the sledge effectually aroused one when disposed to sleep.

On the 13th we travelled over the worst road we had yet met, but on arriving at the Mezen River were able to sledge for some distance up its frozen stream, when we arrived at Khornagora. Here the river is one mile wide, while the banks on either side are high, with fir and birch growing thickly on them. That night we again took to the ice of the Mezen River, and reached Smoyleanitch about an hour before daybreak, to find all the village intoxicated, and celebrating a *prazdnik* or church festival. Again starting, we drove at high speed through hilly pine-covered country, and after some hours came upon a Zirian lying helplessly drunk in the snow. Guessing that he had fallen off his sledge, we picked him up, and two or three miles farther on overtook his sledge, with the horse steadily jogging along the track, quite unconscious or careless of the fact that his master had been jettisoned some time before. We propped up the Zirian on his sledge and took him along with us, and after some time we came up with the party to which he belonged. Telling these people what had happened, and advising them to keep an eye on him, we hurried on. All through the night we kept on, though the snow was falling very heavily, and the roads had become rougher and very steep, with precipitous banks often at the sides of the track, and deep gullies at the bottom of the hills. When one begins travelling in a country of this kind, the mind is apt to be impressed with the risks of driving down such places at a gallop in the darkness, but after a short time the excitement of it becomes exhilarating, and one rushes over the edge of a slope just as we jump into a toboggan at the top of the slide. As a matter of fact it is really safer to gallop hard down a steep hill, as the sledge does not swerve and swing so much as when the pace is steady. One occasionally passed a wretched little hut by the wayside, but I usually cooked my food in the open air, preferring the air, which was a little more than "fresh," to the atmosphere of the huts, which was a great deal worse than stale. Doorkin's food consisted of black bread and fish, with which he seemed quite contented, although very pleased to accept some of the meat I had.

On the 16th we reached Pinega, and found it in a very crowded and busy state, owing to the December fair being in full swing. The usual population is about one thousand five hundred; but on this occasion every house was packed (and very much overpacked) with Russians and Zirians, who had come in from long distances all round to trade their furs—fox, sable, hare, bear, wolf, and reindeer skins and fish, including blubber, which had been brought all the way from Yugorski Schar and that district. I here met with two Germans —Heinrich Landmann and Captain Vogelgesang— who had come from Arkhangel for trading purposes, and could speak English. They proved well-educated and very pleasant companions, and the pleasure of being able to talk in English after four months' silence was a special delight to me. Yet, strange to say, I felt more inclined to use my odd mixture of Samoyad and Russian, which shows what a creature of habit man is.

We had travelled from Ust-Zilma, a distance of seven hundred versts, or about four hundred and seventy miles, in seven and a half days; and I think this speaks volumes for the little Russian horses. We had two sledges, it must be remembered, and one horse to each sledge; we went at a spanking pace nearly the whole of the way, yet they trotted into Pinega apparently as fresh as paint. We never gave them more than two hours at a time for food and rest, and then at long intervals. They were never out of their harness nor put into a stable; in fact, they proved themselves the best nags for cold work that I have yet seen. It was after this satisfactory experience of them that I decided to take them on the Polar Expedition.

Leaving Pinega on the afternoon of the 18th, we

soon found that we had a much better track to travel on; and by the morning of the following day had made forty miles. While going along in single file we heard a loud shouting behind, and looking back saw the Post-sledge coming along at full gallop, and the driver yelling to us to make way. This we did, but an unfortunate peasant who was driving behind us and had fallen asleep did not hear; and as the Post-sledge swerved a little to pass him, the postman, for this I suppose would be the function of the epauletted official in the sledge, leaped up and made a cut with his sheathed sword at the sleeping wretch. Missing the *Mujik*, he vented his indignation by bringing it down with a crash on the unoffending horse. The next moment he galloped past us and was soon lost to sight in the thin forest of birch. I must say that the Russian postal service in winter is wonderfully rapid, considering the badness of the roads in many parts; but then it has the first pick of the horses, and they even take those which a traveller has harnessed to his sledge, if the need should arise.

I crossed the Dvina River on the 20th, at the point where the Pinega runs into it. The village at the junction, Ust-Pinega, which would be in English, Pinegamouth, is the centre of a country undulating in surface, and well grown with pine. I noticed ravens, English sparrows, and the hooded crow in great numbers in this neighbourhood. But we were on a well-known track now, and paused for nothing. In the afternoon we reached Holmogora, where I found the best houses I had seen since leaving England. It was evident that I was at last getting to civilisation; indeed I was only seventy-two miles from Arkhangel. We drove on rapidly, but had a few hours' rest after midnight. My Russian servant, whom I had got at Pinega in place of Doorkin (who returned to Ust-Zilma on reaching Pinega), slept in a dirty little hut near the track, but I preferred a nap on the sledge to breathing the fœtid atmosphere of the hut. We started again about five A.M., and exactly twelve hours later, on 21st December, reached Arkhangel.

I drove at once to the British Vice-Consulate, where I found Mr. Henry A. Cooke, M.A., our Vice-Consul, in the very act of writing a letter to me expressing his regret that he would be unable to remain at Arkhangel to give me a welcome. As it turned out, however, I came in the very nick of time for a hearty, warm, and most hospitable reception, which after my sojourn among the Samoyads and the long sledge journey of two months through the Bolshaia Zemelskija Tundra was very highly appreciated. Mr. Cooke had made arrangements to leave for England two or three days before, but had most kindly altered his plans in the hope of seeing me, having heard from the German gentlemen I had met at Pinega that I was coming on without delay.

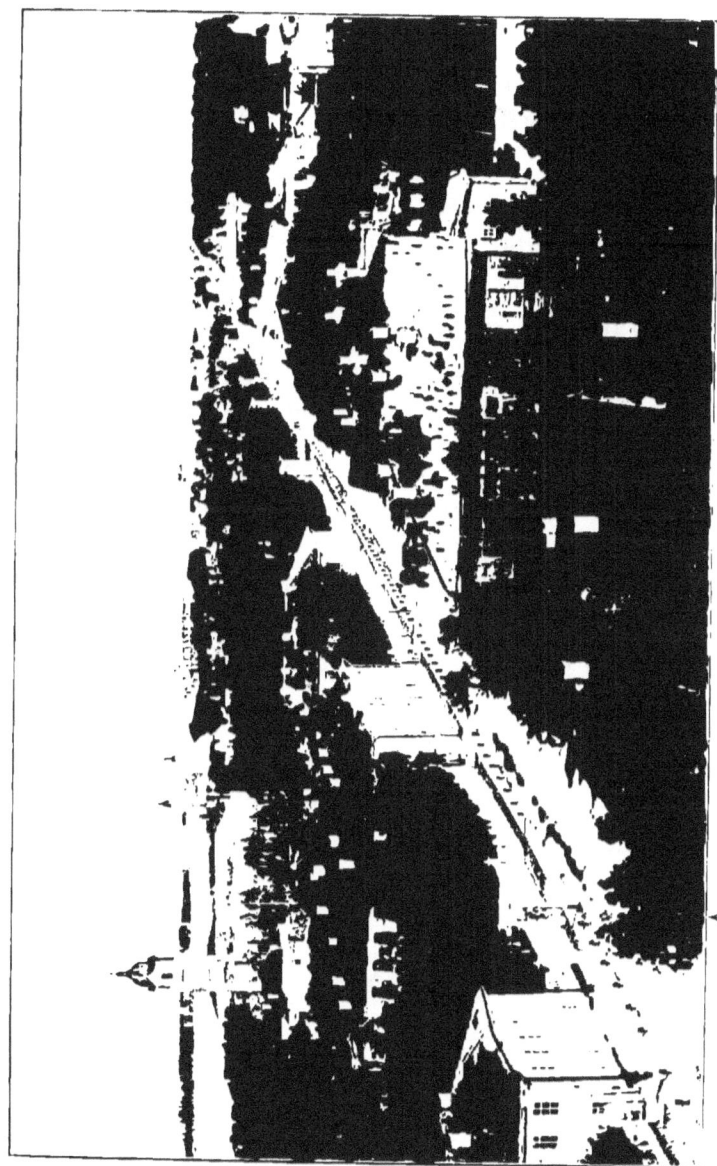

ARKHANGEL IN THE SUMMER.
Entrance to British Vice-Consulate (HENRY A. COOKE, M.A., Vice-Consul).

Almost the first thing he did was to hand me a telegram from my friend Mr. Arthur Montefiore, who had helped me in my preparations for the journey now almost ended, telling me to return home at once and to prepare for the Polar Expedition, as all funds required for this costly undertaking would be provided by an old friend of his, Mr. Alfred C. Harmsworth. This gentleman was determined, I afterwards learnt, to devote a portion of his large fortune to the patriotic purpose of sending an English Expedition to the Arctic Seas with the object of renewing the great work of Polar discovery in which England has always held the lead. I also heard from Mr. Cooke that Mr. Harmsworth had telegraphed to him asking him to despatch a small party of Russians and Samoyads to Yugorski Schar to ascertain my whereabouts, and hasten my return to England. Surrounded by the comfort and hospitality of the Vice-Consulate, I wanted nothing but this glorious piece of news to make me feel that I had made port indeed.

CHAPTER VI

ROUND THE WHITE SEA AND THROUGH LAPLAND—HOME

Object—To compare Lapps with Samoyads, and see dog-sledging—Christmas in camp—Kindness of the Governor of Arkhangel—Onega—Bad weather—Gales and snowdrifts—Buried in the snow—Digging the sledge out—Frost-bites—" Loshadi nieto "—Eaten alive—Kem—Cost of posting—Kandalaksha—The Lapps—The Lapp deer and the Lapp sledge—Costume of the Lapps compared with that of the Samoyads — Kola — The Ispravnik — Captain Louschkin—Days at Kola—Sledging to Kirkeness—Vadsö—Vardo—The return of the sun—Round the North Cape in winter—Christiania—Mr. Alexander Nansen—The Doctor's wife—Norway's champion skater—Mr. Crichton Somerville—Return to England—Courtesy of the Russian authorities—Acknowledgments and thanks.

As I was extremely anxious to compare Lapp life with that of the Samoyads, to pick up any further ideas with regard to conditions of travel under low temperatures, while I had the opportunity, especially with reference to dog-sledging, which I had been told was carried on near Kola, I made up my mind to continue my journey round the White Sea and through Lapland, in preference to going a shorter and quicker way home, *via*

St. Petersburg. I also wished to see more of reindeer, and to settle the question as to whether I could use them on the forthcoming expedition or not.

Staying at Arkhangel until the 29th, making inquiries as to the best route through Russian Lapland, I managed to get away for a couple of days in company with Lieutenant Landmann, an officer in the Russian army, to try for some bear-shooting. Sport was poor, but as Christmas Eve and Christmas Day found us in the field, I made up for it by thinking of the festivities at home, and drinking the healths of friends in England. I was most hospitably entertained everywhere in Arkhangel, and the Governor gave me a document carrying with it the first right to any horses in any village I might come to, and further handed me an Otkriti List, which placed at my disposal the *Zempski* horses, which are only used by police and other officials. Without this latter paper I could not have travelled beyond Kem, where the post-route comes to an end; consequently I consider myself indebted to the courtesy of the Governor of Arkhangel for a useful and interesting journey through Lapland.

On the 29th of December, having bought a horse-sledge for twelve roubles, I started on my journey round the White Sea, passing seven *stantsias* in the night, and arriving at Yuna, one hundred and forty miles from Arkhangel, on the 30th. Even so near Arkhangel as this, one began to experience the difficulty of getting horses, but fortunately the production of the document given me by the Governor, together with a little "bounce" on my own part, brought the desired relays. By four A.M. on the following day we arrived at Onega, two hundred and thirty-six miles from Arkhangel. I there called upon two gentlemen to whom I bore introductions, Messrs. Gernet and Talatieff, the latter of whom spoke English well, and, after enjoying their hospitality, we proceeded on our way to Sorokaze. Owing to heavy snow, the sledge drove into a drift, and we had to get help from the next stantsia, which, as it fortunately turned out, was only two miles away. I camped the night here—Kuzereka—as a perfect blizzard was blowing. The country since I left Onega had been very flat, and stunted pines formed the only vegetation. As it was New Year's Eve, I tried to be festive, but being absolutely alone, the reader can imagine how difficult this was to effect. However I managed to remember a good many friends, whose healths I religiously toasted.

On New Year's Day a heavy gale blew from the north-east, driving the light powdery snow in clouds before it. The high wind made the cold seem more severe than it was, although the thermometer indicated $-19°$ F. However, we started about nine A.M., and reached the next house—sixteen miles off—without mishap. Here our horses were changed, but we had not gone a quarter of a mile before they plunged into a deep drift which had been blown across the track. After struggling for half an hour—heaping up in true Russ fashion all manner of threats on the heads of the unfortunate horses—we got out of it, and for the next seven miles went on tolerably enough. But at this point the track was lost in a drift from ten to fifteen feet in depth. The horses seemed to leap into it bravely, but it was too much for them; they could not go forward a foot, and finally fell down and lay kicking and plunging, at the same time turning the sledge over on its side.

For two hours (they seemed four) we tugged and hauled at the sledge, but could not move it six inches. My Russian man got one of his hands frost-bitten, and I my nose and left cheek. I was so busy over the sledge that I had not felt anything or thought of frost-bite, but the Russian called my attention to the skin turning white, just in the nick of time to prevent a bad sore. After many vain attempts, we got the horses out, and the Russian started off in the direction of Kuzereka, the village we had lately left, as I concluded to get help. But I felt rather doubtful as to his intentions, and was not quite sure that he did not mean to leave me to do the best I could for myself. It was rather an awkward position; but I was determined not to leave my baggage out in the snow, so there was nothing for it but to get into the partly-overturned sledge, light a pipe, rub my nose and cheek (which felt anything but comfortable), and await events. It was bitterly cold, and the wind still blew as hard as ever. Hour after hour passed, and it grew darker and darker, and I began to prepare myself for a night in the snowdrift. This was not a pleasant outlook, as I was not only getting colder and colder, but also more and more hungry. At last, about eight or nine o'clock, I heard a welcome shout, and my Russian attendant rode up on a horse. I canonised him on the spot. He had done his very best, and brought with him no fewer than five men (armed with shovels) and three horses. After much digging and hauling we got the sledge out, and went back together to Kuzereka. The postmaster there was most attentive, assuring me that it was impossible to proceed again that day, the snowdrifts and cold making it dangerous to travel and impossible to reach the next stantsia (thirty miles away). The darkness, too, he declared, was another insuperable difficulty. I was, however, very anxious to get on, and again produced my documents. The postmaster was most apologetic, but remained firm in his opinion on the impossibility of advance. So I resigned myself to the inevitable, seeing that there was no way out of it. The fortnightly post, I learnt, was stopped at the stantsia; and the gale had broken up the ice on the White Sea, along which the track ahead would run for some miles. The men who had come to dig the sledge out were evidently impressed with the weather, for they had swathed their faces and heads so completely with red and blue mufflers and scarves that I could only see their eyes. I believe the precaution to have been needed, but the effect was so grotesque that they would have served admirably for stage-conspirators.

Early the next morning the postmaster sent out some men to cut through the worst drifts, and we started at noon with three horses for the next station. The gale was still high, but by dint of urging our horses forward and busily rubbing our frost-bitten faces, we arrived without mishap at the stantsia. Here we again had the usual trouble to get horses, but some energetic talk in which English and Russian were mixed (as the recipes say) in equal parts, accompanied by the display of my documents, induced the people to find the horses wanted. From this station we travelled all night, passing through flat country, with stunted pines and birch, and skirting the White Sea, now and again coming out of the forest to drive on the frozen water of the sea itself. At noon the wind died down, and soon after we reached a village named Sumpskipesat, where the old trouble of getting horses recurred. My method, however, proved again successful. Up to a certain point these Russian peasants of the White Sea were as independent and impudent as they could well be; but directly they saw that I was armed with special mandates from the

Governor, and would stand no denial or delay, they were ready to crawl at my feet. The last attitude

A RUSSIAN *MUJIK*.
(From a sketch by HERBERT WARD, F.R.G.S.)

is as revolting as the former is offensive, so there was very little pleasure to be got out of our dealings.

However, getting the horses and going on, we reached by the evening the village called Sorozkaja, where the cry of *Loshadi nieto* ("no horses") was again raised, and this time it proved to be true. We had to put up here for the night, and were nearly eaten alive in consequence. This remark, by the way, applies to most of the post-houses, though the rooms seemed clean enough. I attribute it in no small degree to the caulking of the log-houses with moss.

On the following day, 4th January, we reached Kem, after a rather exasperating experience with a bad driver and heavy snowdrifts. I put up at the Potch-house, and then drove out to Popoff Island, nearly six miles off, in the White Sea. Here I found a large saw-mill, and discovered that there was at least one flourishing business in the district.

At Kem I met with reindeer for the first time since leaving Pinega, and learnt that the Lapp deer are much larger than those of the Samoyad, and only one is usually driven at a time. Kem has a fluctuating population, for while there are about one thousand people there in the winter, in the summer it is practically deserted. During this season the men are away fishing in the White Sea, and their wives go on pilgrimage and ultimately join them at Arkhangel.[1] The village is built on both banks of the

[1] The women of Kem are said to bear an unenviable reputation; at any rate, when the writer was staying at the monastery of Sola-

Kem, which is here a wide, rapid, and shallow stream. Down this river an enormous quantity of timber is floated, but as the yellow pine is too small to repay the expense of cutting, it is only red pine which comes down. At Kem itself there is no timber, the only thing approaching wood being patches of low scrub of pine and birch. In March a few head of wild reindeer come down near the village, and are often seen on one of the small islands near the coast, but during the winter they stick to the dense forests inland, which of course they find much warmer. At Kem I was five hundred and twenty-five versts from Arkhangel; we had passed twenty-three stantsias; and the cost of posting had been 44.88 roubles (£4 : 13 : 6). This is not much for six and a half days' travelling. Ever since I left Yugorski Schar I had found it impossible to obtain reliable information as to the route in front of one, and, in fact, both the Bolshaia Zemelskija Tundra and this wild tract

---

vetski in the White Sea, he heard that these Kem ladies, who used to come in their hundreds when their husbands were at the fishing-grounds, and overwhelmed the monks with attentions, had been forbidden the islands. I am not certain, but think that some exception was made in the case of favoured pilgrims, but if so they were strictly confined to the hostel without the monastery walls; or it is quite possible that they were relegated to that adjacent island where everything female is banished and maintained—cows, mares, hens, and the rest. All the milk and eggs you get at the monastery come from this island, for nothing of the female sex is permitted on the Holy Island where Savvati lived and Philip ruled.

on the west of the White Sea are *terræ incognitæ* at Arkhangel.

Leaving Kem on the 7th, I exchanged for two sledges, with a horse harnessed to each, my larger sledge, which required two horses in it. The track ahead was too narrow for the wide sledge, and this obliged me to get narrow ones; but it resulted in a nuisance. For I had to unpack and repack my sledges at every stantsia, changing the sledges with the horses. From here we travelled all through the night, and arrived about 10 A.M. at Poloboryaskaja, which is rather over ninety-six miles from Kem. Here we stayed just long enough to cook and much enjoy a good breakfast; and then started again on the track to Chernoijezkaja, thirty versts from Kandalaksha, where we ultimately arrived at four o'clock in the afternoon on the following day. The country from Kem to this place is impassable during the summer, on account of bogs and the general swampy nature of the country, although here and there, especially in the neighbourhood of Kuda, it is hilly, has occasional lakes, and is wooded with red pine and birch.

Kandalaksha is situated on the northern side of the Kandalaksha Gulf, across the frozen waters of which we drove to the town. It is surrounded by high hills, the one behind the village being called Krestovaia gora ("Crosshill") from a wooden cross erected on its summit (six hundred and fifty feet). The village contains only about a dozen huts and a church, but its situation at the foot of the hills and on the shore of the gulf is very pretty. I heard that bear is plentiful during the summer near here, but could not get information of any bear-holes near the village when I was there.

Leaving Kandalaksha behind us, and following the course of the Niwa River for about thirty versts, we finally arrived at a Lapp hut. Here we found three Lapps, two men and a woman, and I proceeded to bargain for reindeer to take us on our road to Kola. As the deer were feeding at some distance from the hut, several hours were spent in finding them, and I took advantage of the delay to cook myself some food and have a short sleep. We started soon after midnight with three sledges, eight reindeer and one Lapp in attendance, and soon struck the lower end of the Emander Lake, up which we drove. This lake is long and narrow; having on the east side the Hibinski Hills, with the limit of the pines very clearly marked at a line about one-third of the way up. On the west side the hills, though two thousand feet high, are considerably lower than the Hibinski. The scenery here is most beautiful.

As evening drew on, we came to a group of three Lapp huts, fifty versts from our starting-point; and here I bought fifteen pounds of reindeer meat at five

A LAPP MOTHER AND CHILD.
(The cradle of the Samoyad is ruder and more box-like.)

travelling very rapidly and made no long stay anywhere, I had opportunities for forming an opinion on the Lapps, and comparing them with the people with whom I had been living. While the Russian peasant all round the White Sea proved the same uncouth, inquisitive boor I had encountered east of Arkhangel, the Lapps seemed to me an agreeable, well-disposed people, with manners a long way ahead of the Russian peasant. In complexion they are generally fair, with long shaggy hair on their heads,

A LAPP IN HIS *PESK* (WITH BEARSKIN ROUND HIS SHOULDERS).

and often a good deal of hair on their faces. Their cheek-bones are high but not nearly so prominent as those of the Samoyads. They are also much less dirty. Though short they are sturdy, and in some respects they remind me of the Zirians. The general Mongolian appearance is very much less pronounced than that of the Samoyads, although their low stature, flat faces, with the peculiar round outline, often suggested their kinship. On the other hand, they are often fair, while the Samoyads are invariably dark. The Lapp is not such a tough hard fellow as the Samoyad, but his higher civilisation may account for this. I consider, from a good deal of practical experience, that the Samoyad sledge is greatly superior to that of the Lapp; so also is their mode of driving. In fact the Lapp has practically conceded this, for when a small party of Zirians travelled about four years ago from Ishma on the Pechora into Lapland, bringing a number of Samoyads with them, they very soon taught their Lapp neighbours to use the Samoyad sledge and drive after the Samoyad fashion. But the greater number of Lapps still retain their own way, which may be briefly described thus:—to a boat-shaped vehicle about eight feet six inches long and thirty inches broad, square behind and bluntly pointed in front, a single reindeer is harnessed, and is driven with the same arrangement for the rein as the Samoyads employ, but without the "harray" or driving pole. In place of it the Lapp flips the single rein against the flank of the deer. I have had experience of both methods, and much prefer the Samoyad. The boat-shaped sledge shakes one to pieces almost, but I do not doubt that in the mountainous parts of Lapland it has its advantages over the

A LAPP *TALTA* OR SUMMER TENT.
(A relic of the choom.)

Samoyad sledge, being much less easily upset, or perhaps not so readily broken.

The Lapp wears only one fur garment—the *pesk* somewhat similar in appearance to the Samoyad soveek, and having, like that, the hair outside. But his mitts (*guestr*) are never attached to the garment, and this I regard as a distinctly weak point. Moreover, a detachable *Kapperi* (cap) usually takes the place of the Samoyad's hood. His short fur boots are known as *Kadji*, and have been familiarised to us in Norway as Finnesko. They also wear longer boots, like waders in appearance, but made of reindeer skin with the hair removed above the knee. These they call *yerra*.

Again, the Lapp choom is much inferior to that of the Samoyad, and is called a *talta* or *gordi*. Its inferiority may be due to the fact that it is only a summer home; the walls being of thin canvas or cotton roughly supported on sticks. During the winter the Lapp lives in a hut made of timber and earth, and one seldom meets with these except in groups and villages.

My general conclusions were that with regard to clothing, sledges, driving, and general mode of life the Samoyad can give points to the Lapp and beat him easily.

On the 11th we arrived at Kola, having travelled, during the latter stages of our journey, through narrow valleys and along frozen lakes on purpose to avoid the hills which are here troublesome to drive over. The distance from Kem to Kola is five hundred and twenty-five versts, or three hundred and fifty miles ; the cost of the journey was thirty-five roubles, fifty-five kopecks, or £3 : 14 : 9. From Kandalasksha to Kola is two hundred and twenty versts. I paid for reindeer six kopecks per verst per deer, and the same rate for horses. During the whole of my journey through Lapland I never saw the sun, but "enjoyed" a dim twilight for an hour or two during the day. The sun reappears about the end of January, showing for a few minutes each day.

At Kola I found the Governor of Arkhangel had kindly sent on a letter commending me to the officials here, and I accordingly had every attention shown me. Vasili Ivanovitch Smirnoff, the Ispravnik or chief of the police, was particularly attentive ; and from Captain Louschkin, of the Murman coast steamship *Tchishoff*, who speaks English, I also received much hospitality. I learnt from him that the Kola River never freezes, and the sea of the Murmanski coast is always free from ice. I have since heard that it is on this account that the Russian Government intends to establish somewhere on the Murmanski coast a strong naval station, and thus secure a sea-port open all the year round. At Kola I obtained a good deal of further information about reindeer and their food, the building of log-houses, the use of dogs in Lapland, and other matters in which I was particularly interested, and I came to the conclusion that the difficulty of transporting food for the deer would prevent my taking them to Franz Josef Land, thus confirming the opinion formed months earlier among the Samoyads. Everybody seemed glad to give all the information in their power, and I look back to my four days at Kola with a very pleasant remembrance.

Kola itself is a very old place, having been originally founded about six hundred years ago by a party of emigrants from Novgorod. It has, however, been burnt down three or four times, the last time by the English in 1854. Salmon is plentiful in the Kola and Tulama Rivers, and also in the gulf, while herring and cod are obtained outside; and goose, swan, and rabchick offer good sport in the summer. A landslip from a hill behind Kola, which fell about thirteen years ago into the Kola River, now prevents ships of any draught approaching within a mile of the town, but the gulf itself is from one hundred to two hundred fathoms deep. The climate of Kola is naturally severe, and I was not surprised to hear that although barley is grown within a dozen miles of the town, it usually fails to ripen twice out of every three years. The coldest wind is not from the north—for the sea is not only free from ice here, there being that mitigating influence, the Gulf Stream—but from the south-east—in other words, from that ice-cellar the White Sea. Apart from the kindly hospitality which will always make me think of Kola with warm feelings, there was little to note or admire in the place itself; but one exception must be made in favour of the hospital, which is built on an orderly and sensible plan, and is as clean as a new pin. It is a Govern-

KOLA.

ment institution, and the doctor in charge, in common with all officials, wears uniform, sword and all the rest of it. Yet perhaps the most pleasant feature of this attractive little hospital was the fact that when I visited it, there was not one patient within its walls.

From Kola I had to go to Kirkeness to pick up the little coasting steamer in which I proposed to go round the North Cape. The road runs across a hilly and very stony country, the only vegetation of which consists of thin birch scrub and a scattering of stunted pines. On the way one passes through several Lapp villages, if I may so term a group of four or five one-roomed huts, whose only chimney is a hole in the roof.

I usually drove the single reindeer harnessed to my sledge a distance of fifty versts before exchanging him for another, and never once found it distressed by either the weight or distance. At Pasareka, on the banks of the Pass River, a large Lapp pogost or village of twelve or fifteen huts, situated in a valley surrounded by high hills, I found that rare institution, a Lapp school. It is under the protection of the high official who is the lay head of the Greek Church, and Russian is carefully taught to the little Lapps. Here, too, I met for the first time with the Finns, who, with certain exceptions, are exactly like the Lapps. These exceptions include their greater stature, smarter appearance, and more polished manners. Indeed, several of the Finns could only be described as to their appearance and demeanour by the word "gentlemanly." From Pasareka we drove by the Skalmozero Lake to Boris Gleab, a village on the frontier between Lapland and Norway, in this district a very irregular line. As I was extremely anxious to catch the small steamer at Kirkeness, which runs from there to Vadsö,

I promised extra "bakshish" to the Lapp who accompanied me if we got to Kirkeness in time. He was a delightfully energetic fellow, and in this respect different from any of the Lapps I had previously met, and he simply drove like a fiend down steep hills, through narrow gorges, and the only thing I feared might stop me now was a complete smash-up. This, however, we escaped, narrowly enough now and again, and on the 17th January reached Kirkeness at 1.45 A.M. Here I slept on the sledge for four hours, and then cooked my breakfast. The steamer *Varanger* put in an appearance at 8 A.M., and, getting my traps on board, we sailed, an hour later, for Vadsö.

I had bidden good-bye to the rugged stony hills of Lapland and their gorges deep in snow, and I had seen the last for a while of its most valuable inhabitant, my good friend the reindeer. The road from Kola to Kirkeness is one hundred and fifty-eight miles in length, and I had only paid forty-three shillings for the excellent deer I had driven that distance. If there had not been the insuperable difficulty of feeding these splendid draught animals—which, at a pinch, were convertible into steaks and haunches of venison by no means to be despised—I should certainly have secured a number of them for the Expedition to Franz Josef Land; but until they are thoroughly domesticated and stalled, this difficulty in the way of their usefulness to the explorer in the highest latitudes will not be removed. I may here mention, too, that I was disappointed in the dogs of Kola. They are inconsiderable creatures, and only used on rare occasions for draught purposes.

On arriving at Vadsö (the run from Kirkeness to Vadsö takes about six hours, and the fare is two kr. thirty-five öre) I was fortunate enough to come in for a sort of annual *fête*—the first sight of the returning sun. It was the 18th of January, and the whole population, or what seemed to me, at any rate, all the people that could have got comfortably into the houses of the little town, swarmed up the hills behind the settlement, and waited in a state of great excitement for the hour of noon. The darkness had given place to a strange light which grew brighter and brighter towards the south, until, at last, we saw the upper rim of the sun slowly rise over the distant hills. We all greeted it with loud and prolonged cheers in the Norwegian vernacular, and generally behaved as shipwrecked sailors might on beholding a sail bearing down to their rescue. The minutes passed—one, two, three, certainly not ten—and the beautiful golden rim, clear and refulgent, sank again out of our sight. The light waned, and in an hour or two it was dark; but we had seen enough to know that the long winter night had come to an end, and that day by day the sun would remain for a longer time in the sky, until the summer of perpetual day had dawned.

It only remains for me to add that I coasted round the North Cape and down the Norwegian coast in the small steamers that make the mid-winter passage at irregular intervals. Fog and snowstorms add to the dangers of navigation, and make the insurance premium so heavy that the vessels are uninsured; but each creeps round from point to point for only a short distance, and their captains can "smell" their way, thick though the fog be and blinding the storm. I changed steamers at Vardo, again at Hammerfest, and again at Harstad; and at Trondhjem came in touch with the railway. Thence to Christiania was a mere matter of seventeen hours, and at Christiania I felt almost like being at home. Nothing could exceed the kindness I received from Mr. Alexander Nansen (brother of Dr. Nansen), and Mrs. Nansen, the explorer's wife. With Mr. Harold Hagen, the champion skater, I spent many hours in examining and testing the various types of ski, and am indebted to him for enabling me to take part in some ski running near Christiania. To Mr. Alexander Nansen, also, I owe many thanks for the days he spent with me in trying different sledges and ski, and inspecting an equipment similar to that which Dr. Nansen had taken. Nor can I refer to my visit to Christiania without mentioning gratefully the hearty hospitality and many good offices of my countryman, long resident in Norway, Mr. D. M. Crichton Somerville, whose interest in Arctic matters is very great.

Leaving Christiania on 2nd February, I arrived in London *via* Hull on the 5th, feeling as fit as I ever was in my life, and weighing nearly a stone heavier than I did when I left more than six months before. Here my long winter journey from the Kara Sea—two thousand five hundred miles of it by sledge—came to an end, and here, too, I must bring my narrative to a close. But it would be ungracious as well as ungrateful if I did not at this moment emphasise my deep appreciation of the friendliness, hospitality, and courtesy which I everywhere and on every occasion experienced at the hands of the Russian authorities. In the course of this journal of my travels through the Arctic regions of Russia, I have, I think, noted again and again how and when the rough had been made smooth by the good will and kindly offices of the officials of the vast province of Arkhangel—chief among whom, of course, both by reason of his position and the great personal influence he exerted on my behalf, I would mention His Excellency the Governor-General of Arkhangel.

CHAPTER VII

A CHAPTER ON LANGUAGE

The Samoyad speech—Difficulties—Castrén—Parts of Speech—A list of Samoyad words—Mr. Jackson's list—Mr. Rae's list—A contribution from Mr. H. Seebohm—Von Strahlenberg.

WHILE it may be considered as certain that the Samoyad speech is a member of the Finnic family, it should be pointed out that at the present time every one of the numerous Samoyad dialects has undergone distinct modification by contact with other languages, some of which of course are germane, but others, as in the case of Russian, of an entirely different stock. Moreover, we find that while in the pure Finn the language has developed with accretion, and, as far as any language can become crystallised, is now rendered concrete and permanent by its literature, the speech of the Finnic Samoyad has dwindled and is dwindling at an increasing rate. Poor and meagre in the first instance, it has been further impoverished by the fact that all new additions have not only been foreign, but were accompanied by an equivalent loss in tribal purity and idiosyncrasy; and, in consequence, that which is a linguistic gain to a nation whose solidarity and literature are secured, has proved a loss to a nation whose identity is being steadily submerged, and whose literature is yet to seek. Therefore I think we may assume that of all the widespread Finnic group, only the language and the national characteristics of the Finns of Finland will endure; and that any knowledge we can now obtain of the other members of a vanishing race is distinctly worthy of capture.

And with regard to our knowledge of Samoyad speech, it is to the Finlander, Castrén, that our gratitude is chiefly due. Through his investigations, Castrén was the first to arrive at the conviction that from the grammatical point of view the Finns and the Samoyads must not only be reckoned as the same race, but that in the whole wide world no nearer kin can be found for the Samoyad race than the Finnic.

Above all, as he points out, these two resemble one another in this, that the agglutinative process has made far greater progress in them than in the Mongolian and Tungusian or even the Turkish languages; and, secondly, these languages also exhibit, with regard to material, a far greater affinity with each other than with the other Altaic languages. With respect to the nature of the agglutination of the Finnic and Samoyad languages, it must be remarked that it differs very little from the inflection in the Indo-Germanic languages. Of all the agglutinative languages these are nearest to the inflection languages, and form, as it were, a nexus between them. The languages of the Finnic and Samoyad race have, therefore, no complete settled type.[1]

On the basis of the distinctions of language Castrén divides the Samoyads into three great races. These are (1) the Yurak-Samoyads; (2) the Tawgi-Samoyads; (3) the Ostiak-Samoyads, and this last may be again divided into two smaller tribes, the Yenisei-Samoyads and the Kamassinzi. The Yurak-Samoyads extend from the White Sea in the west to the Yenisei in the east, and wander over the treeless tundras along the shore of the Arctic Sea. In their language we can distinguish five different dialects, one of which is the Yurakian.

The Yuraks, who have given their name to the whole branch, are only a single tribe, and Castrén believes their name may be connected with Yugra, Yugrian. The Samoyad languages have chiefly an excess of liquid consonants; while, on the other hand, strongly hissing, sharply aspirated, and other harder consonants occur more rarely in all pure and unspoiled dialects. The aspirate *h* exists in all the Samoyad dialects with the exception of the Tawgi, and as a rule it has the same soft sound as in German. But in Yurak it has sometimes at the beginning of a word the sound of "*k*."

[1] This is probably the case also with the formation of the skull.

In all Samoyad dialects there is a nasal ŋ which Castrén borrowed from the Lapp alphabet. This sound is often original, but not infrequently it arises from the combination of "*n*" and "*g*." A peculiarity of the Yurak and Tawgi languages is specially noteworthy, *e.g.* every initial vowel in the purer dialects can take before it the sound ŋ, which is then represented by the sign ~, *e.g.* Yurak *óka* = ~*óka*, much. In this case ŋ seems only to have had the signification of an aspiration originating from "*h*."[1]

In Samoyad, the different parts of speech are not so clearly defined as in most other languages, the nouns partaking of the character of the verbs and *vice versâ*. No article is used with the noun, nor is there any inflection to mark gender. Another peculiarity is that a noun can be conjugated as well as declined, but

[1] The nasal *ŋ*, the sign of which is borrowed from the Lapp alphabet, has often an original sound, but frequently arises from the combination of *n* + *g* (h). In both cases the pronunciation is the same; if the sound has arisen through combination, it can be resolved into its original sounds and so pronounced that every element is audible, *e.g.* nenecenjad or nenecen + gad. In Yurak and Tawgi every vowel sound in the purer dialects can take the sound *ŋ* before it: for which the sign ~ is employed. In this case the *ŋ* appears only to have had the signification of an aspiration originating perhaps from *h*.

Some of the consonants seem to have three sounds, represented by the ordinary consonant, the ~, and a dot, *e.g.* l, ł, ɫ. The other consonants which have this liquid sound are c, d, n, r, s, t, z. *ł* is especially audible before weak vowels, and is sometimes replaced by *li*.

ł in the Kamassinzi dialect = *lr*, both consonants are distinctly

this conjugation only extends to the Indicative Mood, e.g. *niseam*, "I am a father"; *niseams*, "I was a father."

The Samoyad speech has three numbers: the Singular, Dual, and Plural. In the northern dialects the Dual is certainly used, but its declension is very defective. In Yurak the Dual is formed either by *ha'* or *g'*, *k'*; the plural (originally in Samoyad *t*) by the sharp aspiration (′); this corresponds to the Finnic "*t*," e.g. ~*uda* "hand;" ~*uda'* "hands."

Most of the dialects have seven cases: Nominative, Genitive, Accusative, Dative, Locative, Ablative, and Prosecutive; while some have two more, namely, the Instructive and the Vocative. The Nominative, Genitive, Accusative, and Vocative have the same audible, but are pronounced as a single inseparable sound, and in such a way that the *r* has the preponderance.

In Samoyad *l* = *r* usually, now and then *l*.

    ᴋ only found in Yurak interchanges with *ri*.
    š = Russian *m*, French *ch*, German *sch*.
    ž = French *j*.
    ǯ = French *dj*.
    ꞑ = Spanish *ñ* or French *gn*, Hungarian *ny*.
    ț = Hungarian *ty*, most other languages *tj*.
    đ = Hungarian *gy*.
    ʙ always has *m* or *n* before it.
    ʒ = German *zj*.
    ʒ̧ = French *dz*.

This sign ~ seems to show that the letter has a liquid sound, what the Germans call *mouillirte*.

signification as in Latin and other languages. The Dative, Locative, Ablative signify, respectively, whither, where, whence, and may be used of place as well as of persons and things.

The Prosecutive, while referring to place, connotes distance. The Instructive corresponds to an Instrumental dative, but in most dialects can be replaced by the Locative.

All the Finnic and Tartarian languages have the *same* case-endings for *all* numbers—thus differing from European languages, but the Samoyads, especially the northern tribes in this respect, approximate to the Indo-Germanic group.

The possessive pronouns are very little used, but are, as in Finnic, expressed by personal suffixes.

Personal pronouns—

Man,	I.	pudar,	thou.	puda,	he
mana',	we.	pudara',	ye.	pudu',	they.

The Samoyad languages have an extraordinarily rich supply of pronominal or personal affixes. From their standpoint it is impossible to distinguish the personal affixes for the noun, the verb, and the particles, for they deviate very slightly from one another; *e.g. cf.* the affixes of the noun and verb in the following :—

lâtau,	my plank.	madâu,	I hewed.
lâtar,	thy plank.	mâdar,	thou hewedst.
lâtada,	his plank.	madáda,	he hewed.

Samoyad is very deficient in adjectives, owing to their abstract nature, and most of those in use were originally adverbs. Their numeration is based on the decimal system, but this is evidently a late importation, for the Samoyad numbers proper ended at seven, which number has, for this reason, acquired a special importance in the songs and legends of the people. Again, in all the dialects, there is more resemblance in form in the first seven numbers than in any of the later ones, thus pointing to a common origin.

I may here introduce the following classification of the alphabet, for which I am indebted to Castrén:—

Vowels.

Hard: a, o, u, y.
Soft: ä, ö, ü.
Medium: e, i.

Consonants.

Guttural: k, g, x, h, ŋ, j.
Lingual: l, ł, ļ; r, ŗ, ś, ź, ć, ʒ́.
Dental: n, ṅ, t, ṭ, d, ḍ, s, ṣ, z, ẓ, c, ʒ, ʒ̇.
Labial: p, b, w, f, m.

Those found in Yurak are:—

Vowels: a, e, o (ö), y, i, u, ü.
Consonants: k, g, h, ŋ, j, l, ł, r, ŗ, n, ṅ, t, ṭ, d, ḍ, s, ṣ, z, ẓ, c, ʒ, p, b, w, m.

In Tawgi—

Vowels: a, e, o, i, u (ų).
Consonants: k, g, ŋ, j, l, ł, r, n, ṅ, t, ṭ, d, ḍ, s, ṣ, b, f, m.

I append a list of the numerals and a selected number of words given by Castrén.

Numerals.	Yurak.	Tawgi.
1	˜opoi, ˜ob	˜o'ai'
2	sidea, side	siti
3	nahar når	nagur
4	tét	tata
5	samłaŋ	saŋfakanka
6	mat'	matu'
7	siu, séu	saibua
8	sidendet	site-data
9	håsawaju'	˜ameaitama
10	ju', lúcaju˙	bi'

English.	Yurak.	Tawgi.
Axe	tubka	súŋfa
Back	maha	moku
bad	waebty	buluaŋ
be, to	˜amau	citum
bear	wark	jamada
blood	hém	kam
boat	˜ano	˜andui
body	˜åja	safe
breast	leambara	timi
brother	na	nenne
Carry to	mineu	mendetema
child	˜aleky	nua
church	hahemea	
cold	titi	tici
corpse	hålmer	buedyrbya
Daughter	nenu	kuobtuaŋ
day	jålea	jale
devil	äje	
die	hådm	kû'am
dog	jandu	bâŋ
door	no	˜oa
dress	pany	lû
drive	˜aedalaju	tonuli' ema
Ear	hâ	kou
evening	paeusemboi	kundútu
eye	saeu	saime

English.	Yurak.	Tawgi.
Fat	jur	jir
father	nisea	jase
female reindeer	jahadiei	nami'a
finger	pikitea	feaja
fir	hâdy	ku'a
fire	tu	tui
fish	hâlea	kóle
fish-soup	jewaei	be'a
flesh	~amsa	~amsu
foot	~ae	~oai
forest	puedara	munku
fox	tona	tunte
friend	juꝶu	niruŋ
Girl	piríbtea	kuobtuaŋ
give to	mi'idm	miji'ema
go to	jâdam	meajendem
good	sawa	sawa
grass	~um	nota
ground	yr	mou
grow	~armâdm	baduam
Hair	üöbta	tar'
hand	~uda	jutu
head	~aewa	~aewua
heart	seai	soa
heaven	num	
horse	üöbte	
human being	hüberi	~anasaŋ
Ice	sâlaba	ser
idol	hahe	koika
ill	jíbea	koitalâ
immortal	habtenđe	
iron	jêsea	basa
island	~o	~uai
Judgment	jierutâŋoua	
Kill to	hâdau	kuada'ama
knife	har	tagai
Left	seatanâŋy	badi'e
life	jilêbe	niletem
lord	jieru	bârba
Man	hâsawa	kuájúmu
month, moon	na'	~âŋ
morning	hûwy	kiduatu
moss	narso	đie

English.	Yurak.	Tawgi.
mother	nebea	name
mountain	teal	
Neighbour	jánater	
night	pi	fiŋ
Ptarmigan	hôndie	kafe
Reindeer	ty	tä
reindeer skin	˜ämďor'	fansu
right	mahanaŋy	mantimu
river	jaha	bigai
Sable	to'	
sail	púlabt'	fuala'btu'
sand	tab	jua
sea	jam	jam
sledge	han	kánta
small	núdea	sielaku
smoke	jake	kinta
snow	sira	siru
son	nu	nua
son-in-law	ju	biŋiŋ
speak	lahanádm	buatum
spirit	˜ytarma	
stranger	˜adahʃ	funsâ
sun	hâjer	kou
Tent	mea'	ma'
thunder	hae	kajuaŋ
tree	pea	fâ
Uncle	nineka	isi
Water	ji'	bê'
wind	mearcea	bie
woman	nie	nê
word	wada	buadu
Year	po	fua

I now give the vocabulary collected by Mr. Jackson. It correctly indicates similarity to, and, in many instances, identity with the Yuraks of the Yenisei; while a glance at Mr. Rae's list will show that there is a marked difference between the demoralised Samoyads of the Little Tundra and Mezen, and those who oscillate between the valleys of the Yenisei and Pechora.

MR. JACKSON'S LIST OF WORDS.

VOCABULARY: ENGLISH, RUSSIAN, SAMOYAD.

ENGLISH.	RUSSIAN.	SAMOYAD.
Axe	topór	tupka
Bad	húdo	waywo
bear	medvéd	híbeda
black	chorni	yabsu
blood	kroff	voyaá
book	kníga	páther
boots	sapogí	hortén
bottle	butýlka	pia
box	yáshtchik	lobthé
boy	málchik	[matchika]
bread	kleb	mian
broken	slamaal	mili
butter	máslo	yurr
buy	kupeet	toomthon
Can (tin)		larwatchi
cap	shapka	sohá
claw	kogút	hodda
coffee	káffe	[corf]
cold	hólod	tichi
cooking	virete	yod
Dark	temná	pashami
day	dĕn	yallomur
dead	umera	cohúr
dog	sobáka	píva
drink	peet	garapi
Eat	kúshat	aberdaii
empty	porosnia	kerozhi
evening	vécher	bisharni
expensive	dorogó	zatchmeriem
extinguish	powgoshat	tuhopta
Face	litso	soá
fat	salo	yurr
father	otéts	neeshout or nes sea
fire	ogón	tu

English.	Russian.	Samoyad.
flour	muká	deya
fog	tuman	sinu
food	maha	suroko ya
foot	nogá	raroisé
forest	less	piat
friend	priatil	yúru
from	ot	moní
frost	moróz	techi
Girl	devitsa	persepta
give	dai, daite	meinkantnut / putherathál
go, to	hodit	haium
go on	poshól	haiá
good	horosho	suohor
good-evening	proshtcháité	[proshité]
good-morning	sdravstvuité	toroa
grouse, hazel	rabchik	rabín
gun	rujyó	túni
Half	palavina	piali
hand	ruka	wuda
hasten	skóra	meethurur
have you	Yaist-li-u-vass	ústera
he	on	puther
headman (of village)	starosta	starsun
hill	gorá	haisada
holiday	prázdnik	hibidyali
hoof	kwopwita	tobá
horse	lóshad	unor
how far	kák daloko	huptor
how many or much	skúlko	pshán
hut	izba	méat
I	ya	má
ice	lëd	salabar
if	yesli	mein merru
ill	nezdoróv	nugurúm
iron	jelézo	issia
island	ostrof	orr
it is	eto	tuku
I wish	ya hotchu	mein horiúm
Kill	ubit	hardeish
knife	nójik	há

ENGLISH.	RUSSIAN.	SAMOYAD.
Land	Zemlia	yeá, ya
last	postlaidni	púdna
lazy	lánevoi	leark
leg	noga	ai
less	ménshé	chinnu
little	málo	chánu
long	dolgo	yú
Mad	sumasetsha	solakwa
make	delat	meeritch
man	chelavék	nunekh
may I ?	mójno	mein mrongu
meat	goviádina	amsá
moon	masitch	yerri
morning	útro	ku
mother	mat	nishia
mouth	rot	yerri
my	moi	maan
Name	imia	nim
near	blizko	haii
never	nikógda	shartné muon
new	nóvo	yathera
no	nët	yúngu
noon	polden	monthom
Old	stáro	puhoday
Paddle	lopáta	shiwa
plate	tariélka	perdok
plenty	mnogo	uktior
presently	tot chas	punataton
Quick	skorei	miátarra
Rain	dojd	seroia
red	krasni	narria
reindeer	olen	thena oddi
river	reká	ya or yaha
road	doróga	niáda
rock	kamén	pié
rope	verofka	koroatka
Salt	sol	siare
sea	móré	yom
shallow	melko	tura
shoot	stralit	nearetch
sing	pet	honnen it
sister	sestrá	nápkwoa
sit down	saidite	ondot

English.	Russian.	Samoyad.
sledge	sanki	puán
steamer	parokhód	tuonna
stop	stoi	nuia
strong	krépko	moyu
swan	lábed	lensen
Thick	tolstoi	nenor
thief	vor	teiler
thin	tonki	huten
think (I)	dumau	sénio
to	k'	seru
tree	dérevo	piia
Understand (I)	pamujmayo	nandura
unnecessary	nenujni	nithera
Very	óchen	miá
very good	ladna	miáserra
Walrus	morse	tuóché
warm	tepló	yiba
wet	mókro	sanui
whale	kit	lubraka
what	kto	chuku
white	bélo	suruka
why	ochago	onkachuka
wife	jená	nea
wind	véter	pashami
winter	zimá	ziru
with	s'	wiwa
woman	jenshtchina	habína
work	rábota	muzurish
Year	göd	tutnopa
yes	da	dathrum
yesterday	vcherá	té

Names of some of the Samoyads I lived with :—

Habtise	Moira	Natiya (fem.), and
Parri	Naikwoa	[Vasili
Hongori	Ōshka	Steppan
Tuli	Oilka	Siman]
Narutcha		

(The Samoyad words in the foregoing lists enclosed in brackets are obviously Russian.)

The Samoyads whom Rae met with were those of Mezen and the Malaia Tundra, and in many respects their language differed from those of the purer Samoyads of the Great Tundra. So also was there a slight difference in their chooms and their clothing. But his careful though slight vocabulary has a distinct value, and, as with Mr. Jackson, his method of obtaining it was similar. He spoke the Russian word and obtained the Samoyad equivalent. He was not satisfied with the pronunciation of any one individual, but arrived at it by striking the mean, as it were, of some half a dozen different speakers. Moreover, before he wrote down the word in its final form, he repeated it himself several times, obtaining confirmation of his correctness each time. The system he employed in spelling the words was fairly phonetic.

I append a portion of Mr. Rae's vocabulary.

one	opoi	eight	sidyett
two	sidieh	nine	habéyou
three	nyàr	ten	you
four	tyètt	eleven	opiognia
five	samlak	twelve	sidiegnia
six	matt	thirteen	nyaryegnia
seven	syou	fourteen	tyettegnia

and so on to twenty, which is made up of two and ten, sidyôu. So with thirty, forty, fifty, etc., ninety being habéyou-you, and one hundred your.

Some of the other words may be usefully compared

with those given by Mr. Jackson, and others used to supplement his list.

after	pouna	less	tiàm yo
bad	wàouo	man	héuri
bears	háouèdie	money	njennai
bring	taht	much	oka
cold	tiètsi	more	oko
come	talyàndo	night	pi
day	yalé	no	yàngou
down	tassinié	old	nyàouchi
ebb-tide	hass-yi	please	yabtûndala
flood-tide	oka-yi	quick	mièrkaou
fire	toû	right (as opposed	manyi
fish	hálé	to left)	
God	yliambertje	reindeer	tûr
a god	nûm	rain	soryó
good	sáouo	river	yaha
hot	lómbit	ring	ouda yésia
huts	mia kan	sun	hayar
hand	oudáo	summer	tanhi
head	crouáo	soon	mièrko
half	piéla	spoon	loûtskou
how	sier	silver	njennai
how much?	sià birta?	snow	sirrha
ice	salva	tooth	tjivan
I	man	tent	tjoûm
I will	man ye toutam	thank you	passibo (which is
I will not	nyim mirdal		Russian)
I don't know	man yehrâm	take	mouette
I have	man danyass	up	tjáouna
I want	man harrán	water	yi
I will give	man da goum	winter	serái
knife	harr	when	sia douhtán
land	yáhada	why	amgass
left (as opposed	siàtni	what	amgah
to right)		where	houri
little	tiàmbyôna	yes	tartsa

Mr. Rae does not follow Castrén and other philologists in their identification of the Samoyad tongue with the Finnish, but it should be remembered that the Samoyads with whom he came in contact were closely connected with Russians in trade, and lived in constant touch with them. The Samoyads of the Trans-Pechora and those between the Ob and the Yenisei and this river and the Lena, are very different. However, his vocabulary has its own value, and in spite of the rather rough phonetic system on which it is arranged should be found useful.

I would add here five Samoyad words collected by Mr. Seebohm when he visited the Pechora in 1875. They are the equivalents of sandpiper, willow grouse, swan, goose, and black goose: suitar, hond-jy, chouari, yebtaw, pardén yebtaw. Both in these names and the list taken from Mr. Rae's vocabulary I have not ventured to alter the orthography, although it is obvious that our modern system of reproducing vowel sounds is more exact.

SAMOYAD ROSARY.

Von Strahlenberg, in his *Historico-Geographical*

Description of the North and Eastern Parts of Europe and Asia (Editions 1730 and 1738), gives a curious and valuable Polyglot Table of thirty-two "Tartarian Nations;" and to the Samoyads of the Pechora, he attributes the following equivalents of these numerals:—

one	ob	six	maat
two	side	seven	siw
three	niar	eight	siniet
four	thiet	nine	niensei
five	samlei	ten	ju

It will be interesting to tabulate these numerals with those given by Von Strahlenberg as used by the Ostiaks who live on the Ob near Narym; the Ostiaks living in the basin of the Ob near Tomsk; the Samoyads who live between the Yenisei and the Lena; those dwelling in the lower valley of the Yenisei; and those who inhabit the valley of the Kann.

A CHAPTER ON LANGUAGE

English.	Samoyads of the Greater Tundra.	Ostiaks of Narym.	Ostiaks of Tomsk.	Samoyads between Yenisei and Lena.	Samoyads of the Lower Yenisei.	Kanskoi (Khotowa).
One	ob	oker	ockr	gree	noye	opp
Two	side	schidæ	tzidæ	sitti	side	tzida
Three	niar	nakor	nagur	nagor	nehe	naghor
Four	thiet	thett	thita	kietta	tetta	thæta
Five	samlei	nomblach	ssoombulang	samfolenka	saborika	ssoumbulang
Six	maat	mocktin	mucktu	motto	motto	muctu
Seven	siw	hælsch	ssellgie	seiba	sea	seigbe
Eight	siniet	stagwet	ssidyniet	sitteretta	sidetta	schidætæ
Nine	niensei	okresiawet	ockr-Venjet	nayma-tomma	essa	togus
Ten	ju	pawoget	kiæht	by	by	bud

There are several words in the above table which might be reasonably written with greater similarity. Thus, *side* (two), if written *sidé*, would give us the two sounds which the whole series, we may fairly infer, represents. So *by* (ten) is probably a Russian literation which should read in English *bu*.

CHAPTER VIII

SAMOYAD FOLK-TALES [1]

1. The two sisters and the old woman of the island—2. The seven maidens of the lake—3. The old man of deceit.

1. *The Two Sisters and the Old Woman of the Island*

IN one and the self-same tent dwell two women, the one young, the other old. The younger has two children, both girls, but the old woman is childless. The young woman busily makes her children clothes; the old one lies down and does nothing.

---

[1] These Folk-tales I have taken from the German edition of M. Alexander Castrén's *Ethnologische Vorlesungen über Die Altaischen Völker herausgegeben von Anton Schiefner* (St. Petersburg, 1857), vol. iv. Their great merit lies in a simplicity so absolute that it might be taken for mere crudity, or even literary incompetence on the part of the transcriber. But a careful study of these tales will show that the limit of descriptive terminology is imposed on the one hand by a meagre syntax; and, on the other, by the bare and unvaried geographical environment in which the tales arise. The features of the Tundra are few; the landscape monotonous, the fauna restricted; the people are primitive and their fashions permanent. Their life is made up of incidents common to all, and there is absence of variety in the experiences which can befall them. Yet the Samoyad's motives and ideas are shown here in that low

One day the childless woman says to the other : " Let us go and pick shoe-grass."[1]

The other answers : " I have not time ; I must sew my children's clothes." However, she goes. And as they gather grass there in the field, the childless woman takes her knife and stabs her who has two children. She kindles a fire, cooks the flesh, and eats it. She eats not the head, but will eat that another time.

She then returns to the tent, and the children ask, " Where is our mother ? "

" Your mother picks shoe-grass, she will come, I suppose, when she has time," answers the old woman, and lays herself down to sleep across the door, so that the children may not slip out ; she means to eat them up also when she awakes. While she sleeps there,

moral key which seems befitting such a people ; and every illustration is obviously derived from an environment which is characteristic enough, if distinctly barren of variety. How completely the wealth of description at the disposal of the Samoyad has been utilised and even exhausted may be gathered from that incident in the first tale, when the girls are told by the Old Woman of the Island that they will find in the boat, axes, knives and borers—these three tools forming the entire stock of Samoyad implements.

I may add here that the few songs of the Samoyads, though metrical, exhibit no system, definiteness, or anything that may be called a law of versification. The subject of these crooning songs is chiefly the old and universal theme of love, here shown in its most primitive aspect—the abduction of women.

[1] The Finns also have a custom in the winter time of placing grass inside their shoes, in order to make them warmer. The grass used for this purpose the story calls here shoe-grass.

the elder maiden creeps softly out of the balagan.¹ The old woman sleeps on, and the maiden goes to the door. There she sees the head of her mother, and thinks—

"The old woman has eaten my mother; when she wakes she will also eat up me and my sister." So she catches two live birds, places them in the balagan, and runs away with her sister.

The old woman sleeps on for seven days,² then wakes, goes to the balagan and now will eat up the children; but she finds only the two birds.

"Ye have not escaped me," mutters the beldame, and she begins to run after the maidens. She runs seven days, and then overtakes them, and will lay hold of the younger maiden, who lags behind. The elder maiden, however, throws a grindstone behind her. At once a river flows along, and steep cliffs rise on both banks of the river. The old woman remains standing on the other side of the river and the maidens escape. The river flows seven days and then flows away. So the old woman runs after the children again; she runs for seven days, and then overtakes the maidens. She is just going to lay hold of the younger when the elder threw a firestone (flint) behind her, and at once a high

---

[1] A kind of linen tent or curtain, which one needs as a protection against the mosquitoes; in Samoyad a balagan is called a *jéser*.

[2] The series of original numbers ceases in all Samoyad and Finnic dialects with seven, which number has received, for this reason, a special importance in the songs and tales of the people.

mountain rises up, and the old hag remains standing behind the mountain.

After seven days the mountain disappears and again the old woman begins to run. She runs for seven days and then overtakes the maidens and will lay hold of the younger. The elder throws a comb behind her, and there rises a thick forest, so thick that the old woman cannot come through. But after seven days the forest vanishes, and then the old woman began again to run after them.

When the children had run three days, they came to a place where not long since a tent had stood. Seven crows now sit there and eat reindeer dung.

The elder maiden says to one of the crows: "Little mother, show us the way to a place where men dwell?"

The crow answers: "Go ye still farther and farther on, and then ye will come to the blue sea. There ye will find seven sea-gulls, and they will point out to you your way to men."

The maidens ran again for seven days, came to the blue sea, and found the seven sea-gulls. These were eating seal flesh.

The elder maiden said to one of the sea-gulls: "Little mother, whither shall we go to find men?"

The sea-gull answers: "Go ye along the sea-coast, there there is an island between two seas. On the island lives an old woman; she will carry you over the strait."

The maidens ran seven days, came straight to the island without trouble, saw a tent, and began to call for a boat. Then the old woman comes out of the tent, and asks the maidens—

"What is my face like?"

"It shines like the sun," answers the elder maiden.

"What is my breast like?"

"Beautiful as reindeer spleen!"

"My hands and feet (arms and legs) what are they like?"

"Thick and fat like the flesh of the sea-horse!"

Then the old woman called aloud, and a beaver swam to the maidens and carried them over the strait.

But scarcely had they reached the island, when the horrible old beldame came hurrying after the maidens. Standing on the bank, she begged the other old woman to carry her across the strait.

Then the old woman from the island asks the terrible old hag—

"What is my face like?"

"Thy face is ugly, it is like the hind part of a beast!" answers the horrible old woman.

"What is my breast like?"

"Like the dugs of a bitch!"

"My arms and legs, what are they like?"

"They are like spoon-handles!"

"What sawest thou on the way?" further asked the old woman of the island.

"Seven crows," answers the beldame.

"How do they live?"

"Very badly. I think that they are no longer alive. Their food was reindeer dung."

"What sawest thou further?"

"Seven sea-gulls."

"How do these live?"

"Badly, they eat only seal's flesh."

Then the old woman of the island screamed out, and a sturgeon swam up to the horrible old woman.

And then the old woman of the island said, "Place thyself on the sturgeon."

"How can I sit here?—the back is sharp and pointed; I cannot sit here. Tell me, how came the maidens across the strait?" asks the old woman.

"On this same sturgeon," replied the old woman of the island.

Then the horrible old hag puts herself on its back, and the sturgeon swims far from the island. He swims farther and farther, and at last the old woman is drowned.

Now the maidens lived with the old woman on the island for a long time.

But at last the elder one begins to grow weary,

and she says to the old woman: "Show us another place, where men dwell."

The old woman says: "Go ye along the footpath on the island until ye come to the shore; by the shore is a shallow, and in the shallow a copper-boat. Place yourselves in the boat; without oar, without sail, it will bring you to where people live. But in the boat there are many dangerous tools—axes, knives, and borers. Touch not these; and do thou"—she says to the elder sister—"look after the younger that she touches none of them with her hands. If you take these things in your hands, they strike you dead, and the boat stands still. Sit ye quite still, therefore, and ye will arrive; then speak ye to the boat: 'Boat, go back to the place whence thou hast come,' and then my boat will return home again."

So the maidens followed the footpath and came to the shore; on the shore there was a shallow, and in the shallow a boat. In the boat there were axes, knives, and gimlets. Then the maidens pushed the boat into the water and climbed into it themselves.

The boat runs by itself; it goes over many seas, and comes at last to a river, and begins to glide along up the stream. On the river bank grow trees of every kind, birches, firs, and black alder trees. At one place grow two big larch trees, one on each side of the river. Their tops have grown together; and the river runs through between the trees.

"See, what high bushes!" says the elder sister.

Then the younger takes a knife to cut a branch from the tree. The knife strikes her dead, and she dies, and the boat stops by the bank.

The elder maiden lifts her dead sister out of the boat and says: "Boat, go thou back thither, whence thou hast come."

And immediately the boat goes back.

The elder maiden now goes to bury her dead sister, and carries her to a pine forest.

She asks her sister by means of the magic drum: "Where shall I bury thee, sister; somewhere here?"

The sister answers: "Bury me not in the pine forest, for there folk come and frighten me."

She carries her farther, sees a birch-wood, and asks again by means of the magic drum: "Shall I bury thee here?"

The sister answers: "Bury me not in the birch-wood, for there folk come, hew down birches and frighten me."

She carries her still farther, comes to a fir-wood, and asks by means of the magic drum: "May I bury thee in the fir-wood?"

The sister answers: "Bury me not in the fir-wood, for there children come, break branches, and frighten me."

Then is the sister weary of the carrying, and, seeing a birch copse, says: "There I bury thee; my hands ache, I cannot carry thee any longer." She comes to the copse, finds a wolf's den there, and puts her sister in the den. She herself goes on her way, farther and farther away, on and on for several months.

It becomes winter, but she still goes on, ever walking. At last she comes to a footpath, and follows it and arrives at a river, on whose banks stand two sledges. Reindeer are yoked to them; to one sledge a speckled, to the other a dazzling white reindeer. But there are no men to be seen.

So the maiden thinks: "I shall wait here for the men: they will surely come, as they must have gone into the forest." She waits all the day through, she waits until evening. And in the evening two men come out of the forest.

One of them asks the maiden: "Wilt thou not drive on the sledge with us to our home?"

"No," answers the maiden, "I will go on foot; for I am ashamed in the presence of men."

The older man, who had a dazzling-white reindeer, says to his companion: "Take the maiden and put her on the sledge."

"I will have no one on my sledge," he replied. "Take her thyself."

Then the older man, who had the dazzling-white reindeer, took the maiden on his sledge and drove home with her. Here stand rows of tents, and over all these tents rule only two masters, each of whom has a son. The men who came out of the forest were their sons. The maiden begins to live here; the elder of the two men takes her to wife. They live long together.

One day they begin to break up the tents, and drive for one day, two days, three days; then they make a halt. In the night a storm comes on and the wolf drives away the reindeer. So, on the following day the two sons set out to look for the reindeer, and they drive in different directions. Suddenly the reindeer of the older man shows signs of fear, and he begins to look about to see why they have taken fright. He espies a wolf's den, hears the wolves howl, hears also a sob; he listens and listens,—it is a woman who is sobbing.

He calls out: "Weep not, my child, thy father brings thee meat!" Then he drove home again.

His father asks: "Hast thou found the reindeer?"

The son answers: "The reindeer I found not," but he says nothing of the wonder that he had seen. In the night, however, he tells all to his wife, and relates how the wolf-cubs howl and the woman weeps.

The wife answers: "Must it not be my sister who weeps there? I buried her there. Let us go thither."

So on the following day they all drive to the wolf's den, and when they come to the place the wolf has run away, but the cubs and the woman are there. They killed the cubs, but the woman they took and led her to the tent. She is like a mad woman, she only screams. They make a fire and place her near the fire. She looks at the flames, and after she had gazed at them a long time, she seems to wake and says, " Have I slept long ? "

" Long, sister ; very long. We sailed with the boat which the old woman on the island had given us, and thou didst stab thyself and die. I buried thee in the wolf's den, and there my husband heard thee weep but yesterday."

So the younger sister now lived in the choom, whither they had brought her, and she became the wife of the younger son with the speckled reindeer.

2. *The Seven Maidens of the Lake*

Two Samoyads live in a solitary place, busily catching foxes, sables, and bears. It chances one day that one goes on a journey, but the other remains at home. As he travels, he sees an old woman chopping birch-trees. He went up to the old woman and said, " How are you chopping, old woman ? you chop all round, and you will not fell the tree then. Cut from both sides ! Let me hew ! "

He took the axe from the sledge, began to hew at another part, struck from both sides and so felled the tree. He placed the tree on the sledge and brought it to the old woman's choom and laid the tree on the ground.

Then the old woman says, "Hide thyself so that no one sees thee."

So he hides himself, and the old woman remains standing on some high ground. Then seven maidens come up to her.

"Who has hewn this tree for thee? Thou hewest not like this. Who is with thee?"

The old woman said: "No one is with me; I have felled the tree myself."

The maidens went away immediately, without even entering the tent, and the Samoyad comes out of his hiding-place, and goes up to the old woman. The old woman says: "In the gloomy forest there is a lake, a big lake; go to it. When thou reachest it, the seven maidens will be swimming, having left their clothes on the bank. Go up softly, take one of the maidens' clothes and hide them."

The Samoyad went, came to the lake, took the best-looking clothes and hid them.

The seven maidens swim about, then come to the bank and begin to dress themselves, but one girl's clothes have vanished. So she threw herself into the lake again, and the others went away. But the lone maiden weeps in the lake, for she knows not who has taken her clothes. At last she cries out, "I will be the wife of him who has taken my clothes when he gives back the clothes to me."

But the Samoyad trusts not the maiden, and holds back still.

Then in the lake the maiden thinks and again calls out: "Our old woman has a sister still older; she has a son. If he has taken my clothes, then I will be his wife."

Then the man comes forward, and the maiden sees him.

"You are, indeed, the nephew of our old woman! Give me my clothes, then I will be thy wife."

"If I give thee thy clothes, then thou wilt return to heaven. How, then, can I get possession of thee?"

"Truly I will be thy wife! Give me my clothes, for I am cold."

"Not far from here there are seven Samoyads, who all live together in an out-of-the-way place, and go about and kill many people. When they come home they take their own hearts out and hang them on the tent-poles. Get their seven hearts for me, then I will give thee thy clothes, else thou gettest them not, even if thou shouldest die in this place."

"I will get the hearts, so give me my clothes."

"I will give them not until thou tellest me how thou wilt get the hearts of the seven sons."

"In the night I will go and take them privily."

"Then thou takest them not; for many have tried

but no one has yet succeeded. Come nearer to me, and then I will teach thee how thou canst get them into thy power."

So the maiden swam nearer to the bank, and the Samoyad said—

"They have robbed me of a sister, and we must get her to help. Go thou to my sister where she keeps watch over the hearts, and ask her for them." Thus they agreed together, and he gave the maiden her clothes.

When she had dressed herself, he asked how long a time it would be before he should get the hearts. "Within five days I will come to thee with my Raid[1] and my choom," the maiden replied. So the Samoyad went back to his tent to his companion.

His old comrade asks, "Where hast thou been, what hast thou seen?"—"I have been nowhere; I have seen nothing," was the reply.

His companion says, "Thou hast certainly been with our father's sister! The seven brothers without hearts have killed our mother, and they kill thee too if thou goest there: never go to the old woman."

So five days pass, and on the fifth day the maiden comes swiftly with her Raid and choom, and becomes his wife.

"Let us go to the seven brothers," says the wife. "We shall see whether we cannot get possession of

[1] Raid (Lapp, Raido) is a team of deer.

their hearts." So they came to their tent; but the brothers had gone out, and there were only women in the tent. The husband and wife go into the tent, but no one can see the wife. The man is seen, however, and he says to his sister: "Where do the seven brothers lay their hearts when they come home?"

"They hang them there on the tent-poles at night, for they always sleep without them." The sister continues: "They trust me, and when they come home in the evening I take a dish and go from one brother to the other. Each lays his heart in the dish; and then I hang the hearts on the poles. Now, take thou the dish, and take the hearts off the poles and place them on the dish. In the morning they will ask thee for their hearts, but throw thou the hearts of the six younger brothers wherever thou wishest—for they may die— but go with the elder brother's heart to him and say, 'If my mother comes to life again, then I will give thee thy heart, otherwise I will not.'"

Towards night the Samoyad goes home with his wife. His wife says, "Go thou not to them; let me take the hearts, and I will go alone." So in the night she returns. The seven brothers are eating their supper and no one sees her. They finish their meal, spread out their reindeer-skins and lie down to sleep. Then the sister takes the dish, and each one lays his heart upon it, and she goes and puts the hearts in the appointed place.

"Why puttest thou our hearts away so carelessly?" asks one of the brothers.

"She will guard them well," said the eldest brother.

But when they went to sleep, the woman carried off the hearts and came to her husband with them.

When the morning dawned, the husband went with the hearts to the brothers; they were already on the point of dying. They all begged for their hearts, but he threw them on the ground, and as he threw them down the brothers die. So died the six younger brothers. But he threw not the eldest brother's heart on the ground. So when he again and again begged for his heart, the man said: "Thou hast killed my mother, make her alive again, then I will give thee thy heart."

"Give me my heart first, then I will bring her to life again."

"If thou makest her not alive again first, thou gettest not thy heart." Then the eldest brother says to his wife: "Go to the place where the dead woman lies and there you will see a bag; bring me this bag, for in the bag is her spirit." The wife fetches the bag.

"Go to thy dead mother, shake the bag and let the spirit breathe over all the bones; then she will come to life again."

He came to his mother, and did as the Samoyad had commanded him, and the mother received her life again. So he sent his mother to his tent and he himself went to his sister and there he found the

Samoyad still alive. But he threw his heart on the ground; so that he also died.

After the brother had gone home with his sister he went again to his father's sister, and found her again in the same place in the forest.

She says, "Have the seven not yet killed thee?"

"No, but we have rather killed them; but how are you getting on?"

The father's sister said: "Thy wife's knife is here, I will give thee the knife, do thou give it to thy wife, and beg her to do what she likes with it, and I myself will come to you soon."

The Samoyad goes home, gives the knife to his wife and begs her to do what she likes with it. The wife takes with it the hearts of all those who were in the tent, also her husband's heart and her own, and throws them into the air. And when their father's sister came, and saw that all were without hearts, she said, "All are without hearts, they live not, yet they are not dead; what am I to do? I will go to the big lake and perhaps I may find some one there again." So she went and found the six sisters again bathing in the lake; and taking the best clothes, she hid them, and heard them weeping and moaning there.

"We know not which way our sister has gone." And swimming about, they came to the bank again. Now one cannot find her clothes, so she throws herself into the lake and the rest go away.

But the maiden weeps, "I would be the wife of him who has taken my clothes, and would make alive again all his beloved dead ones, if I could only get back my clothes. We have caught many hearts in the air and I can help the dead with these."

Then the old woman comes forward: "See, here are thy clothes."

"Give me the clothes," cries the maiden, "everything that I have promised, I will do."

"Give thou me all the hearts you have found, then I give thee the clothes," said the woman: "for you live in the air, but your sister is now on earth. When she asks you for anything, can you help her?"

"If she lives, we will do everything that she wishes."

So the maiden gave up the hearts and the old woman the clothes. Then the old woman went to the tent where the men without the hearts had lived, who had gone up to the land of the spirits; and she gave them all their hearts, and all became *clean* and *holy*.

"Now," said the woman, "let us go to the land of the spirits, to our sisters."

So they caught reindeer, set off on their journey, and drove through the air. Then they suddenly came upon a thick mist, so that they could see nothing. Seven days they went through the mist, then they came to a warm, a very warm and happy place. And there they live still to this day.

3. *The Old Man of Deceit*

By a river lived an old man and an old woman; these two alone, and they were Samoyads. Higher up the river lived Ostiaks in yourts, at a place where there were several yourts near one another, like a village. The old man lived in the extremest poverty, he had neither weapons nor tools, but only an axe. One evening the old man, after he had eaten his supper, went out of the tent; and he saw ptarmigan run on the snow. He took a log and threw it at the ptarmigan, but hit them not.

The ptarmigan began to speak: "Why wishest thou to take away our life? Go into the tent and kill thy wife. Thou art poor; if thou killest thy wife, then thou wilt be rich."

So the old man took his axe, went into the tent and killed his wife.

Then he begins to weep: "What have I done? why have I killed my wife? all our lifetime we have lived happily together, and now I have killed her."

All night long he weeps. Morning came,—God gave the light. Then the old man prepares a small dog-sledge, sat his wife up in the sledge as if she were alive, and drove her down the river, following its course. At last the river flows into a wide stream, and he goes up the stream until he comes to a village where dwelt an Ostiak prince (*Hahe-jieru*). He left the dead body by a hole which had been made in the ice for fishing. He himself went to the prince, who had two beautiful daughters. Now the prince let the old man eat and drink as much as he pleased, until he was filled.

Then said the old man: "I have eaten and drunken here, while my wife is perhaps frozen outside the meanwhile."

"Why didst thou not tell me, old man, that thou hadst thy wife here; perhaps she is frozen."

So the prince says to his two daughters: "Go ye to the old woman and bring her hither, that she may warm herself."

The daughters ran, and the younger one ran the faster.

"Why runnest thou so fast? thou wilt hurt the old woman," called out her sister.

However, she kept on running and came to the sledge, drew it quickly by the thongs, and the old woman fell into the hole.

So the maidens went home to their father the prince, and told him that the old woman was drowned. The prince searched for the old woman with long poles, but found her not.

The old man stayed with the prince, weeping night and day, and moaning aloud over the loss of his wife, until at last the prince says: "My ears suffer from this noise. I will give thee my eldest daughter instead of the old woman." So there was a wedding. The prince gave the old man a yourt, and there they lived a long time, and the woman bore a son. The prince her father was pleased at this and gave a big feast; and they ate and drank greatly. All became drunk except the prince and his daughter's husband, who still went on drinking. And at last the prince falls down also.

Now the old man begins to cry out: "I alone stand on my legs; they all lie there drunk, although we all have drunk alike. These folk are good for nothing. I have killed my wife, and yet am a better man than all these. I live now in wealth, since I have taken my wife's life."

"What," said the younger maiden, "hast thou thyself taken the life of thy wife?"

The old man went up to the maiden, struck the maiden with his hand, so that she became speechless. And the guests having slept, went home, and so did the old man.

But the younger maiden remained speechless, and could eat nothing, and soon she began to die.

The prince says: "Where can I find any one who could heal her? Go," said he, "to my son-in-law, and ask whether he knows not where such an one is to be found."

And the son-in-law came to the prince, but said that he knew not any one who could heal her.

"Then," said the prince, "I have heard that near us live seven Ostiaks; they have a mother, who is said to be very wise. Son-in-law! drive thou with good dogs to her."

So the old man yoked some good dogs and set off, and came to the seven Ostiaks, and begged the mother to come with him to the prince to heal his sick daughter.

The old woman got into the sledge, and together they went to the prince. When they arrived the prince said, "Canst thou not heal my sick daughter?"

"I do not know. If men have hurt her, there is healing; if the sickness comes from God, she cannot be helped. But it seems to me as if men had hurt her."

So the old woman takes her magic drum, strikes it, and then left off: "By God," said she, "I have not found the cause of the sickness, and death (*Häbcep*) has done her no harm."

The old woman sat down beside the old man and began to beat the drum again, striking with much strength, and throwing herself from side to side. At that moment the old man was cutting sharp pegs, and as the old woman flung herself on one side a peg went through one of her ears, and came out at the other. So she died on the spot.

"What means this?" exclaimed the prince. "My daughter is on the point of death, the old woman has died, and the seven Ostiaks will attack me."

Again the prince begs the old man: "If thou wilt take this old woman to her sons, and canst speak such words so that they do not attack me, then I will give thee half of my wealth."

So the old man again yoked some good dogs to the sledge, put the old woman on the sledge, as if she were alive, and drove off with her. He drives into dark woods, where two Samoyads are shooting with bows at a squirrel. They shoot, but hit not.

The old man halts, picks up their arrows, and says: "Why shoot ye so badly? let me shoot, then I will take the squirrel as a gift to the prince." So he goes to the old woman, sticks an arrow through her ears.

"What," says he, "you have shot the mother of the seven Ostiaks; the arrow went in at one ear and came out at the other."

The Samoyads come and see, grieve very much, betake themselves to the prince, and beg for mercy.

"Go ye," says the prince, "drive the old woman to the Ostiaks, and make it up with them as well as you can."

The Samoyads beg the old man to take the woman to the Ostiaks. "We will give thee what thou wishest —foxes, sables, fat, clothes, and other things, if thou wilt only take the old woman to the Ostiaks!"

"I will undertake it, only deceive me not." So the old man drives off again, and at last comes to where the seven Ostiaks live. Standing by the dead body, he drew the arrow out of her ears and stuck a twig in. Then he covered the old woman with snow, and went up to the seven Ostiaks. They came to meet him and go to their mother, and look at their mother, and see the twig in her ears.

"What! thou hast killed our mother?"

"What say ye?"

"Seest thou not the twig which sticks out of her ears?"

"That is," said the old man, "because the prince gave me wild dogs; it is clear that during the drive through the wood a twig ran into her ears."

The Ostiaks said, "The fault is thine and it will go badly with thee."

Then they raise the mother from the sledge and tell the old man to return home. So he went, and coming to the place where the two Samoyads were shooting at the squirrel he found them again, and they had brought with them what they had promised. One sledge was full of foxes and sables, another with clothes of various kinds. So he took the sledges and drove home with them, and lived for a time with the prince.

But the maiden lies at the last gasp, and so the prince speaks to him: "Heal thou my younger daughter, and take her for thy second wife!"

And the old man replies: "Bring her to me, and I will try her."

So she was brought to him and they went to rest;

the maiden was placed in a special room, and all forbidden to go to her. Alarmed by her calling out aloud, however, the elder sister goes; then her husband's command occurs to her and she turns back. But her younger sister immediately runs out—healthy, active, and with ready tongue. The prince rejoiced exceedingly, and gave her to the old man.

After the wedding they live for a long while at the same place; the younger wife says no word of that which has befallen her, and two sons are born to the old man, one of the elder, the other of the younger sister.

Then the old man says to the elder sister: "Go to thy father and ask him for a boat; I wish to see my former dwelling-place."

So the wife goes and asks for the boat and gets permission from the prince for her husband to choose from among his boats the one which suits him best. The old man now took a boat and went off on his journey alone until he came to the place where he had taken the life of his wife. He drew the boat to the shore and went into the village near that place where he formerly lived. All the neighbours knew him and ask, "Where hast thou been so long?"

"In the neighbourhood of the Ostiak Prince yonder, I have been."

"What do they do in that country?" ask the neighbours.

"Nothing good: that is why I have come away. It is said that the Harjutsi-Samoyads[1] will come and plunder us; now we must save ourselves from them."

"How can we save ourselves?"

"Make two pits," says the old man, "and hide yourselves in them. Cover the pits with big trees, then I myself will cover the trees with earth. Lay in the one pit your reindeer and all your property, cover them well with earth and go yourselves into the other as many as ye are."

So the neighbours did just as the old man told them; the one pit they covered themselves, and the other was covered by the old man. But the old man himself started again on his journey and returned home.

After he had lived again for a time with the prince, he asks the prince for boats to go home in once more.

"There," says he, "I have my property in its old place, and there I could live."

Thereupon he took his two wives, sons, all his goods, and betook himself in three boats to his old dwelling-place. He settled down in the village where formerly his neighbours had lived, and puts his goods in their store-rooms.

"See," says one of the daughters, "what a splendid yourt our husband has here."

"But," said he, "let us also look at my goods, which I have hidden in the earth."

[1] A Samoyad tribe within the Obdorian Volost.

The pit is opened, and here there is property of all kinds,—foxes, sables, ermines, gold, clothes, and much more besides. And they carried everything into the store-rooms, until all the store-rooms were filled.

"Now there," said the old man, "is riches for you. I am old and soon I descend to the grave; but what I have gathered for you, you may spend after my death as you will."

A SAMOYAD DOLL.

APPENDIX A

NOTES ON THE ORNITHOLOGICAL RESULTS OF MR. JACKSON'S JOURNEY

By JOS. RUSSELL JEAFFRESON, F.R.G.S.

No one interested in Ornithology, especially that of the Palæarctic birds, can read the story of so successful a journey as that of Mr. Jackson without envying him his fortune in passing through a district which has, during the last half century, been regarded by many naturalists as the Land of Promise. Of course it must be borne in mind that Mr. Jackson's aim was not Natural History, but to test his equipment; otherwise he would have arranged his arrival at Habarova some two or three months earlier, and would then have had the opportunity of working during the breeding season.

But when I remember the date on which he reached Habarova, I must say that the greatest praise is due to him for the splendid use he made of his time and his gun before the autumn migration took place. The mere list of his birds will confirm what I say, although I speak also from my acquaintance with Mr. Jackson during a number of years, and my knowledge of his being a most ardent and admirable sportsman.

Mr. Jackson's journey being confined to a march westward from 60 E. long., he has not brought us back any birds or notes from the country between the Kara River and the mouth of the Ob and Yenisei—which would have completed a chain of evidence, the extreme links of which have been contributed by Mr. Seebohm; but in traversing the Great and, to Englishmen, unknown Tundra, he has been able to extend and confirm the very interesting observations of that gentleman in the valley of the Pechora, even though the line of Mr. Jackson's route was well to the northward.

In opening the parcels of skins, I found much of my task already done for me; they had been treated in so workman-like a manner that, in spite of the difficult and laborious sledge journey on which they were subsequently taken, they looked as if fresh from the bird. I may say at once that I have nothing new to report nor anything of particular rarity, but I regard the "bag" as most valuable in its confirmation and proof of the geographical distribution of many species. The greater part of Mr. Jackson's journey was performed in winter, and we are to that extent the losers; for he could have had little opportunity then of adding to the number he collected in the short time before that season set in. He records taking some Snowy Owls which had stayed late on the Tundra—tempted thereto by the lemmings, probably—but it is to the first six weeks, and very busy weeks they must have been, that we owe what we have. Of Geese he brings the Bean Goose, and of Swans—not Bewick's—but the common variety of that region; and the nesting-place of the Curlew Sandpiper still remains a problem to be solved. For although this bird is itself a regular visitor to our shores its breeding-place is quite unknown. In my opinion Novaia Zemlia, or possibly Yalmal, holds the secret; and I am inclined to the former, if only on the ground that if the bird bred on Yalmal some stragglers would have nested to the westward and even the southward. Neither did any naturalist I know think that Kolguev was the site: Kolguev is too inconsiderable, and too near the Little Tundra of Russia, and, moreover, too frequently visited to have been likely.

Mr. Jackson reports that every stream and patch of open water on the Great Tundra is the resort of thousands of birds; that the pools between the rolling tundra and the sandy marshes abutting on the streams form the home of hundreds of those waders, who love such secluded nesting-places, and are here to be found in their most northern habitat. When, too, he reached the tree limit of the Tundra, he noted the northern game-birds and many species besides. Two months earlier he would have found in the larch and pine forests the Woodpeckers and Grossbills; but as it is, the number of interesting skins he has secured, and his notes on their former owners, lead us to hope great results in Ornithology from Franz Josef Land. Will he bring us back the Knott's and the pigmy curlew's eggs and those of Ross's Rosy Gull? I have little doubt that the latter birds breed on Franz Josef Land; and less that Mr. Jackson will find them, if they are to be found.

I now append the list, and may well leave it to speak for itself:—

BIRD LIST.

(*Professor Huxley's Classification, as adopted by* Mr. H. E. DRESSER, F.L.S., F.Z.S., *in his "Birds of Europe."*)

Aves CARINATÆ

ÆGITHOGNATHÆ

Order PASSERES

Suborder OSCINES

Section OSCINES DENTIROSTRES

Family TURDIDÆ

Subfamily TURDINÆ

1. Missel-Thrush (*Turdus viscivorus*, Linn.)
2. Song-Thrush (*Turdus musicus*, Linn.)
3. Redwing (*Turdus iliacus*, Linn.)
4. Fieldfare (*Turdus pilaris*, Linn.)
5. Siberian Thrush (*Turdus sibiricus*, Pall.)
6. Blackbird (*Turdus merula*, Linn.)

Subfamily SAXICOLINÆ.

7. Common Wheatear (*Saxicola œnanthe*, Linn.)]
8. Stone-Chat (*Pratincola rubicola*, Linn.)
9. Red Start (*Ruticilla phœnicurus*, Linn.)

Subfamily PHYLLOSCOPINÆ.

10. Chiffchaff (*Phylloscopus collybita*, Vieill.)

Family MOTACILLIDÆ.

11. Rock Pipet (*Anthus obscurus*, Lath.)

---

1. Killed on Waigatz Island.
2. Killed on Waigatz Island.
5. Killed near Pustozersk.
7. Common on the shore at Waigatz Island.
11. Common on the shore at Waigatz Island.

Section 3.—OSCINES CONIROSTRES.

Subfamily FRINGILLINÆ.

12. Siskin (*Chrysorostris spinus*, Linn.)
12A. Brambling (*Fringilla montifringilla*, Linn.)
13. Snow-Finch (*Montifringilla nivalis*, Linn.)

Subfamily EMBERIZINÆ.

13A. Snow Bunting (*Plectrophanes nivalis*, Linn.)

Section 5.—OSCINES CULHIROSTRES.

Family STURNIDÆ.

14. Starling (*Sturnus vulgaris*, Linn.)
15. Siberian Jay (*Perisoreus infaustus*, Linn.)
16. Jackdaw (*Corvus monedula*, Linn.)
17. Magpie (*Pica Rustica*, Scop.)
18. Hooded Crow (*Corvus cornix*, Linn.)
19. Raven (*Corvus corax*, Linn.)

12A. Sometimes wanders in winter as far as our isles, where it is met with in small flocks.

13A. This hardy little bird seems to have been met with all through the author's journey, as its name constantly occurs in his notes.

16. Seems much whiter in its collar in all the skins than the common English specimen. One was undoubtedly *Corvus dauricus* by its white vent.

17. About half a dozen beautiful skins of this bird were brought back by Mr. Jackson; they seem identical with those killed in Asia and America.

18. This hardy scavenger seems quite to have taken the place of the ordinary crow in many places. Mr. Jackson saw it everywhere, and far into winter it still remained north to see what it could pick up in the way of starving lemmings or small birds.

19. Found all over Western Siberia, but still with all its hardihood is seldom found wandering north of 68° N. lat.

Order II.—ACCIPITRES.
Suborder STRIGES.
Family STRIGIDÆ.

20. Barn Owl (*Strix flammea*, Linn.)
21. Snowy Owl (*Nyctea scandiaca*, Linn.)

Family FALCONIDÆ.

22. Sea Eagle (*Haliætus albicilla*, Linn.)
23. Peregrine Falcon (*Falco peregrinus*, Tunstall).
24. Sparrow Hawk (*Accipiter nisus*, Linn.)

Order V.—ANSERES.
Family ANATIDÆ.

25. Grey Lag Goose (*Anser cinereus*, Meyer).
26. Bean Goose (*Anser segetum*, Gmel.)
27. Pink-footed (*Anser brachystrynchus*, Bail.)
28. Bewick's Swan (*Cygnus bewicki*, Yarr.)
29. Mallard (*Anas boscas*, Linn.)
30. Pintail (*Dafila acuta*, Linn.)
31. Widgeon (*Mureca penelope*, Linn.)
32. Goldeneye (*Clangula glaucion*, Linn.)
33. Steller's Duck (*Somateria stelleri*, Pall.)
34. Smew (*Mergus albellus*, Linn.)

---

20. This specimen was labelled as being killed near Arkhangel.

21. This hardy bird seemed to be little affected by the Arctic cold, and Mr. Jackson relates how even in the depth of winter he saw them flitting about like white ghosts on the Tundra on the look-out for lemmings—their staple winter food.

22. Seen fishing, not shot.

23. Found dead on the Tundra in the snow, and one other seen during the expedition.

28. Killed on Waigatz Island.

33. About a dozen most perfect skins of this lovely bird were brought home by Mr. Jackson.

34. This bird sometimes wanders as far as our islands in winter. Mr. Jackson's specimen was the only one seen by him on his expedition.

Order II.—GALLINÆ.

Family TETRAONIDÆ.

35. Willow Ptarmigan (*Lagopus albus*, Gmel.)
36. Hazel Grouse (*Bonasa betulina*, Scop.)

Order IV.—LIMICOLÆ.

Family CHARADRIIDÆ.

37. Golden Plover (*Charadrius pluvialis*, Linn.)
38. Grey Plover (*Squatarola helvetica*, Linn.)
39. Ringed Plover (*Ægialetis curonica*, Gmel.)
40. Oyster-catcher (*Hæmatopus ostralegus*, Linn.)
41. Red-shank (*Totanus calidus*, Linn.)
42. Snipe (*Gallinago cœlestris*, Frenzel).
43. Curlew (*Numenius arquata*, Linn.)
44. Wimbrel (*Numenius phæopus*, Linn.)
45. Little Stint (*Tringa minuta*, Leisl.)

Order V.—GAVIÆ.

Family LARIDÆ.

Subfamily STERNINÆ.

46. Arctic Tern (*Sterna macrura*, Naum.)
47. Glaucus Gull (*Larus glaucus*, Faber).

---

35. About a dozen very perfect skins of this bird were brought back.

36. This superb game-bird, though unknown in England, is well-known to all Arctic sportsmen, as it is found in nearly all the Arctic and Hyperborean lands. It is well-known in Norway under the name of Hyerper.

38. Killed near the Pechora.

40. Essentially a summer visitor to the North. I noticed in Iceland in 1891, and in Faröe in 1894, they were the first to leave of their family.

45. The egg of this tiny bird is a great prize, and totally unknown in the cabinets of private collectors. The only authentic eggs being those taken by Middendorff. The specimen killed by Mr. Jackson is marked east coast of Waigatz Island.

48. Iceland Gull (*Larus leucopterus*, Faber).
49. Kittiwake (*Rissa tridactyla*, Linn.).
50. Herring Gull (*Larus argentatus*, Gmel.).
51. Silurian Herring Gull (*Larus argentatus*, Gmel.).
52. Great Black-backed Gull (*Larus marinus*, Linn.).

Subfamily STERCORARIINÆ.

53. Skua (*Stercorarius catarrhactes*, Linn.).

Order VI.—TUBINARES.

54. Fulmar (*Fulmarus glacialis*, Linn.).

Order VII.—ALCÆ.

Family ALCIDÆ.

55. Guillemot (*Lomnia troile*, Linn.).
56. Little Auk (*Mergulus alle*, Linn.).
57. Puffin (*Fratercula arctica*, Linn.).

Order VIII.—PYGOPODES.

Family COLYMBIDÆ.

58. Red-throated Diver (*Colymbus septentrionalis*, Linn.).

---

52. Some of the largest skins of this lovely sea bird I have ever seen.

56. A large number were seen on the edge of the ice at the mouth of the Kara Sea.

THE ANTLERS OF THE REINDEER. (One-tenth natural size.)
From photograph by Messrs. GUNN AND STEWART, Richmond, Surrey,
and 162 Sloane Street, London, S.W.

APPENDIX

WEATHER OBSERVATIONS KEPT BY F. G. JACKSON, F.R.G.S.,

Date.		Barometer.		Thermometer F.				Wind.
		A.M.	P.M.	A.M.		P.M.		
				Max.	Min.	Max.	Min.	
				°	°	°	°	
Sept.	1	29.70	29.78	38	32	36	30	N.E.
,,	2	29.90	29.98	36	30	30	24	N.E.
,,	3	29.98	29.80	50	35	32	40	N.
,,	4	29.78	29.75	45	32	35	32	W.
,,	5	29.70	29.65	47	32.5	37	30	N.E.
,,	6	29.60	29.55	45	35	34	21	N.W.
,,	7	29.58	29.51	36	31	35	22	N.W.
,,	8	29.55	29.58	41	28	34	20	W. 2 N.
,,	9	29.48	29.30	40	28	35	29	N.E.
,,	10	29.30	29.10	37	30	35	33	S.E.
,,	11	28.95	28.85	36	33	33	24	E. 1½ S.
,,	12	29.4	29.57	33	28	31	25	N.W.
,,	13	29.62	29.55	41	20	20	7	N.W.
,,	14	29.58	29.58	35	18	32	25	W.
,,	15	29.13	28.80	35	32	35	20	S.E.
,,	16	28.90	29.00	36	30	32	21	S.E.
,,	17	29.15	29.20	28	22	32	25	S.W.
,,	18	29.20	29.15	33	24	30	21	S.W.
,,	19	29.20	29.22	30	26	26	9	N.E.
,,	20	29.48	29.51	28	22	32	21	N.E.
,,	21	29.60	29.80	33	25	25	17	N.E.
,,	22	30.1	29.81	34	18	35	26	E.
,,	23	30.10	30.10	36	26	41	36	S.W.
,,	24	29.80	29.80	45	40	41	36	S.W.
,,	25	29.98	29.85	45	37	44	33	S.W.
,,	26	29.60	29.58	52	48	44	42	S.W.
,,	27	29.84	29.62	50	40	42	32	N.E.
,,	28	29.71	29.71	43	37	41	32	S.W.
,,	29	29.48	29.45	45	34	38	32	S.
,,	30	29.51	29.60	37	33	35	33	S. 2 W.

September 1893 to January 1894

Weather Notes.

Gale (strong) dropping a little towards evening. Sky overcast.
A stiff breeze. Snow-storms at intervals.
Wind dropped. Sunny and pleasant. Little wind.
Calm. (Nearly a dead calm.) Sunny day.
Blowing half a gale. Snow-storms with bright intervals.
Very little wind. Bright and sunny; a little snow in the wind.
Breezy. Sky overcast with snow-storms frequently.
Strong gale, falling towards night. Gleams of sunshine at intervals.
Gentle breeze, bright and sunny all day. [sun gleaming sometimes.
Strong, increasing to gale at night. Sky overcast with heavy clouds, and
Strong gale with rain and fog, increasing as the day went on.
Gale with driving, fine snow; died down during afternoon. Sky cleared
 and sun shone. Still, frosty evening. [Sunny, calm day.
Very light wind. Bright, sunny morning; variable airs after 11 A.M.
Very light wind till about 2 P.M. when a W. breeze got up. Bright morning,
 cloudy afterwards. [all day.
Strong gale with fine, driving snow, with rise in temperature. Continued
Bright morning, no wind and sunny. Gale from S.E. with sleet and hail
 got up at 1 P.M., and blew and snowed the rest of the day.
Bright sunny day with occasional snow scuds. Brilliant aurora.
High wind (gale) from S.W. with very frequent snow-storms. Sky overcast.
Gentle breeze with heavy snow from 1 P.M. to 6 P.M. [after 8 P.M.
Strong breeze till 3 P.M. when it died down. Bright and sunny. Snow
Faint breeze all day. Bright and sunny.
A light breeze till 2.30 when the wind increased and blew rather hard; sky
 overcast all day, threatening snow.
Moderate breeze. Fog till 2 P.M. when it cleared off till 5 P.M.
Strong breeze; rain in morning; warm, foggy, with overcast sky; wind
 W. after 5 P.M.
Warm fog till 2 P.M.; light breeze till 5 P.M.; then blowing stiffly and raining.
Little or no wind till 5 P.M., then a heavy gale from S. 2 W. Very warm
 for season. [most of the day.
Dead calm; variable airs till 4 P.M.; then breeze from N.E.; overcast sky
Light S.W. breeze in morning and afternoon, falling to a calm in even-
 ing; rain during night; a little fog early in morning.
S. breeze with rain till 4.30 P.M. when it shifted to S. 2 W. and blew a gale.
High gale from S. 2 W. still blowing with sleet and snow, continued all day.

Date.	Barometer.		Thermometer F.				Wind.
	A.M.	P.M.	A.M.		P.M.		
			Max. °	Min. °	Max. °	Min. °	
Oct. 1	29.60	29.81	34	33	34	32	S. 2 W. N.W.
,, 2	30.30	30.40	34	32	33	30	N. 2 W.
,, 3	30.45	30.28	35	30	33	28	S. 2 E.
,, 4	29.90	29.80	36	33	34	32	S. 2 E.
,, 5	29.80	29.80	38	33	37	33	W. 1 N.
,, 6	29.80	29.71	38	35	37	33	N.
,, 7	29.60	29.62	36	33	32	29	N.
,, 8	29.78	30.00	32	30	30	20	N.E.
,, 9	30.21	30.35	26	24	24	22	N.E.
,, 10	30.40	30.40	25	22	22	20	N.
,, 11	30.10	29.90	25	22	24	18	S. S.W.
,, 12	29.80	29.80	24	21	22	16	N.E.
,, 13	29.85	29.65	24	18	18	9	N.E.
,, 14	29.70	29.55	20	18	18	12	E.N.E.
,, 15	29.60	29.70	16	14	14	20	E.N.E.
,, 16	29.50	29.10	23	20	20	17	E.N.E.
,, 17	29.15	29.58	15	12	13	10	N.
,, 18	29.70	29.72	23	13	20	10	N.
,, 19	29.60	29.60	27	20	26	23	W.
,, 20	29.51	29.42	27	24	20	17	W.
,, 21	29.45	29.50	21	18	16	4	N. 2 W.
,, 22	29.50	29.48	15	5	10	4	N. 2 W.
,, 23	29.30	29.30	15	10	10	-2	W.
,, 24	29.32	29.60	-3	-13	6	-13	N.
,, 25	29.70	29.88	15	10	10	5	N.
,, 26	29.90	29.80	17	12	9	-14	N.
,, 27	29.78	29.50	-5	-21	15	-5	N. S.E.
,, 28	29.32	29.30	25	15	32	25	S.E.
,, 29	29.30	29.40	32	26	25	22	S.
,, 30	29.50	29.30	33	32	33	30	S.E.
,, 31	29.25	29.15	34	32	33	30	S.E. S.W.

Weather Notes.

Wind shifted to N.W. from S. 2 W., and is blowing half a gale with snow-storms, increasing towards night again to a full gale, but barometer rising. Overcast sky.
Blowing very stiffly; cloudy overcast sky with occasional snow-storms.
Nearly a calm till 5 P.M. Sky overcast, with sunny intervals. Snow-storms.
Half a gale with heavy rain and fog continued all day.
Fog and rain with a stiff breeze till 4.30 P.M. Sky overcast all day.
Calm in early morning. Breeze from N., later increasing to gale. Sky overcast all day.
Full gale still blowing from N. with heavy rain. Heavy overcast sky.
Blowing a gale from N.E. with frequent snow-storms. Sky overcast.
Blowing half a gale; overcast sky; 6° or 7° of frost all day. Snow occasionally.
Gentle breeze; cloudy overcast sky with occasional snow-storms.
Breeze from S. with snow till noon; changing to S.W., blowing half a gale towards night with heavy snow.
Strong breeze; occasional sunshine. No snow fell to-day.
Gentle breeze; cloudy sky; occasional snow-storms.
Breeze. Constant snow showers. Cloudy sky.
Faint breeze till 6 P.M., when a strong breeze got up. Sunny and bright till 4 P.M., then cloudy.
Strong, with snow increasing as the day went on. Snowed and blew hard all day. [midday.
Strong breeze with a little snow occasionally. Sunny for two hours at
Light breeze; no snow to-day. Sky overcast.
Strong gale, with driving, fine snow; continued all day.
Gale, with driving fine sleet and snow all day, ceasing to blow about midnight.
Dead calm with variable airs, till about 4 P.M. then N. 2 W. breeze. No snow to-day; overcast sky.
Stiff breeze with keen frost and occasional sunshine.
Light breeze with occasional snow-storms; overcast sky.
Very light breeze; severe frost all day; sunshine all day; fog at night.
Very light breeze; cloudy and overcast. Frost less severe.
Light breeze, clear sky, but foggy near the ground.
Light breeze; clear sky and sunshine till 6 P.M., then S.E. stiff breeze with heavy snow.
Breeze with heavy snow nearly the whole day.
Very light breeze; snowy sky with frequent snow-storms; very warm.
Moderate breeze. Heavy snow all day. [towards night.
Breeze till afternoon with heavy snow, then S.W. blowing half a gale

Date	Barometer		Thermometer F.				Wind
	A.M.	P.M.	A.M.		P.M.		
			Max. °	Min. °	Max. °	Min. °	
Nov. 1	29.32	29.60	30	15	20	11	N. 2 E.
,, 2	29.72	29.82	12	8	8	5	N. 2 E.
,, 3	29.75	29.70	7	5	8	6	N.E.
,, 4	29.60	29.10	16	8	30	20	N.E.
,, 5	28.95	29.20	28	18	18	4	S.W.
,, 6	29.32	29.35	8	3	14	3	S.W.
,, 7	29.50	29.35	15	9	9	−1	S.W.
,, 8	29.40	29.40	−1	−11	8	−11	S.W.
,, 9	29.48	29.50	10	5	7	−4	N.E.
,, 10	29.42	29.15	8	−10	...	...[1]	S.E.
,, 11	29.10	29.00	7	−3	−3	−8	S.E.
,, 12	29.20	29.32	−8	−15	−9	−15	N.W.
,, 13	29.30	29.30	−8	−11	−9	−11	W.
,, 14	29.30	29.30	−2	−8	−3	−12	W.
,, 15	29.40	29.30	0	−7	0	−10	S.E.
,, 16	29.70	29.78	−4	−10	5	−7	N.W.
,, 17	29.65	29.35	10	−3	25	20	S.
,, 18	29.35	29.40	33	27	27	22	S.
,, 19	29.48	29.48	25	21	25	23	S.
,, 20	29.5	29.15	28	12	16	12	S.
,, 21	29.30	29.30	15	10	10	−1	S.W.
,, 22	29.20	29.30	12	−1	11	−3	S.W.
,, 23	29.62	29.76	11	−4	12	10	S.W.
,, 24	29.72	29.50	10	0	8	5	E.
,, 25	29.30	29.2	10	−4	−4	−10	E 2 S.
,, 26	29.15	29.25	−1	−8	−8	−10	S.W.
,, 27	29.40	29.45	−8	−12	−12	−18	S.W.
,, 28	29.48	29.50	−4	−14	−3	−14	W.
,, 29	29.50	29.40	−7	−5	−4	−9	N.E.
,, 30	29.30	29.28	−3	−6	−6	−14	N.E.

[1] Travelling rapidly till 1.30 A.M. that night.

Weather Notes.

Moderate breeze with snow-storms; much colder; heavy snowy sky.
Very light breeze with snow till noon; heavy snowy sky.
Gale with snow till noon.   Dark snowy sky all day.
Full gale with heavy, fine, hard snow all day.
Heavy gale; snow after 4 P.M.   Heavy overcast sky.
Very faint breeze; sky cleared; sunshine all day; no snow.
Light breeze till 4 P.M., when it began to blow hard, increasing to a gale in the evening.   Snow-storms.
Light breeze with snow till noon, afterwards clear and sunny.
Light breeze; overcast sky with occasional light snow-storms.
Stiff breeze with heavy snow, and increasing to a gale at night.
Light breeze till 6 P.M., then came on a gale with snow.
Stiff breeze, clear sky, no snow, keen frost ($-15°$ F. most of the day).
Very faint breeze, overcast cloudy sky; no sun, no snow.
Very faint breeze, overcast cloudy sky; no snow, no sun.
Very light breeze; sunny for an hour till 11 A.M., then overcast; snow in the evening.
Light breeze and sunny, changing to S.W. in afternoon with cloudy sky.
Gale with snow continuing the whole day.
Gale; it lulled early in the morning, but blew hard again after 11 A.M. with snow.
Gale with heavy snow all day; sky clearing a little late in the evening.
Gale with heavy snow till 3.30 P.M., when the wind changed suddenly to N. and blew hard from that quarter with fall of temperature and clearing of the sky with barometer rising.
Gale (wind remained N. only a few hours) during the whole day; clear sky; no snow till night, then heavy.
Light breeze; some sun, but sky overcast most of the day; a little snow.
Faint breeze; overcast sky; little snow in the evening.
Very faint breeze till night, then it began to blow; overcast sky all day.
Very light breeze with some snow.   Heavy overcast sky, clearing in the evening.
Very light breeze; overcast sky with a little snow.
Variable faint breezes, S.W. being the chief direction; overcast sky, snow at night.
Stiff breeze, sun shone occasionally.   Peculiar reflection of sun at sunset, like three suns.   Horizon like portions of the rainbow, but ruddy; duration fifteen minutes about 10° right and left, 5° high.
Moderate breeze; overcast sky, no snow.
Moderate breeze; overcast sky, no snow.

Date.	Barometer.		Thermometer F.			
	A.M.	P.M.	A.M.		P.M.	
			Max. °	Min. °	Max. °	Min. °
Dec. 1	29.25	29.30	...	...	...	...
,, 2	29.30	29.25	...	...	...	...
,, 3	29.32	29.45	...	...	...	...
,, 4	29.70	29.70	−20	−28	−29	−35
,, 5	29.95	30.00	−27	−36.5		
,, 6	30.2	30.15	...	...		
,, 7	30.20	30.5	...			
,, 8	30.00	29.95	...			
,, 9	29.90	29.90	...			
,, 10	29.60	29.40	...			
,, 11	29.60	29.70	...			
,, 12	29.70	29.80	...			
,, 13	29.80	29.70				
,, 14	29.90	29.80				
,, 15	29.50	29.60				
,, 16	29.62	29.78				
,, 17	29.80	29.32				
,, 18	29.10	29.20				
,, 19	29.55	29.72				
,, 20	29.80	29.65				
,, 21	29.60	29.75				
,, 22	30.82	29.80				
,, 23	29.70	29.60				
,, 24	29.45	29.45	...			
,, 25	29.45	...	...			
,, 26	...	...	...			
,, 27	30.30	30.40	...			
,, 28	30.20	29.80	−28			
,, 29	29.70	29.50	...			
,, 30	29.5	28 80	...			
,, 31	28.55	28.90	...			

By a most unfortunate accident, the book containing the thermometrical observations for December and January has been lost. It will be seen, however, from the occasional entries, gathered from the *Journal*, that a prolonged period of low temperatures ensued.

A. M.

Weather Notes.

Light breeze, clear sky with sun for an hour or two at very low altitude.
Light breeze with some snow. Heavy overcast sky all day.
Very faint breeze, heavy overcast sky ; no snow.
Very faint breeze, clear sky for about two hours, then overcast (Temp. − 28° F. and − 35° F.)
Breeze fairly strong ; clear sky occasionally.
Breeze—light—clear sky most of the day.
Breeze—light—clear sky until towards 7 P.M., then overcast.
Stiff breeze, clear and cloudy sky alternately ; a little snow in the evening.
Light breeze, cloudy sky with a little snow.
Light breeze, overcast sky ; no snow.
Light breeze, overcast sky ; no snow.
Light breeze, heavy snow till afternoon, then clear sky.
Light breeze, overcast sky with heavy snow during the night.
Light breeze, heavy snow most of the day ; heavy overcast sky.
Light breeze, overcast sky with heavy snow.
Faint breeze with a cloudy overcast sky, with heavy snow occasionally.
Light breeze till afternoon, increasing to a gale at night ; overcast sky.
Light breeze (gale abated) with heavy snow day and night.
Very light breeze, snow occasionally.
Stiff breeze with heavy snow most of the day and night, the breeze dying down about 5 P.M.
Very light breeze, cloudy sky, no snow.
Heavy snow nearly the whole day ; very light breeze.
Heavy snow till noon ; overcast all day.
Very light breeze, overcast sky ; no snow.
Moderate breeze with heavy snow ; overcast sky.
Light breeze, clear sky, no snow.
Moderate breeze, overcast sky, colder (− 28° F.)
Overcast sky, stiff breeze at night with snow.
Wind gale ; heavy snow ; warm cloudy sky.
Moderate breeze ; a little snow ; cloudy sky ; warm.
Light breeze till noon, then heavy snow with wind increasing to a very strong gale with low temperature—decreasing in force with a clearing of the sky towards midnight.

Date.		Barometer.		Thermometer F.			
		A.M.	P.M.	A.M.		P.M.	
				Max. °	Min. °	Max. °	Min. °
Jan.	1	29.30	29.60	−19	−23	...	...
,,	2	30.00	30.40				
,,	3	30.50	30.10				
,,	4	30.15	29.90				
,,	5	29.82	29.90				
,,	6	30.15	30.20				
,,	7	30.2	29.70				
,,	8	29.90	30.10				
,,	9	30.28	29.52				
,,	10	29.50	29.50				
,,	11	29.20	29.90				
,,	12	30.00	30.10				
,,	13	30.10	29.90				
,,	14	29.80	29.60				
,,	15	29.40	29.10				
,,	16	29.20	29.10				
,,	17	29.50	29.50				
,,	18	29.60	29.55				
,,	19	29.35	29.21				
,,	20	29.35	29.15				
,,	21	28.80	29.55				
,,	22	28.70	28.60				
,,	23	28.90	29.25				
,,	24	29.30	29.30				
,,	25	28.70	28.70				
,,	26	28.85	28.80				

Weather Notes.

A very heavy gale with a low temperature (blizzard) which drove the powdered snow in clouds before it, but not much fell (Thermometer $-19°$ F. to $-23°$).
Strong gale, clear sky, wind drove the loose snow before it, but none fell; very cold.
Strong breeze, clear sky, snow in the evening.
Light breeze, clear sky, no snow.
Strong breeze, clear sky.
Light breeze, clear sky.
Strong breeze, cloudy sky, no snow.
Light breeze, clear sky.
Very light breeze overhead (fifty feet from ground), fog, no snow.
Very light breeze, clear sky.
Variable airs, a little snow.
Light wind with fog.
Moderate breeze, overcast sky.
Strong gale towards night, heavy overcast sky.
Stiff breeze, overcast sky.
Little wind, clear sky.
Stiff breeze off the land, sky clear.
Moderate breeze, overcast sky with a little snow.
Very little breeze, heavy snow.
Half a gale later in the day, E. breeze, overcast sky all day.
Heavy gale with fog and snow till 7 P.M., then W. and fog cleared.
Heavy gale with fog and snow throughout day, except at intervals.
Heavy gale, fog and snow. Gale dropped towards afternoon, and fog and snow cleared off.
Moderate breeze, clear sky part of the day; no snow.
Heavy gale; snow-storms; fog.

APPENDIX C

TOPOGRAPHICAL NOTES TO ACCOMPANY THE MAP OF THE GREAT TUNDRA

By F. G. JACKSON, F.R.G.S.

Oct. 13, 1893.—Leaving Habarova, we crossed typical rolling tundra, and at three miles distance came to the Nikolski River. Passing over this, we found the ice in the shallow lakes not always safe, and after an immersion in one of the lakes, reached the Oyo River and camped.

Oct. 14.—Keeping a southerly course, in order to cross a rapid but otherwise unimportant stream higher up, I was impressed with its precipitous and lofty bank, which, as I was to find, was a common characteristic.

Oct. 15.—Course S. 2 E. At noon we reached and crossed the Gushina River; and then the Tundra, which had been rolling, and consequently in summer fairly dry on the ridges, became very flat and evidently, before frost set in, unbroken swamp. From the Gushina we could see the Arctic Ocean.

Oct. 16.—Starting at 10 A.M. we crossed the Talata River. This is a shallow stream, and runs swiftly down a wide channel, having high and steep banks. About twenty versts to the westward we camped, being then about eight miles north of the Korotaika River. For this we made a south-easterly course, as we were still so near the sea as to find the snow soft and the ice on the rivers doubtful. Between the Talata and the Korotaika Rivers the dead level was exchanged for typical rolling tundra; but the blinding snowstorm in which we crossed it made it impossible to see for more than a quarter of a mile on either side.

Oct. 17.—On examining the Korotaika we found the ice near the banks in a rotten condition, but that in midstream—indeed, within ten yards of the bank—sound. The channel of the Korotaika is at least one mile wide, although the water-channel of autumn did not exceed a width of three hundred yards. There was, however, a second channel, which, at our camp, was about seventy yards broad. The depth of the main channel was some twenty feet, and the banks are low. In the spring, when the ice breaks up, the volume of water which it conveys into the sea must be very large. About two miles to the north of our camp, on the right bank, there was a pleasant break in the otherwise unbroken monotony of the tundra in the shape of patches of uraa scrub, which reached a height greater than I had yet seen—thirty inches. It is precisely the same plant as that observed at Waigatz and on the tundra behind Habarova, but it grows here to quite two and a half times the height. On Waigatz I did not see a single bush either of this or any other species exceeding one foot in height. A tributary of the Korotaika, on the right bank, is the Viséha River, the banks of which are low like those of the Korotaika, and the channel two hundred yards wide.

On the 18th October we crossed the Korotaika (only one sledge going through), and entered on a stretch of tundra almost a dead level, with low ridges at rare intervals. The 19th was spent in camp, waiting for the return of a Samoyad who had been sent back after deer.

Oct. 20.—We made a south-westerly course over tundra uncompromisingly flat, passing a Samoyad burying-place on a solitary eminence. We camped after making fifteen miles, and one mile to the westward of the Peretayaha River, a small and unimportant stream. Oct. 21.—Tundra flat, and eight miles from camp crossed the Talata River (No. 2), and camped two miles (Oct. 22) east of the Tambiha River. East and west of this large shallow lakes become more frequent. Oct. 23.—Six miles west of the small Tambiha River we struck the Nosiyaha River, only a little larger; camped on 24th and 25th, waiting for missing deer, and I took advantage of the delay to drive over in my sledge, with three deer in the traces, to some low ridges which I had noticed about eight miles to the south, and where I found that the Nosiyaha River rose.

Oct. 26.—Struck camp early and made south-west to the Haiputhra Guba, through dead-level country. On coming to the Ya-ya-ha River I found that it did not empty into the sea, as laid down on the maps, but is an affluent of the Haiputhra, at least eight miles from the coast. Crossing the Haiputhra, I camped about four miles from the sea and one mile east of the Eraya River. Bearing north-west from us there rose out of the perfectly flat waste a single hill—perhaps fifty feet high—while south-west a range of low hills gave an unusual aspect to the landscape.

Oct. 27.—Following the coast, we crossed the Eraya River, small and unimportant, and subsequently the Hanna-wa-yaha, the channel of which is nearly two hundred yards broad, though at this season only occupied by a wasted stream. Two small rivers, the Sonsida and Lobbagon-wa-yaha, were passed shortly afterwards, and finally camped about two miles south of the Charna-yaha. Between this and the Eraya the tundra becomes undulating, with well-developed ridges.

Oct. 28.—Crossing the Charna-yaha, we soon came to the Ikvit and Nahwúl Rivers—the latter of which flows through very low-lying country—and Lake Ozurko, across which I sledged and found it to be roughly circular with a diameter of three-quarters of a mile. Made about twenty miles eastwards.

Oct. 29.—Crossed the Nahwúl-yaha (No. 2), and thence the route lay across a chain of large lakes. The country here again became very flat, and abounded with wide lakes or meres. The uraa scrub (called by the Samoyads "miroa") gradually increases in height as one travels west, and in this district it was quite four feet above the soil. Camped six miles east of the Pasanka-yaha.

Oct. 30.—Made about fourteen miles through soft snow (temperature had risen suddenly), and across low country and many wide meres. Crossed the O'zero and its tributary the Pasanka near the affluence, and found the O'zero's channel about three-quarters of a mile wide. This is a great summer camp of the Samoyads, and affords them abundance of a fish they call "Shaipk," undoubtedly different from that which they catch on the Korotaika and call "O'myl." At this point the sea is about ten miles distant, but we are travelling on such low ground that we can only see—and we can see this all day—its reflection in the northern sky.

Oct. 31.—The tundra remains a dead flat, but some six miles to the south there runs a ridge of hills, at least a hundred feet high. Crossed and camped on the left bank of the small river Gostroma, having passed another Samoyad burying-place.

Nov. 1.—Came to and crossed the Piatsowor-yaha which the Samoyads declare to be a very long river. When and where I crossed it the channel is only about one hundred and fifty yards wide, and the water merely runs along the centre of this as a shallow stream. Eight miles west of this river I came to the raised beaches and old sea-floor described in the narrative. The whole of it is now covered with grass, which in many places grows in large pools of salt water. West of this interesting relic of a gulf, I crossed a long ridge and entered another and smaller amphitheatre of raised beaches and old sea-floor, finally reaching the Grishna, Nútnia, and Baichúrka Rivers. The southerly range to which I have previously referred suddenly rises, about seven miles south of the old gulf, into three high peaks, which I mention as excellent landmarks.

Nov. 3.—A third series of raised beaches was met with, about six miles from the sea, and soon after crossed the Pustoi River, an affluent of the Pi-yaha, which we found to have a channel about two hundred yards in width, with a good quantity of water between its low, muddy banks. Westward of the Pi-yaha the country is very flat and, like the old gulfs already mentioned, strewn with driftwood. The Cirilofka River, the next we came to, differed from those we had recently crossed in having high banks, though only about a hundred yards apart. The river itself is deep and rises in the Pitkoff Mountains, the southerly range of which I have spoken and which gradually becomes more important as one travels west. In this longitude it reaches a height of five hundred and sixty-three feet, the greatest elevation I had encountered. West of the Cirilofka is the Kriviraka River, with a channel about two hundred yards wide, but little water at this time of the year. For some time now we had been travelling through low country, with a very swampy flat area between us and the coast, and typical undulating tundra to the south.

Nov. 4.—Four miles west of camp struck the Alexa River, which is narrow with sloping banks; the Rumanoa, about eighty yards wide, and full of water; the Kaminka, almost as wide and well filled; and the Muroa, seventy yards wide from bank to bank, the stream occupying a channel about forty yards wide. All these streams rise in the Pitkoff Hills, and in spring evidently, judging from the signs of flood which met me everywhere, are formidable rivers.

Nov. 5.—Left camp on Muroa River, and travelled over tundra of undulating type, crossing first an affluent of and next the Drisvanka itself. It is about eighty yards wide at this point, and its banks are high. The Drisvanka is about twelve miles long, and rises in the Pitkoff Hills. The most remarkable point about all these rivers is the width, depth, and relative importance they attain in their very short courses. This is naturally due to the damming of the lower part of the rivers with ice and the sudden melting of the snows of the hills and upper valleys. The pressure exerted in the spring must be very great, and when resisted by the still frozen rivers must necessarily bank up the water and melting snow and result in severe floods.

On Nov. 6 we crossed the following rivers: Uriúne and Siribrinka (the former with high and the latter with low banks), the Urefka (Samoyads called it Hulthui), which rises in the southern slope of the Pitkoffs and winds round their south-western extremity. Where we crossed, it was a hundred yards wide, and had as much water as the low banks could contain. Between these rivers the tundra was alternately undulating and flat. Wherever it is the latter, it abounds with large shallow meres. The uraa scrub again was met with in the valley, if I may use this expression, of the Urefka.

On the 7th, a short distance west of the Mika and Yigur Rivers, another old gulf, with its raised beaches strewn with heavy driftwood, was encountered. West of this, again, is the Yekhi-yaha, a small river, which is tidal for about seven miles from the sea. The Pusto River, seventy yards wide at this point, was passed on the 8th, and on the same day the Pesanka—the Samoyads called it Nurota— was successfully negotiated. This river, although not more than fifty yards across, has a longer course than the majority of the rivers met with; and its passage is somewhat difficult, owing to the height and almost precipitous sides of the right bank. Our sledges came down this with the speed and in the manner of a toboggan descending a slide, and we were fortunate in escaping with nothing beyond a good shaking all round. The right bank of these tundra rivers is usually high and the left bank low.[1] To the west of the Pesanka the country is gouged out with deep gullies, more or less occupied by rough scrub, and as I was driving a Norwegian sledge, only six inches above the ground, the nature of the surface was a consideration.[2]

For some time, on the 9th, we travelled parallel with a range of hills, which we ultimately crossed about fifteen miles north of the Urtuna River. Their greatest elevation was shown to be one hundred and ninety feet by the aneroid. This was the highest land we had traversed since leaving Habarova, and the Samoyads called the range Heisada Hoi, *heisada* meaning hills. At this point Pustozersk is about one hundred versts to the westward in direct line.

Nov. 10.—Leaving camp about 11 A.M., Ivan Berzumoff

---

[1] Compare Nordenskiöld, *Voyage of the Vega*, chap. vi. "It is the general rule that where rivers flow through loose, earthy strata in a direction deviating considerably from that of the parallels of latitude, the right bank, when one stands facing the mouth of the river, is high, and the left low. The cause of this is the globular form of the earth and its rotation, which gives rivers flowing north a tendency towards the east, to rivers flowing south a tendency to the west. This tendency is resisted by the bank, but it is gradually eaten into and washed away by degrees, so that the river-bed, in the course of thousands of years, is shifted in the direction indicated."

[2] The innumerable gullies and grooves cut deeply in the more undulating parts of the Tundra are as much due to the expansive action of ice as to the mechanical energy of water. Every year, of course, the water which flows in the bed of the gullies and that which saturates the surrounding plains is frozen hard, and thus not only are the channels gouged wider and deeper, but the earth itself, on the sur-

and I made a forced march to Pustozersk (I was driving the Norwegian sledge—ten feet six inches long, eighteen inches wide, and six inches high—with three reindeer harnessed to it). Kuia we reached at 5 P.M., after passing through rough hilly country, plentifully covered with uraa scrub, four feet high, and possessing many lakes of considerable size and—a more novel feature—of considerable depth. Striking the Kuia River eight miles from the village, we sledged down the frozen surface of the river to Kuia itself. Two hours later we started again for Pustozersk, now forty versts distant, and on reaching the Pechora River—having had to find our way by compass, owing to the blinding snow which a heavy westerly gale was driving before it—we ascended its rough, hummocky ice for nearly twenty miles, until we came to a fisherman's hut. We roused its solitary inmate, got directions for the track, and eighteen miles farther on reached Ussia, three miles from Pustozersk, about 1.30 A.M. We had crossed the Korzur, and both the Bolshaia and Malaia Kunzuki Rivers, and having travelled by a devious route, made a total day's run of about one hundred and ten miles.

---

face and below it, is lacerated and displaced in a million directions. Then comes the sudden thaw, and, of course, with it the mechanical force of the water which rushes impetuously along the river channels, carrying with it as much of the already disintegrated soil as is within reach. And at the same time, on the surface of the plains and down below the surface out of sight, as far as the zone of perpetual frost, there is water trickling everywhere—tiny rills of melted ice and snow ever uniting and becoming more and more important, making wider the crevices and deeper the shafts in which they have been locked, and thinner and ever thinner the intervening walls of earth. And then at last, either this year or next year, the soil is displaced and carried away—somewhere, anywhere, as long as it is downhill, and a new wrinkle has appeared on the face of the earth. This is what takes place at the annual bursting of the water-pipes of the land, and in no part of the world can it be seen to greater advantage than on the Tundras.—A. M.

These brief topographical notes of the Trans-Pechora country, no adequate map of which is in existence, and of which no account is to be found in the English language, may prove, I hope, of some use in studying my sketch-map.

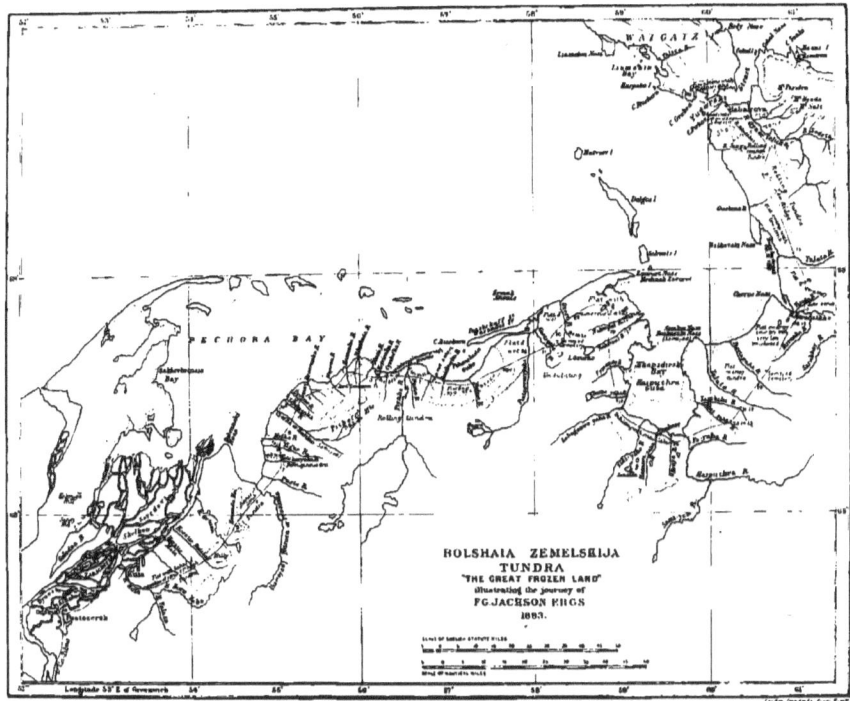

APPENDIX D

THE JACKSON-HARMSWORTH POLAR EXPEDITION: ITS OBJECT, METHOD, AND EQUIPMENT[1]

THERE seems to be a fashion in geographical discovery as in everything else. For many years, dating from the discovery of the Great Lakes, Africa has been the vogue. "What news from Africa?" has been asked this century, much as it was asked twenty centuries ago. And there has been no lack of reply, or of the heroic in the telling of the tale. But this prolonged interest, sustained during a number of years at high pitch, has itself, to some extent, proved destructive of the passion for Tropical Africa. Wearied of fevers and forests, of Arabs and ivory, the pendulum of taste has swung back with a vengeance. The fashion has indeed changed, but only, as is usual in history, to reassume an old form. For the age of Polar exploration—of doing and daring, of discovery, and, too often, of defeat in the world of Ancient Ice—has come to us again; and the sources of the great ice-currents which sweep out of the Polar Basin are again sought as eagerly as, through a score of centuries, were the ultimate sources of the Nile.

---

[1] I have been requested by Messrs. Macmillan to conclude this book with an account of the organisation of the expedition which Mr. Jackson had in view throughout his former journey; and on which he has since sailed. The account is necessarily brief, but owing to my official connection with the expedition, may be regarded as reliable as far as "weights and measures" are concerned.—ARTHUR MONTEFIORE.

There is an attraction in the far North which no tropical country can supply. The desolate landscape, the winter darkness, the great difficulty of supporting even existence; the highly specialised fauna; the few and diminutive plants, these contribute much; and more attractive even than they are the vast regions which are as yet utterly unknown, where continents may stand rigid, or seas rise and fall; but, chiefest of all to compel our interest and retain our service, is that long chronicle of human effort and endurance, which has invested the ice-pack and the iceberg, the solitary peaks and vast glaciers, with the association of something richer than romance; with nothing less, in fact, than that story of human failure, of heroic endurance, of admirable endeavour, which those of the past have handed down to us of the present—a story which cannot but stimulate while it seems to sanctify our quest. These are the conditions, and these the influences, which make for that passion, which, once it has entered into the breast of the Arctic voyager, shall scarcely be allayed.

Perhaps it was Nansen who helped the revival to become effective. That rush across Greenland—from a starting-point which forbade return, towards a goal whose avenue of approach might so easily have proved unapproachable—commended itself to us, less for its geographical importance than for its boldness and pluck. Moreover, it was successful. The omen was good, and the spirit of enterprise was responsive; and so, almost before we knew it, we were committed to an age of Arctic discovery. Men, as aforetime, were not to fail for leaders; nor leaders for the generosity of private patrons. And the world, too, was just in the mood to give that sympathy and support, without which scientific discovery would be shorn of half its ethical value. More recently, too, the explorers have been bolder. For we have Peary, with his great object of conclusively proving Greenland to be an island, and from its northern termination to push forward over the Sea of Ancient Ice to the region of the North Pole ; and Nansen, this time as the darling of a nation, intent on thrusting a ship—such as the world had never yet seen — into the fearful embrace of oceanic ice, if haply he might thus drift into the vicinity of that mathematical point in which the northern end of the earth's axis terminates.

But while Nansen represents the individuality of Norway —as Nordenskiöld did that of Sweden, and Peary that of America—England has had, in recent years, no representative in the field. From the twenties to the sixties in this century she was the leader in Arctic exploration ; among the nations easily chief. Vast sums of money, both private and public, were lavished on enterprise after enterprise ; ship after ship was despatched from these shores, until we had manned a great Arctic fleet. Discovery followed fast on discovery, even though "disaster followed faster." Always to the fore in geographical adventure, we compassed the northern ends of the earth with a completeness which no nation ever equalled. Science gained, and the nation gloried. Was not this something ? Surely England may suffer much tribulation, and yet be England still ; but, as some one has well said, " The loss of a spirit of adventure among her sons is not one which she can endure."

Yet, with the return of that great expedition, which, under the able command of Sir George Nares, was declared to have proved the Pole impracticable and thereby disappointed a nation set on achievement, there comes a period where we vainly look for our country in the Arctic regions. Whether this was owing to the great cost of that expedition, or to the blank dismay created by its result, I cannot say. But whether the Government again fits out a great scientific expedition or not, the progress of geographical discovery will go on unchecked. Indeed, the mode of the age seems to tend in the direction of private enterprise, and against the employment of naval resources and public funds. Livingstone and Stanley — men totally unlike the other, except in their independence and impatience of official control — showed what the civilian can do for geography under difficulties of the most stupendous kind ; and, in the Arctic area, Peary and Nansen succeeded them. It is almost unquestionable that private enterprise has always done the lion's share of pioneering, and the encouragement afforded us in Polar exploration by the examples of Felix Booth, Lady Franklin, Oscar Dickson, and others, is great indeed. England herself, it might be justly maintained, owes her Empire to private enterprise.

It is not unnatural, therefore, that we should find the new English expedition to the Polar Seas led by an Englishman, who, while he has had great experience of travel, is a civilian ; and that the whole cost of this expedition should be borne by an Englishman, who, partly from the pure love of Arctic exploration, partly for the cause of that science which knows no nationality, but chiefly for the good name and fame of his country, is happy to devote many thousands of pounds to a voyage of discovery.

The Polar Expedition, of which Mr. Frederick G. Jackson is the leader, and Mr. Alfred C. Harmsworth the patron, has for its immediate objective that little-known country, Franz Josef Land. This lies in a higher latitude than any other known land in the eastern portion of the Polar Basin. It was first discovered by the Austro-Hungarian Expedition, under remarkable circumstances in 1873 ; then too, and for the only time, it was pierced by a sledging party for a distance of about one hundred and twenty-five geographical miles ; and although the experience of the Austrians, under Weyprecht and Payer, had seemed to declare it as almost unapproachable, the fact that in three successive seasons it was approached, that in two of these was actually reached by Mr. Leigh Smith, and in the fourth successfully departed from by the Leigh Smith Expedition, has rendered it beyond question the most advantageous route in the eastern Polar Basin for any advance in a northerly direction. Its southern shores lie along the latitude of 80° N.; up Austria Sound, a natural avenue leading north, Payer, the commander of the land party of the Austro-Hungarian Expedition, advanced in seventeen days to Cape Fligely, 82° 5′ N. lat.; and he did this with comparative ease, and without special advantages in the way of equipment. Standing on the summit of Cape Fligely, one thousand feet above the sea-level, he saw the land there reaching away northward—high blue mountains beyond the eighty-third degree, and within a few miles of the farthest point yet attained anywhere. To the northwestward more high land rose above the open water, itself bearing but little ice on its bosom, though to the northward encompassed with floes. In the immediate locality, however, bears and foxes were plentiful, and seals played in great numbers at the edge of the ice; in short, there was no lack whatever of that animal life for which the explorer looks so anxiously. Given fresh meat, there should be no thought of scurvy; for scurvy is a form of anæmia, and by the use of meat from which the blood has not been drained it should be successfully defied.

Was ever prospect more fair? Here, at the eighty-second degree, to have *terra firma* at one's feet, and to behold *terra firma* sixty and seventy miles to the northward, on the direct road to the great unknown but discoverable area; here, too, to find an abundance of the animal life so essential to the health of the explorer; hither also to have come by a route so practicable, and with so slender an expenditure of time. Clearly the gulf which trends so deeply into Franz

Josef Land, or, should that country prove insulated land masses, this strait which divides islands of such extent—this Austria Sound—holds open a route northward inferior to none. It is amazing that no explorer had seriously adopted it before Mr. Jackson published his views, his objects, and his methods, two years ago.

In selecting Franz Josef Land as his point of departure for the exploration of the unknown regions of the North Polar Basin, Mr. Jackson was fortified by the opinions of our greatest living Arctic authorities, as well as by the experience of the only two expeditions which have visited that region. Admiral Sir George Nares, for example, has said that "the extreme importance of Eira Harbour (Franz Josef Land) as a base for future journeys northward has been proved; it is an admirable position, with plenty of animal life and open water, and no doubt some good use will be made of it at no very distant time."

Admiral Albert Markham, in his recent *Life of Sir John Franklin*, considers that "a good steamer, specially designed for ice navigation, would easily succeed in reaching Eira Harbour, or even Austria Sound, every year. This being assumed, it is evident that Franz Josef Land should form the objective, and be the direction in which future Arctic exploration should be carried out. But to ensure useful results, it is essential to pass a winter in that little known land, so that exploration can be carried out by sledging parties during the spring and summer." He further says that "it may be assumed that Franz Josef Land is of great extent, and it is not at all improbable that the dimensions of this little known land will be found, when explored, to equal in size the large continent of Greenland." Admiral Sir Erasmus Ommanney has declared that "as all other points afford no hopes of penetration to the northward, we must now accept Franz Josef Land as the base for future operations." And Sir Allen Young points out that "Franz Josef Land now appears to be the only land extending far to the north by which such journeys can be made."

In the paper he read before the Royal Geographical Society, shortly before he sailed from England, Mr. Jackson summed up the advantages of Franz Josef Land under four heads, and it would be useful to reproduce them here.

"I. The accessibility of Franz Josef Land late in the summer when approached along the meridian of 45° E., or some meridian between that of 45° and 50° E. This accessibility has been proved, in my opinion, by the voyages of Mr. Leigh Smith and the little Dutch ship *Willem Barents*.

"II. The northward extension of Franz Josef Land to a latitude as high as 82.5° at Cape Fligely, and some twenty or so miles further if we accept Payer's view that Cape Sherard Osborne is continuous with that portion of the country he called Prince Rodolf's Land. The long stretch of *terra firma* forms a safe route for advance or retreat, and provides all we need in the way of sites for our depôts and cairns.

"III. The still further extension to the north of what, perhaps, I should call the Franz Josef Land group. Standing on Cape Fligely, Payer saw, sixty or seventy miles to the north, the high outlines of an ice-covered land of apparently large extent. This he called Petermann Land, and this land lies undoubtedly in a latitude as far north as any yet reached. There is absolutely nothing known of it beyond this, but it is a reasonable hypothesis to maintain that a land of such elevation would probably reach at least to the eighty-fourth degree north latitude, and who knows how much farther?

"It is this land which we shall try to reach after we

have safely landed, and, in the early days of the following spring, marched over the ice of Austria Sound, a gulf which penetrates the country to Cape Fligely ; or, if this be not so favourable to us as it proved to Payer, along the shores that reach down to the Sound.

"IV. The fourth consideration is provided by the observations of Payer, confirmed by the winter experience of Mr. Leigh Smith. And this consideration is a strong one—the great abundance of animal life on the southern shores of Franz Josef Land during the winter, as well as in the summer. In the winter and spring, of course, this is due to open water. It is owing to this that I regard with equanimity the winter seasons of this northern land. Given fresh meat and enough of it, I believe we shall be able to combat that form of anæmia which we call scurvy. Blood to the bloodless ; and it is man's unfailing tendency to become bloodless if he sojourns long in the extremes of the Arctic.

"I should mention, in passing, that my friend Dr. Neale, who was surgeon to Mr. Leigh Smith's party, had a most anxious and difficult work before him to keep that party in health. With little food, no furs, no special equipment, he kept between twenty and thirty men in health all through the long winter in the North ; and I attribute his success to his insistence on fresh meat, and the ingenious way in which he froze and used the blood of the game his party killed. It is quite possible we should have heard more of this remedy before now, but two things have been against our doing so : the one is the fact that much Arctic exploration has been carried on where game is scarce ; and the other is the mistake that some explorers have made in taking so many men with them. It would be almost impossible, even in a country exceedingly rich in game, to provide for the daily wants of a hundred and fifty men. In fact, expeditions have been too large; but the day of large expeditions is, I believe, gone; and Nansen sails into the ice with thirteen men, and we disembark on Franz Josef Land with no more than eight or nine."

It will be seen from the foregoing that Mr. Jackson's method lies in the chain of depôts which he proposes to establish at short intervals as long as land may be found extending northward. His plan prescribes a base and a line of communication which may be extended indefinitely, and he preserves and recognises that great Arctic canon, "Keep your line of retreat open." Arriving at Franz Josef Land in the autumn of 1894, he goes into winter quarters almost immediately, and devotes the months of darkness and inevitable delay to preparing for his march in the following spring. When the sun returns, and the furious gales of early spring subside, Mr. Jackson hopes to advance up Austria Sound, establishing depôts as he marches and cacheing his provisions. Every article of the equipment and the great bulk of provisions have been specially prepared with a view to this marching, either overland or across the frozen waters of the Sound. For the first time in the history of Arctic exploration the greater part of the instruments, implements, and two of the boats have been constructed of aluminium; a metal which, for lightness and strength combined, has no equal. The party will carry its provisions and stores on sledges, and the sledges will be drawn by dogs, and (if this should prove practicable) by the hardy little Russian ponies which have been taken with the expedition. Moreover, the aluminium boats, built in sections, can each be transported on a single sledge, and will be ready at hand should both land and ice suddenly terminate and open water lie before them. I believe that we have provided for every emergency that can arise, and, while the event only too often belies the expectation, I believe we have anticipated most of the difficulties and accidents for which human foresight can provide. The sequel cannot be told yet—it may be years before the complete story of the expedition can be written—but I am now merely concerned with its organisation, its objects, its methods, and its equipment.

Much has been written about the expedition and the mission upon which it has been sent, which is somewhat beside the exact truth, and I may therefore be excused if I here reproduce a letter which Mr. Harmsworth wrote to me a short time before the expedition sailed:—

12 CLARGES STREET, PICCADILLY, W.

MY DEAR MONTEFIORE,—To write "a few words" on a subject one has at heart very deeply is not easy; but I will be as brief as possible in my explanation of the reasons I had in mind when I decided on fitting out the present Polar expedition.

From the time when, as a youngster, I read the story of Franklin, I have always been fascinated by the great mystery of the North. Julius von Payer's book and the concluding chapter of Admiral Markham's *Sir John Franklin* decided me to contribute to the best of my ability to the exploration of Franz Josef Land, in itself a field for a vast amount of scientific work, and, in the opinion of many of the most distinguished Arctic men, the best road to the North Pole. Having, owing to the efforts of yourself, been made aware of Mr. Jackson's wonderful energy and his recent work in the Arctic, I offered him the leadership of the expedition, and secured an ally in whom I place the utmost confidence.

As to Mr. Jackson's chances of reaching the Pole, I shall say nothing. For my own part, I shall be entirely satisfied if he and his companions add to our knowledge of the geography and the fauna and flora of Franz Josef Land and the area lying immediately north of it. With "beating the record" North I have very little sympathy. If Mr. Jackson plants the Union Flag nearer the Pole than the Stars and Stripes (who head us by four miles only) I shall be glad, but if he came back, having found the Pole but minus the work of the scientists, of which our expedition consists, I should regard the venture as a failure.

I have emphasised this point particularly. Our venture is not a North Pole, but a Polar expedition, a distinction with a vast difference. The advice and assistance given us by such authorities as the President of the Royal Geographical Society, the Council of the Meteorological Office, the Committee and Superintendent of the Kew Observatory, Captain Creak, R.N., of the Hydrographic Department of the Admiralty, Mr. B. Leigh Smith, Sir Leopold M'Clintock, Admiral Markham, Sir Allen Young, Mr. R. H. Scott, F.R.S., Mr. J. Coles, F.R.A.S., of the Royal Geographical Society, Mr. W. Harkness, F.C.S., of Somerset House, Sir George Thomas, Bart., and Dr. W. H. Neale, and the interest evoked throughout the world have been very gratifying to all the brave fellows who have elected to be left on Franz Josef Land for two—perhaps for four or five—years.—Yours faithfully, ALFRED C. HARMSWORTH.

Here, then, we find the reasons which actuated Mr. Harmsworth in fitting out the expedition, and the commission with which he has entrusted Mr. Jackson. Geographical discovery and scientific records constitute the first and sufficient aim, and, as I have elsewhere said, in the achievement of these it is that there must also come those perils and adventures of which the world has never yet tired of hearing. Mr. Jackson's commission is to bring back the former, and I have no doubt that it will be his lot to encounter the latter.

Of the leader himself, the previous chapters will have given some idea, but I should like to add in this place, as one who has known him during the past nine years, that no man has more impressed me by his energy, his activity, his natural alertness and precision. For fifteen years Mr. Jackson has been a traveller in all parts of the world, and has made two journeys to the Arctic regions. On the day he sailed from England, I do not think that one more physically fit could have been found in this country. Six feet one in height, well knit of frame, slight but sinewy, and with his muscles like whip-cords, Mr. Jackson has great capacity for physical exertion and endurance. Methodical in his habits, exact in his calculations, devoted to the pursuit of natural history, and fully alive to the many important questions which the incidents of travel in the Arctic regions may present, I regard Mr. Jackson—not merely as one of those keen sportsmen who have gradually developed into ardent naturalists—but as a man who possesses in himself the highest qualities we desire in a pioneer, a comrade, and a leader.

The second officer in command, and the nautical astronomer to the expedition, is Mr. Albert Armitage, a lieutenant in the Royal Naval Reserve, and, until recently, a second officer in the Peninsular and Oriental Service. An observer of ability and experience, a man accustomed to command, possessing high scientific attainments and a remarkably powerful physique, Mr. Armitage adds to these qualifications an enthusiasm and zeal beyond praise.

The medical officer is Mr. Reginald Kettlitz, M.R.C.S., L.R.C.P. Devoted to his profession, and possessed of a valuable experience which comes to few of his age, Mr. Kettlitz has, like all other members of the party, special physical and mental qualifications for the post he occupies. Moreover, in addition to looking after the well-being of the party, it will fall to his lot to observe and collect evidence of the geological problems presented by Franz Josef Land, and in this he will be assisted by the mineralogist and surveyor.

In Captain Schlosshauer we have obtained not only a worthy representative of the Mercantile Marine, but also a man of marked physical power; moreover, as an old backwoodsman in the Rocky Mountains, he has had an experience of rough camping life under severe climatic conditions, which cannot but stand him in good stead while serving with the expedition.

Highly qualified as a botanist, and well known to the chief European scientific institutions as an enthusiastic and reliable collector, I regard Mr. Harry Fisher, who, previous to his departure, had been botanical curator to the Museum of the University College, Nottingham, not merely as one of the most scientific members of the expedition, but as a man of remarkable force of character.

In the topographical surveyor, Mr. H. A. H. Dunsford, we have a man who has had a varied experience of roughing it in many parts of the world. Particularly useful for our purpose was the experience he obtained during several years of practical surveying in the more northern and remote parts of Canada, during which he was exposed to an essentially Arctic climate, and habitually carried on surveying operations under extremely unfavourable circumstances.

In Mr. F. J. Child, the mineralogist to the expedition, we possess a scientific man of exceptional abilities, whose attainments in the science of chemistry are of the utmost value. Moreover, Mr. Child has the gift of manual dexterity, and can work in metals and other substances with technical skill. An ardent amateur photographer of some eight years' steady application, he has also been appointed photographer to the expedition, although, of course, several members are capable of taking satisfactory photographs. I may add that Mr. Child has invented a novel form of message balloon, and, sooner or later, Mr. Jackson will probably avail himself of this and send an aerial messenger south.

Mr. Sidney Burgess accompanies the expedition as commissariat officer, but as he has seen service on more than one occasion in the Arctic regions in the capacity of surgeon to a whaler, his practical experience of Arctic life and his skill as a surgeon make him a very desirable addition to the party.

Lastly, in Mr. John Heyward, the youngest member of the expedition, but not the least energetic or capable, the party will probably find they have an excellent steward and handy man for many if not all their departments of work. Mr. Heyward worked under me in the organisation of the expedition, and I have the highest opinion of his personal character and mental capacity.

I now pass to a description of the instruments, apparatus, clothing, provisions, and stores of the expedition, an account which, though necessarily brief, may place the reader in possession of the more essential facts of the organisation of the expedition.

But in the first place I must say a few words about the ship. The *Windward* is a well-known whaler, built on the good old plan, sturdy and very strong. She has made many voyages into Arctic seas and had many battles with heavy ice, but up to the present she has always proved herself not merely a comfortable and sea-worthy ship, but extremely well fitted for ice-navigation; short for her tonnage, quick to answer her helm, carrying a good spread of canvas, and equipped with steam power, the *Windward* is, in most respects, the ideal ship for Arctic exploration. Powerfully built of oak, teak, and greenheart, armoured about her bows with heavy plates of iron, and protected by the usual ice-sheathing, there is no reason why she should not sustain in this her latest voyage the reputation won in those previously made. Her gross tonnage is 321; net registered, 245; from stem to stern she measures $118\frac{1}{2}$ feet; her greatest beam is $28\frac{3}{4}$ feet; greatest depth, $16\frac{1}{2}$ feet; and when we have taken away the space required for the accommodation of the crew and the exploring party of nine which she bears to their destination, her carrying capacity would be equal to about seven hundred cubic metres.

I do not propose, of course, to give here a list of the remarkably complete sets of instruments which the expedition has taken with it, but I should like to mention that Franz Josef Land, the point of departure selected by Mr. Jackson for his route into the unknown polar area lying north of it, must obviously necessitate a large amount of sledging for at least a considerable part of the journey; and this has modified and, in several instances, determined the nature of the scientific equipment. Some instruments which would have been useful if the party were to remain on board ship have not been taken, and some instruments which would have assumed a more bulky form, and perhaps have given a greater nicety of result, have been most carefully reduced in weight and size to make them suitable for a land march. The wisdom of this step needs little showing, for it has been found on several previous occasions that when large and complicated instruments have been taken on board the ship, only a very few of them have proved suitable for the necessarily rough work of sledging, and the rest have consequently been left behind. It will be seen, then, that the outfit of the Jackson-Harmsworth Polar Expedition is essentially adapted to the conditions and accidents of sledge journeys. On the other hand, as a very complete depôt is to be erected somewhere on the south coast of Franz Josef Land, together with a carefully designed and equipped observatory, an opportunity will arise for using such delicate instruments as the Unifilar Magnetometer and Barrow's Dip Circle, which are accordingly taken. The same considerations apply to the geological, botanical, and mineralogical equipment. But it may be noted in passing, that in order to have everything as light and strong as possible, every advantage has been taken of the progress recently made in the application of aluminium to the manufacture of instruments of delicacy and accuracy ; thus we have two six-inch and one four-inch aluminium sextants which gave the greatest satisfaction when tested, and only weighed 1 lb. 7 ozs. and 10 ozs. respectively. The sextant-stands taken are also of aluminium, and weigh only five pounds. For astronomical observations the folding artificial horizons are of aluminium ; the fittings of the plane tables are of the same metal ; as also are the pocket compasses, field telescopes, and binoculars, and the like. It is worthy of notice, too, that among the compasses the expedition has taken a spirit compass of an entirely new type which, having been tested at a temperature of $-70°$ Fahrenheit without freezing, may be expected to be useful in a measure which the spirit compasses taken on previous occasions have never attained. It is hardly necessary to add that the thermometers, aneroid barometers, and various registering instruments have been specially prepared and graded for the conditions they are expected to encounter.

Strength and portability are the chief characteristics of the geological and botanical instruments and apparatus, and the special requirements of an Arctic expedition have modified the very complete equipment of the mineralogist, for while he can carry out at the depôts, or at the headquarters on the south coast of Franz Josef Land, the most careful experiments, he carries with him on the march a graded series of miniature outfits which are capable of producing highly satisfactory results, though occupying but a minimum of space.

Naturally enough, the claims of photography have received most anxious attention, and as photography in the Arctic regions is exposed to very different conditions to those we have in temperate climates, certain special and novel preparations have been made. First, of course, with regard to chemicals and developers, plates and films; and next, with reference to special screens for reducing the glare, special telephotographic lenses for photographing far-distant objects, devices for reducing the strong contrast that snow and dark rock may be expected to offer, and the like.

In the medical chests have been placed not only a large variety of drugs in compressed tabloid and other forms, but also a whole series of surgical appliances to meet with every possible form of contingency. Particular attention should be drawn to the citrate and acetate of soda, and the calcium chloride, as new departures in the treatment and prevention of scurvy, for these are strongly recommended by Dr. A. E. Wright, Professor of Pathology at the Army Medical School, Netley, on the ground that it is in the deficiency of soda and potass salts, and therefore in the acid condition of the blood, that the origin of scurvy may be found. The calcium chloride is expected to counteract the tendency to the non-coagulability of the blood which is usually exhibited in scurvy. Lime-juice, moreover, both in liquid and tabloid form, has been taken, but Mr. Jackson hopes that the animal life which Franz Josef Land possesses may contribute that supply of fresh meat which is, after all, the surest preventative of this dread disease.

It would be ungracious if I did not, before passing from this brief consideration of the scientific equipment of the expedition, acknowledge the advice and assistance offered by Captain Creak, R.N., of the Hydrographic Department; Mr. Charles Chree of the Kew observatory, and Mr. Baker of the same establishment; Mr. John Coles, curator to the Royal Geographical Society; my valued friend the late Mr. W. Topley, F.R.S., for his geological help; Professor Boulger, F.L.S., F.G.S., for his assistance in supervising our botanical equipment; and Dr. W. H. Neale, medical officer to Mr. Leigh Smith's expedition to Franz Josef Land, for his valuable advice in connection with our medical equipment.

I now pass from the instruments to the apparatus, the most important items of which are the light boats and sledges. For the first time on record an expedition has left England equipped with two aluminium boats for service in the Arctic regions. Directly it was decided by Mr. Jackson to make his expedition largely a sledging expedition, it became obvious that something very different from the old whale-boats of the past would have to be taken on the march. No small band of explorers could hope to drag these heavy, cumbersome, though in other respects magnificent boats across the rough hummocks of oceanic ice. Terribly familiar are those records which tell how the old explorers manfully but hopelessly struggled, for months at a time, with these heavy boats against unyielding piled-up masses of ice. So it was resolved to utilise the metal aluminium in the construction of special boats for conveyance by sledges, and as soon as the resolution was made, we were at once faced by perhaps the greatest difficulty we experienced in the organisation of the expedition. Week after week rolled by, month after month, and manufacturer after manufacturer tried and promised, and successively failed, until at last we had almost given up the hope that it would be possible to get what we wanted made in England. But before trying elsewhere we made yet one more effort, and fortunately found in Birmingham the man who, as the event proved, could make strong, light, practicable aluminium boats, weighing not more than one hundred and forty-eight pounds—a contrast indeed to the two thousand pounds and even three thousand pounds weight of the old-fashioned boat! As it is, these boats, built in sections, with interchangeable bows and sterns, will each compactly go upon one sledge, and even when loaded with masts and sails and oars, will not exceed one man's load. It is obvious, of course, that these aluminium boats can never be expected for a moment to take the place of a whale-boat in buffeting with the ice or sea ; but that is not the object. The aluminium boats are taken because they can be transported readily and rapidly over the widest stretch of ice, and can be trusted to for crossing those intervening spaces of open water which recur from time to time even in the most densely packed ice-fields. The expedition has, of course, several whale-boats with it in case of accident to the ship, or if the party should need them after they have left the ship, or on a prolonged voyage among loose ice But midway between these heavy boats and those of aluminium, come several light Norwegian fishing-boats, wooden in substance and of the form familiar to us in the famous Viking boats of old. These boats, wooden-riveted, low in the gunwale, and high at stem and stern, are those in which the hardy Norse fisherman sails to-day out of his fiords to fish in the open sea. Crank they look and crazy, but there is no question as to their strength and their sea-worthiness. Their weight too is so small that they may be almost placed on a par with those made of aluminium, for they do not scale more than two hundred pounds each, and consequently can be carried on one sledge.

Even from this the reader will have gathered how important a part the sledges play in the equipment, for they will carry these boats across the ice, and they will also bear the provisions, the stores, the instruments, the clothing, and all the essential impedimenta of the expedition. When Mr. Jackson went on his journey along the shores of the Kara and Barents Seas, he took with him two or three types of sledges, with the special object of determining their respective suitability to rough marching, and he gave the palm, as

Peary has done in the other hemisphere, to that long, narrow, Norwegian type which is now so familiar. Seventeen of such sledges have been taken. Uniformly eighteen inches wide, and six inches high, the largest is thirteen feet six inches long, and the smallest nine feet six inches. The lightest weighs sixteen pounds, and the heaviest twenty-three pounds, while a load of three hundred pounds would not try the strength of the lightest. Made of hard usk wood (ash wood), and well seasoned, these sledges are lashed together with raw hide, and in their pliability lies their greater strength. The runners are merely Norwegian ski, and offer little friction to the snow. The sledges will be ordinarily pulled by the Western Siberian dogs, of which no fewer than thirty were obtained by Mr. Jackson at Habarova on his way out, through the kind services of Mr. Henry Howard, C.B., at that time acting as our Minister at St. Petersburg. Mr. Howard enlisted the sympathy and support of Mr. Edward Wardropper of Tiumen, and this gentleman employed the Russian Raving to obtain them from the Samoyads on the Ob. For their own rapid progress the members of the expedition will trust to Indian snow-shoes, and, when the snow is in good condition, to the Norwegian ski.

It was intended, and I hope circumstances have enabled the party to carry the intention out, to erect somewhere on the south coast of Franz Josef Land, in all probability at Eira Harbour or Cape Flora, a completely fitted and permanent depôt, which should be the headquarters of the party, and in which all reserve stores and apparatus might be securely housed during its absence. To form this depôt a Russian log-house was taken out from Arkhangel in separate pieces, and from a personal inspection of this house, erected for our examination, I can only say that if the party have been able to land it and erect it securely, they have a house of dimensions, strength, and suitability which cannot be surpassed. From Arkhangel, too, they took a store-house and stable, built on the same good fashion of heavy logs, each fitting and mortising into the other; the one for their reserve provisions, and the other for those four little Russian ponies which Mr. Jackson has enlisted on the chance of being able to utilise them, sturdy and hardy as they are. But in addition to these are the light treble-walled houses designed and built by the Rev. E. L. Berthon, who also supplies several of his collapsible boats. These houses are made of special air-tight canvas and light planks of wood; they are lined with felt, and air is admitted from the outside under the double floor, escaping into the room through the stove as heated air. Similar to these in principle is the observatory with its revolving roof, and only slightly different the round stable, the dogs' kennels, and the store-room. All these houses are built on the collapsible principle, so as to facilitate their being landed even under difficulties, and erected without delay. The collapsible principle is also applied to the travelling tents, which have double walls, and yet only weigh thirty pounds apiece; for they shut up somewhat like a Chinese lantern, being crescent-shaped when closed.

With respect to the clothing, I can fortunately be brief, because it has been described in the foregoing pages by Mr. Jackson himself. Impressed with its suitability to withstand the low temperature and piercing winds of the Arctic regions, Mr. Jackson has adopted the Samoyad costume, almost without modification — for all the members of the expedition are equipped with militzas, rukavitza, soveeks, pimmies, and lieupthieu; but in addition they have for foot-wear—perhaps the most vulnerable point in the Arctic costume—heavy elk-skin boots from Finmarken, the lighter Finnesko from Norway; long sealskin boots to withstand the wet and sloppy snow, and long leather boots for the same conditions in summer. The boots specially used for *skilobning* have also been taken. But reindeer-skin constitutes almost the only material employed in this department, for not only are the garments made of it, but the sleeping-bags, the rugs, blankets, and tent linings, and the spare skins for mending and making clothes, are all of reindeer-skin. Double-breasted leather jackets will keep out the wind when the days are comparatively mild, and "Jaeger" is worn next the skin. Gabardine tunics will be worn over the militza during the prevalence of wet snow and rain storms, in order to prevent the hide, which is of course outside, from subsequently freezing hard. Many little devices, too, have been added for special occasions, and it would take the whole space I am occupying with this account were I to give a list of the multitude of etceteras, each of which would, under various circumstances, conduce greatly to the comfort, the well-being, and the success of the explorers.

In dealing with the foods, I may say that the chief considerations which guided us were those of their quality, vitalising power, preservation, and portability. Many articles were rejected because we could not satisfy ourselves as to their keeping properties; others, because we were able to ascertain that much of their vitalising power had been exhausted in the course of preparation; and yet others because more convenient and compressed forms could be obtained. In all this work we were most generously helped by Mr. W. Harkness, F.C.S., of Somerset House.

I have looked over my stores lists, and find many hundreds of entries, which of course it would be absurd to reproduce here; but regarding the stores as a whole, I may select a few articles as illustrating the variety and quantity of food finally selected, the greater part of which was calculated for four years' provision. Under the head of meat, fish, and soups, I find that the expedition has taken about sixteen thousand pounds weight, and this is distributed in varying proportions between roast beef, roast mutton, rump steak, veal, pressed beef, mutton chops, German sausages, veal cutlets, tripe and onions, and sheep's tongues; ham, bacon; fresh herrings, Findon haddocks, and sardines with tomatoes; pea, mulligatawny, mock turtle, and real turtle soups. With regard to biscuits and flour, the explorers have ten tons with them, and about a ton of oatmeal. Some four thousand pounds of highly compressed vegetables have been taken, and to these we must add one thousand pounds of Spanish onions, and four hundred pounds of tomatoes. No fewer than one thousand four hundred pounds of cheese have been sealed down in specially constructed air-tight tins, and the same weight of sugar. Butter to the amount of one thousand five hundred pounds; jams and syrups to that of one thousand pounds; and four hundred and fifty pounds of honey must also be included. Among other items I may mention eight hundred pounds of highly compressed coffee, and one thousand one hundred tins of milk. It is hoped, of course, that the expedition will be able to live largely on bear steaks and seals' flesh, and in order to reduce these into eatable condition, one must not forget the mincing machines, nor the seventy dozens of sauces and pickles for disguising the somewhat unappetising flavour of those creatures. Invalids have not been forgotten, and a large quantity of beef-tea jellies and concentrated meat-juice —so highly concentrated, in fact, that a two-ounce bottle contains all the albuminous matter of four pounds of best English beef—have been included in the stores, together with many dozens of highly concentrated essences of beef and other invalid foods.

But we not only had to provision the nine explorers for four years, but also to fit out the crew and provision them against the contingency of being delayed on their return;

and as the crew of the *Windward* numbered twenty-three souls, their provisions for a year and a half also bulk largely in the estimates. For example, of meat, fish, and soups they have just under sixteen thousand pounds weight; of biscuits, some three tons; of flour, one thousand six hundred pounds; of rice and barley, one thousand one hundred and twenty pounds, and the same quantity of peas; of butter, over one thousand pounds; of tea, coffee, and cocoa, nearly five hundred pounds, and among their minor stores I notice over three hundred pounds of marmalade, and more than that weight of tobacco.

The ponies and dogs have also been provided for, but the former only for two years, and we have calculated that they can be kept in health and working condition on twelve tons of hay, and five tons of mixed provender; while, for the dogs, rather over seven tons of different sorts of biscuits and special foods have been taken.

These, then, form the chief articles of food with which the expedition is provided, but it must not be forgotten that there are, for the sake of that variety which is such an incentive to appetite, smaller quantities of many different preparations which have been included; and that in every case special air-tight tins, and other precautions of a stringent character, have been taken to preserve this food. Moreover, it has been specially prepared for our purpose, and certain modifications been introduced into the methods usually employed. Neither pains nor expense has been spared in the matter, and the great care and trouble taken by the chief caterers to the expedition must be gratefully acknowledged, for without their loyal co-operation, of course, we could not have ensured, what we now believe we have ensured, a quantity of food the best and most suitable for the purpose that could possibly be obtained.

Finally, it only remains for me to add that the S.Y.

Windward, flying the blue ensign, and the burgee of the Royal Thames Yacht Club, left the London Docks on 11th July 1894, and passed down the river to Greenhithe, whence she finally sailed on the following day. Arriving at Arkhangel on 31st July, she took on board further stores, a complete winter outfit for the crew, the Russian log-house, and the four Russian ponies. Mr. Jackson and his colleagues were entertained by the Governor-General, the Naval Commander-in-Chief of that station, and the port authorities, on three occasions; and on 5th August the S.Y. *Windward* sailed from Arkhangel amid a scene of great enthusiasm, and on the following morning I took my leave of the party as they fairly entered the White Sea. From that day to this we have only heard of them, of course, indirectly. A few days later, it seems, they called at Habarova, and took on board the dogs, which were safely delivered to them there by the Russian Raving; in the middle of August the *Windward* was sighted at the edge of the ice-pack by some Norwegian sealing sloops; and Mr. J. Russell Jeaffreson, returning from Iceland by way of the Faröe Islands, was told by the captain of the *Betsy* walrus sloop, whom he met at Thorshavn, that about the end of August he had sighted the *Windward* in N.L. 70° 45', and 44° E. longitude, steaming up an open lead in the ice, with apparently no barrier to the northward.

That is the sum of what we know; for the present we must trust that all is well, and that Mr. Jackson and his gallant companions are fulfilling the high expectations they have aroused—aided in no slight degree by the completeness of the resources placed at their disposal. And in the meanwhile we well may echo the wishes of that Arctic veteran, Mr. Clements R. Markham, C.B., the President of the Royal Geographical Society, who concluded his farewell letter to Mr. Jackson with the following words:—

"In your hands for the time is the Arctic fame of your country; and I feel sure that you will rise to the high level of your great undertaking, and worthily uphold British credit and renown. Accept my most heartfelt wishes for your well-being, for your success, and for your safe return."

Last View of the S.Y. *Windward* steaming North in the White Sea.
(From a photograph taken by Herbert Ward, F.R.G.S.)

INDEX

ABSENCE of trees, 15
Abstinence from smoking, 89
Acknowledgments, 279
Adjectives in Samoyad, 195
Allium sibiricum (Linn.), 16
Alphabet, the Samoyad, 195
Aluminium boats, 280
  ,,   the use of, 271
A.M.—Note on the gullies of the Tundra, 269
Antlers of the reindeer, 73, 243
Appearance, physical, of the Lapps, 177
Appearance, physical, of the Samoyads, 58
Arctostaphylos alpina (Spreng.), 16
Arkhangel, 162, 287
  ,,   Governor-General of, 166, 188, 287
Armitage, Mr. Albert, 274
Auk, Little (*Mergulus alle*, Linn.), 242

BARGAIN, a Samoyad, 24
Barter, 92
Bays, lost, 129
Beaches, old, 129
Begging, absence of, 30
Berzumoff, Ivan, 100
Blackbird (*Turdus merula*, Linn.), 238
Blencathra, the, 3, 102
Boats, aluminium, 280

Bolshaia Zemelskija Tundra, 13, 97, 98
Bolvanski Noss, 14, 39
Bonnet of the Samoyad woman, 66
Boris Gleab, 184
Box, snuff-, 89
Brambling (*Fringilla montifringilla*, Linn.), 239
Branches of the Ural-Altaic Family, 50
Bread, Samoyad, 76
Breaking in reindeer, 124
Broken harrays, 84
  ,,   sledges, 84
Buckles, Samoyad, 67
Bunting, Snow (*Plectrophanes nivalis*, Linn.), 239
Burgess, Mr. Sidney, 275
Burial-places, Samoyad, 45, 83, 119, 147

CALCULATING sticks, 90
  ,,   ,,   Dr. G. Harley, 90-92
Camp, Christmas in, 166
Canadian snow-shoe, the, 133
Captain Louschkin, 181
  ,,   Schlosshauer, 274
  ,,   Vogelgesang, 160
Carex dioica (Linn.), 16
  ,,   *glauca* (Murr.), 16
  ,,   *leporina* (Linn.), 16
  ,,   *pallescens* (Linn.), 16

Carex rigida (Good.), 16
,, saxatilis (Linn.), 16
,, vaginata (Murr.), 16
Cases in Samoyad, 103
Castren, 189, 190
,, vocabulary of, 190
Chaddi, 56, 85
Character of the Samoyads, 96
Charms, Samoyad, 68
Charnavaha River, 122, 256
Chernoijezkaja, 174
Chiffchaff (*Phylloscopus collybita*, Vieill.), 238
Child, Mr. F. J., 275
Children, dress of Samoyad, 70
Choom, Samoyad, 28, 82
,, ,, furniture of the, 29
Christiania, 187
Christmas in camp, 166
Chrysanthemum Leucanthemum, 16
Chulkis, Samoyad, 115
Cladonia rangiferina, 16
Clothing outfit for the expedition, 283
Coast, the Murmanski, 181
Colour of the reindeer, 72
,, Samoyad's skin, 60
Contents, list of, xiii.
Cooke, Mr. Henry A., M.A., 154, 162
Cost of a journey, 145, 181
,, Samoyad dog, 77
Crosses, wayside, 142
Cross-foxes, 102
Crow, hooded (*Corvus cornix*, Linn.), 239
Curiosity, an object of, 139, 151
Curlew (*Numenius arquata*, Linn.), 241

DECEMBER 1893, weather observations, 250
Deer. *See* reindeer
Deschampsia cæspitosa (Beauv.), 16
Dirtiness of the Samoyads, 33, 57
Diseases of the Samoyads, 94
Diver, Red-throated (*Colymbus septentrionalis*, Linn.), 242

Dogs, Samoyad, 77
,, cost of, 77
Dolga Bay, 36
Doorkin, Cyprian, 156
Dress of Samoyads, 27, 63
,, Samoyad children, 70
Driving a Norwegian sledge, 130
,, reindeer, 115
Drunken Zirian, a, 158
Duck, Steller's (*Somateria stelleri*, Pall.), 240
Dumb show, 56
Dunsford, Mr. H. A. H., 275
Dvina River, 161

EAGLE, SEA (*Haliætus albicilla*, Linn.), 240
Eating "marbles," 138
,, method of, 75
Eccentricity, a solar, 146
Emander, Lake, 175, 176
Empetrum nigrum (Linn.), 16
Endurance of the reindeer, 73
Eraya River, 122, 256
Eriophorum polystachyon, 16
,, *vaginatum* (Linn.), 16
Exchange value of stores, 93
Expedition, the Jackson-Harmsworth Polar, 263

FALCON, Peregrine (*Falco peregrinus*, Tunstall), 240
Family, the Ural-Altaic, 49
Farewell to Mr. Jackson from Mr. C. R. Markham, C.B., 288
Feast, a Samoyad, 40
Feet of the reindeer, 74
Festuca ovina, 16
Fieldfare (*Turdus pilaris*, Linn.), 238
Filth of the Samoyads, 33, 57
Finch, Snow- (*Montifringilla nivalis*, Linn.), 239
Finding quarters, 19
Finnic Group, the, 50
First survey of Waigatz Island, 13
Fisher, Mr. Harry, 275

Folk-tales, Samoyad—
  1. The Two Sisters and the Old Woman of the Island, 208
  2. The Seven Maidens of the Lake, 218
  3. The Old Man of Deceit, 226
Franz Josef Land, 266, 268
Fulmar (*Fulmarus glacialis*, Linn.), 242
Furniture of the choom, 29

GAIT of the Samoyad woman, 66
Game, a Samoyad, 63
Geographical distribution of the Samoyads, 52
Gnaphalium sylvaticum, 16
Goldeneye (*Clangula glaucion*, Linn.), 240
Goose, Bean (*Anser segetum*, Gmel.), 240
Goose, Grey Lag (*Anser cinereus*, Meyer), 240
Goose Land, 7
Gostroma River, 122, 257
Governor-General of Arkhangel, 188
Grasses, 16
Great Migration, the, 106
Great Tundra, the, 13, 97, 98
  ,, Topographical Notes to accompany Map of, 254
Group, the Finnic, 50
Grouse, Hazel (*Bonasa betulina*, Scop.), 241
Guestr, the Lapp, 180
Guillemot (*Lomnia troile*, Linn.), 242
Gull, Glaucus (*Larus glaucus*, Faber), 241
Gull, Great Black-backed (*Larus marinus*, Linn.), 242
Gull, Herring (*Larus argentatus*, Gmel.), 242
Gull, Iceland (*Larus leucopterus*, Faber), 242
Gull, Silurian Herring (*Larus argentatus*, Gmel.), 242

Guns, Samoyad, 80
Gun-rests, 80

HABAROVA, country round, 15
  ,, description of, 13
  ,, landing at, 8
  ,, spelling of the name of, 23
  ,, tide at, 101
Hagen, Mr. Harold, 187
Haiputhra River, 122, 256
Hammerfest, 187
Hannawayaha River, 122
Harley, Dr. George, note on calculating sticks, 90-92
Harmsworth, Mr. Alfred C., 164
  ,, ,, letter from, 272
Harness, reindeer, 115
Harrays, Samoyad, 119
  ,, broken, 84
Harstad, 187
Hasovo, the, 52
Hawk, Sparrow (*Accipiter nisus*, Linn.), 240
Height, tables of, 61
Heisadahoi Hills, the, 133, 260
Heyward, Mr. John, 276
Hibinski Hills, the, 175
Hills, the Heisadahoi, 133, 260
  ,, the Hibinski, 175
  ,, the Pitkoff, 130, 258, 259
History of the Samoyad, the, 54
Holmogora, 162
Holy Island, the, 83
Hospitality, Russian, 142
Houses for the expedition, 283

"ICE-BLINK," the, 1
Ice movements round Waigatz, 45
Ichvit River, 122
Illustrations, list of, xvii
Important stream, an, 38
Instruments, scientific, 277
Ishma, 154
Island, Popoff, 172

Island, the Holy, 83
Juncus articulatus (Linn.), 16
  ,, *biglumis* ,, 16
  ,, *bufonius* ,, 16
  ,, *squarrosus* ,, 16
  ,, *trifidus* ,, 16
  ,, *triglumis* ,, 16
Ivan Berzumoff, 100
  ,, at home, 137

JACKDAW (*Corvus monedula*, Linn.), 239
Jackson, Mr. Frederick G., F.R.G.S., 273
—— Topographical Notes, 254
—— Vocabulary of, 199
Jackson-Harmsworth Polar Expedition: its object, method, and equipment, 263
January 1894, weather observations, 252
Jay, Siberian (*Perisoreus infaustus*, Linn.), 239
Jeaffreson, J. Russell, Notes on the Ornithological Results of Mr. Jackson's Journey, 235
Jewellery, Samoyad, 67
Journey, cost of a, 145, 181

KADJI, the Lapp, 180
Kamassintzi, the, 52
Kandalaksha, 174, 175
  ,, Gulf, 174
Kanskoi, numerals of the, 207
Kapperi, the Lapp, 180
Karagasses, the, 52
Kara River, attempt to sail to the, 104
  ,, Sea, 43
Kem, 172-174
Kettlitz, Mr. Reginald, M.R.C.S., L.R.C.P., 274
Khornagora, 158
Kindness of parents, 63
Kirkeness, 183
Kittiwake (*Rissa tridactyla*, Linn.), 242

Koibals, the, 52
Kola, 180-182
  ,, River, 181
Koropatki, 112
Korotaika River, 111, 112, 254, 255, 257
Krestovaia gora, 174
Kuda, 174
Kuia, 134, 261
Kuzereka, 167

LAKE EMANDER, 175, 176
  ,, Skalmozero, 184
Landing at Habarova, 8
Landmann, Heinrich, 160
  ,, Lieutenant, 166
Lapp costume, the, 180
  ,, physical appearance of the, 177
  ,, school, a, 184
  ,, sledge, the, 178
  ,, *talta*, the, 180
Lasso, the Samoyad, 78
Learning the Samoyad speech, 49
Lemming, the, 17
Letter from Mr. Alfred C. Harmsworth, 272
Lieupthieu, Samoyad, 64
Line, the tree-, 148
Load of a reindeer, the, 109
Lobbergonway Yaha River, 122, 256
Lodkas, unfitness for sea voyages of, 10
Lost bays, 129
Louschkin, Captain, 181
Luzula campestris (Willd.), 16
  ,, *spicata* (DC.), 16

MADAME OKATOV, 150, 156
Magpie (*Pica Rustica*, Scop.), 239
Málaia Zemlia, 98
"Marbles," eating, 138
Markham, Mr. Clements R., C.B., farewell words, 288
Marriage, 81
Massailskaja, 176
Meaning of "Waigatz," 25

Meaning of the name "Samoyad," 49, 53
Medical outfit, 279
Meeting the ice, 2
Method of eating, 75
  ,, killing the deer to be sacrificed, 56
  ,, washing, 58
Mezen River, 158
Midveat Retchka River, 42
Migration, the Great, 106
Militza, the Samoyad, 64, 113
Minusinsk, the, 3
Molinia cærulea (Moench.), 16
Money, 91
Montefiore, Arthur, xii. 164, 263
Murmanski coast, the, 181

NAHWUL RIVER, 122, 256, 257
Nansen, Mr. Alexander, 187
  ,, Mrs., 187
Nayesdnik, the, 6
Nikolski River, 15, 102, 106, 254
Niwa River, 175
Nordenskiöld, note, 260
Norwegian sledge, driving a, 130
Nosiyaha River, 122, 256
Nouns, Samoyad, 192
November 1893, weather observations, 248
November 1893, topographical notes, 257
Numbers in Samoyad speech, 193
Numerals, Kanskoi, 207
  .. Ostiak, 207
  ., Samoyad, 196, 203, 207

OBJECT of curiosity, an, 139, 151
October 1893, topographical notes, 254
October 1893, weather observations, 246
Odour of the Samoyads, 58
Okatov, Madame, 150, 156
  ,, Roman, 150, 156
Old beaches, 129

Onega, 167
Orestes, the s.s., 3
Ornaments, Samoyad, 67
Ornithological Results of Mr. Jackson's Journey, 235
Ostiaks of Narym, numerals of the, 207
  ,, Tomsk, numerals of the, 207
Outfit, winter, 21
Owl, Barn (*Strix flammea*, Linn.), 240
  ,, Snowy (*Nyctea scandiaca*, Linn.), 17, 240
Oya River, 102
Oyster-catcher (*Hæmatopus ostralegus*, Linn.), 241

PAPAVER nudicaule, 16
Parents, kindness of, 63
Pasareka, 184
Pass River, 184
Pechora River, 135, 136, 140, 141, 143, 144, 149, 150, 261
Peel, Miss Helen, 103
Pesk, the Lapp, 180
Photographic apparatus, 278
Piatsoworyaha River, 128, 257
Pimmies, Samoyad, 64, 114
Pinega, 159
Pink-footed Goose (*Anser brachystrynchus*, Bail.), 240
Pintail (*Dafila acuta*, Linn.), 240
Pipet, Rock (*Anthus obscurus*, Lath.), 238
Pitkoff Hills, the, 130, 258, 259
Plans for the winter, 9
Plates, tin, 94
Plover, Golden (*Charadrius pluvialis*, Linn.), 241
Plover, Grey (*Squalarola helvetica*, Linn.), 241
Plover, Ringed (*Ægialetis curonica*, Gmel.), 241
Poa pratensis (Linn.), 16
Poloboryáskaja, 174
Pony, the Russian, 147, 157
Popham, Mr. F. Leybourne, 3, 103
Popoff Island, 172

Posanka River, 132, 257
Post-sledge, a, 101
Preface, vii.
Priestly functions of the Samoyads, 85-88
Pronouns in Samoyad, 194
Provisions for the expedition, amount of, 284
Ptarmigan, Willow (*Lagopus albus*, Gmel.), 241
Pterinea, 15
Puffin (*Fratercula arctica*, Linn.), 242
Pustozersk, 140
Putting a baby to bed, 109
Pzaitch, the, 34

Rae, Mr., vocabulary of, 204
Raven (*Corvus corax*, Linn.), 239
Red-shank (*Totanus calidus*, Linn.), 241
Redwing (*Turdus iliacus*, Linn.), 238
Reindeer, the, 70
,, antlers of the, 73, 243
,, breaking in, 124
,, colour of the, 72
,, driving, 115
,, endurance of the, 73
,, feet of the, 74
,, flesh as food, 75
,, food of the, 71
,, harness, 115
,, rounding up the, 78
,, the load of a, 109
,, verst, a, 74
Religion, 84
Revival of Arctic Exploration, 263
River Charnayaha, 122, 256
,, Dvina, 161
,, Eraya, 122, 256
,, Gostroma, 122, 257
,, Gushina, 110, 254
,, Haiputhra, 122, 256
,, Hannawayaha, 122
,, Ichvit, 122
,, Kola, 181
,, Korotaika, 111, 112, 254, 255, 257

River Lobbergonway Yaha, 122, 256
,, Mezen, 158
,, Midveat, 42
,, Nahwul, 122, 256, 257
,, Nikolski, 15, 102, 106, 254
,, Niwa, 175
,, Nosiyaha, 122, 256
,, Oya, 102
,, Pass, 184
,, Pechora, 135, 136, 140, 141, 143, 144, 149, 150, 261
,, Piatsoworyaha, 128, 257
,, Posanka, 132, 257
,, Sonsida, 122, 256
,, Talata, 34, 111, 122, 254, 256
,, Tambiha, 122, 256
,, Tulama, 182
,, Vischa, 112, 255
,, Yaha, 122, 256
Robe of the Samoyad woman, 65
Roman Okatov, 150, 156
Rounding up the reindeer, 78
Rukavitza, the Samoyad, 64
Rushes, 16
Russian hospitality, 142
,, pony, the, 147, 157
,, vocabulary, 199

Sacrifices, Samoyad, 86
Sacrificial pile, 35
Salix lanata, 16
Samoedia, 55
Samoyad, adjectives in, 195
,, alphabet, 195
,, bargain, a, 24
,, bread, 76
,, buckles, 67
,, burial-places, 45, 83, 119, 147
,, cases in, 193
,, character of the, 96
,, charms, 68,
,, choom, 28, 82
,, colour of the, 60
,, costume, 27, 63
,, dirtiness of the, 33, 57
,, diseases, 94

Samoyad dogs, 77
,, feast, a, 40
,, folk-tales, 208, 218, 226
,, game, a, 63
,, geographical distribution of the, 52
,, guns and gun-rests, 80
,, history of the, 54
,, jewellery, 67
,, lasso, 78
,, marriage, a, 81
,, meaning of the name, 49, 53
,, nouns, 192
,, numbers in, 193
,, numerals, 196, 203, 207
,, odour of the, 58
,, ornaments, 67
,, physical appearance of the, 58
,, priestly functions of the, 85-88
,, pronouns in, 194
,, religion of the, 84
,, sacrifices, 86
,, sacrificial pile of the, 35
,, ski, 69
,, sociability of the, 61
,, speech, 189
,, spelling of the word, 49, 54
,, timidity of the, 10
,, toast, 62
,, tombs, 83
,, toys, 63
,, treasure-chest of the, 30
,, trial, a, 94
,, unselfishness of the, 63
,, vocabulary, 199, 204
Saxicava arctica, 15
Schlosshauer, Captain, 274
School, a Lapp, 184
Scientific instruments, 277
Scirpus cæspitosus (Linn.), 16
,, pauciflorus (Linn.), 16
Scurvy, a story of, 99
Sea, White, 170
Sedges, 16

Seebohm, Mr. Henry, 205
September 1893, weather observations, 244
Sewing, 80
Siskin (Chrysorostris spinus, Linn.), 239
Skalmozer Lake, 184
Skin, colour of the Samoyad's, 60
Ski, Samoyad, 69
Skua (Stercorarius calarrhactes, Linn.), 242
Sledge, a post, 161
,, broken, 84
,, driving a Norwegian, 130
,, Samoyad, 117. 281
,, ,, woman's, 118
,, the Lapp, 178
Smew (Mergus albellus, Linn.), 240
Smirnoff, Vasili Ivanovitch, 181.
Smoking, abstinence from, 89
Smoyleanitch, 158
Snipe (Gallinago cælestris, Frenzel), 241
Snow-shoe, the Canadian, 133
Snuff-box, Samoyad, 89
,, spoon, 90
,, taking, 89
Sociability of the Samoyads, 61
Soil of the Tundra, 15
Soiots, the, 52
Solar eccentricity, a, 146
Solitude of the Tundra, 126
Somerville, Mr. D. M. Crichton, 187
Sonsida River, 122, 256
Sorokaze, 167
Soveck, the Samoyad, 65
Speech, learning the Samoyad, 49
,, Samoyad, 189
Spelling of the name "Samoyad," 49, 54
Spoon. snuff-, 90
Starling (Sturnus vulgaris, Linn.), 239
Start, Red (Ruticilla phænicurus, Linn.), 238
Stefan, 96
Sticks, calculating, 90

Stint, Little (*Tringa minuta*, Leisl.), 241
Stone-Chat (*Pratincola rubicola*, Linn.), 238
Stores, exchange value of, 93
Story of scurvy, a, 99
Strong current, a, 101
Sumpskipesat, 170
Swan, Bewick's (*Cygnus bewicki*, Yarr.), 240

TABLES of heights, 61
Talata River, 34, 111, 122, 254, 256
Talta, the Lapp, 180
Tambiha River, 122, 256
Tawgi, the, 52
  ,, vocabulary, 196-198
Teeth, whiteness of the, 59
Tern, Arctic (*Sterna macrura*, Naum.), 241
Thrush, Missel- (*Turdus viscivorus*, Linn.), 238
Thrush, Siberian (*Turdus sibiricus*, Pall.), 238
Thrush, Song- (*Turdus musicus*, Linn.), 238
Tide at Habarova, the, 101
Timidity of the Samoyads, 10
Tin plates, 94
"Tit-bits" of food, 75
"Toast," Samoyad, 62
Tombs, Samoyad, 83
Tools, Samoyad, 80
Topographical Notes to accompany Map of Great Tundra, 254
Toys, Samoyad, 63
Treasure-chest of the Samoyads, 30
Tree-line, the, 148
Trees, absence of, 15
Trial, a Samoyad, 94
Trondhjem, 187
Tulama River, 182
Tundra, Bolshaia Zemelskija, 13, 97, 98
Tundra, soil of the, 15
  ,, solitude of the, 126
  ,, vegetation of the, 16

UNSELFISHNESS of the Samoyads, 63
Ural-Altaic Family, the, 49
  ,, ,, branches of the, 50
Ussia, 137
Ust-Pinega, 161
Ust-Zilma, 149, 153

VACCINIUM *Vitis-Idæa* (Linn.), 16
  ,, *uliginosum* (Linn.), 16
Vadso, 186
Vardo, 187
Vasili Ivanovitch Smirnoff, 181
Vasili and his babba; their costume, 26
Verst, a "reindeer," 74
Vischa River, 112, 255
Vocabulary, Castrén's, 196-198
  ,, Mr. Jackson's, 199
  ,, Mr. Rae's, 204
  ,, Russian, 199
  ,, Samoyad, 199, 204
  ,, Tawgi, 196-198
  ,, Yurak, 196-198
Vogelgesang, Captain, 160
Voronoff Noss, 36

WAIGATZ ISLAND, 83
  ,, ,, first survey of, 13
  ,, ,, ice movements round, 45
  ,, meaning of, 25
Wash, a welcome, 139
Washing, method of, 58
Wayside crosses, 142
Weather observations—
  September 1893, 244
  October ,, 246
  November ,, 248
  December ,, 250
  January 1894, 252
Wheatear, Common (*Saxicola œnanthe*, Linn.), 238
Whiteness of the teeth, 59
White Sea, the, 170
Widgeon (*Mareca penelope*, Linn.), 240

INDEX

Wiggins, Captain Joseph, 3
Wimbrel (*Numenius phæopus*, Linn.), 241
Windward, the S.Y., 276
    ,,   sailing of the, 287
Winter, arrival of, 105
    ,, travelling outfit, 21
Woman, bonnet of the Samoyad, 67
    ,,   gait, 66
    ,,   robe, 65
    ,,   sledge, 118

YAHA RIVER, 122, 256
Yeniseians, the, 52

Yerra, the Lapp, 180
Yon-pa-ha-pai, 89
Yugorski Schar, the, 5
Yuna, 166
Yurak vocabulary, 196-198
Yuraks, the, 52

ZIRIAN, a, 112
    ,,   a drunken, 158
    ,,   woman, a, 113
Zirians, the, 149
    .. by Henry A. Cooke, M.A., 154

THE END

Printed by R. & R. CLARK, LIMITED, *Edinburgh*.

www.ingramcontent.com/pod-product-compliance
Lightning Source LLC
Chambersburg PA
CBHW030018240426
43672CB00007B/1000